A History of
Abbotswood

GUILDFORD'S MOST UNUSUAL ESTATE

A History of ABBOTSWOOD

Guildford's Most Unusual Estate

Michael Drakeford

PHILLIMORE

2008

Published by
PHILLIMORE & CO. LTD
Chichester, West Sussex, England
www.phillimore.co.uk
www.thehistorypress.co.uk

ISBN 978-1-86077-521-5

Printed and bound in Great Britain at
CAMBRIDGE UNIVERSITY PRESS

Contents

Sponsors

The author is grateful for the sponsorship provided by many organisations and individuals. This book is a commentary on an important part of the history of Guildford, and it is hoped that it will interest many inside and outside the town. The records and photographs used have been offered to the Surrey History Centre in Woking for safe keeping in perpetuity.

Baker Tilly
Churchouse Financial Planning Limited
Guildford Borough Council
Surrey Advertiser
Tony Vokes

Supporters of Local History in Guildford

Corporate

Clyde & Co.
Deeks and Steer plc
Abbotswood Tree Care
Bruffell Williams
Charles Russell
Chelsea Building Society
H.A. Fox-Jaguar
Hill Clements
Howard Morley & Sons
McAllisters Recovery Limited
Merrow Interiors
PKF
Savills
Sutton Green Golf Club
The Guildford Society
The Arts and Crafts Movement in Surrey
Transport Maintenance

Private Individuals

John and Maria Acoumis
Arthur and Gill Basford
Gerald and June Bedford
David and Veronica Campbell
Ian and Eileen Chapman
Andy Corner and Sian Powell
Stewart and Margaret Davies
Tony and Jane Derbyshire
Georgina, James and Peter Drakeford
Peter Dudley
Robert and Claire Elphick
Ragnor Eynon
Fereydoon and Nahid Farkhondeh
Peter and Eluned Ferguson
Ken and Pat Fisher
Cllr Matt Furniss
Paul and Pam Gillingham
Peter and Samantha Gissel
Jean Grieves
Paul and Natasha Halliwell
Peter and Olivia Harwood
Graham and Sue Hibbert
Cllr Andrew Hodges
Betty Jaeger
Alan and Debbie Jenkins
Dr Rosemary Jenkins
Paul and Wendy Kenyon
Michael and Christine Kirby
Niels and Elizabeth Laub
David and Celia Leck
Reeve and Bridget Martin
Anne Milton MP
John and Lesley Myles
Terry and Sue Newman
David and Sue O'Flaherty
David and Anne Pardo
Peter and Amanda Regan
Ian and Rosemary Spence
Bernard and Carol Stevens
Rab and Ruth Suttill
Bob and Joan Thomas
Peter Tolhurst and Yuko Nozawa
Jean Trickett
Sir Anthony and Lady Vineall
Dylan and Nicky White
Alan K. Williams

Acknowledgements

Bill Hancock – For background information regarding title deeds, and the Abbotswood Residents Association Limited.

Peter Drakeford – For producing the first 'history' of Abbotswood as a part of a GCSE project.

Carol Stevens – For information about the architect, Burlingham, and the Arts and Crafts features in The Hurst.

Residents – For valuable information about the various houses, the provision of their deeds, and for letting me take so many photographs.

The Taylor family – For the details of the family history and in particular Jonathan Taylor, son of Charles, Peter Kirwan-Taylor, son of John, Anthony Turnbull, son of Joyce, James Suenson-Taylor, grandson of Jesse, Ben Moorhead, grandson of Harold, and Georgina Macpherson, granddaughter of John.

Pat and Russell Burlingham – For their comments about their father and his work.

Michael Onslow, 7th Earl of Onslow, for providing the foreword.

Illustration Acknowledgements

All illustrations are taken by either Michael Drakeford or supplied by current residents, except for:

Pat Burlingham, 39, 48, 54 60, 201, 204-6; Lyn Clark, 29; Peter Doresa, 240; Peter Drakeford, 152; Knight Frank, 87, 89, 90, 129, 218; Sarah Gall and Domestic Building Research Group, 25; Guildford Institute, 242; Diane Haigh, 146, 153; Shirley Hewitt, 76, 245; Roderick Hole, 40; Philip Hutchinson, 17; London and Manchester Assurance Co. Ltd, 35, 41; Georgina Macpherson, 38; Oonagh Monckton, 70; Royal Institute of British Architects, 72; David Rose and the *Surrey Advertiser*, 1, 8; Savills, 120; Seymours, 86; Geraldine Stewart, 244; *The Sunday Times*, 246; Surrey History Centre, 4, 5, 6, 7, 9, 15, 42, 45, 55, 57, 221, 248-58; Jonathan Taylor, 37; Walter Thomson, 59; Town and Country Homes, 46.

Foreword

The Arts and Crafts movement was one of the cultural revolutions of the late
19th century. Its influence and progress continued well into the 20th century.
Guildford is lucky in that it has major areas of the town built in its style. This
author has created a record of them; some are under threat from developers
but the unique record that he has made will be a great help to those who wish
to preserve and keep them. These buildings are as much a part of our social
history as Clandon Park in which I grew up, the Cathedral, the Town Hall,
the Royal Grammar School or the Abbot's Hospital. They all need our tender
loving care!

Onslow, 2008

Introduction

Guildford is a most attractive town, lying on an escarpment of the North Downs. It has been the county town of Surrey for centuries and has a rich heritage evident through the Norman castle and keep, the 'cobbled' high street, the Guildhall and a myriad of old houses throughout the town. The ancient church of St Mary's dates back to Saxon times. Guildford had its own mint, issuing coins from about A.D. 950 until after the Norman Conquest.

Much has been done to preserve the identity of the town by the Guildford Society and others. Nevertheless, the march of time is held

back by no one. Today, planners are facing immense pressures from the government to allow additional housing for the growing population of southern England. All too often we see the older houses in Guildford either demolished for housing, being converted into flats, or having their gardens ripped up for additional housing.

There is obviously a housing need that has to be fulfilled, and the worst of all worlds would be for our countryside to become a concrete jungle. In order to achieve an acceptable solution it is inevitable that the density of housing in already built-up areas will increase, but my plea, through this book, is that any development should be undertaken in a sensitive way, and that the character of Guildford and similar towns should be maintained for the generations to come. We do not want more of the unfortunate projects of the 1960s and 1970s that still scar our towns and villages.

This book will primarily record the history of Abbotswood, a unique estate in Guildford containing two listed properties. Today, it is a prosperous middle-class suburb within a wealthy town in the 'Stockbroker Belt' comprising mainly large four-six bedroom houses. The occupations of the house owners include that of doctor, scientist, accountant, lawyer, businessmen and retired people, all of whom have clearly achieved much – it remains the sort of place to which many aspire. This concise description of its inhabitants has changed little in nearly one hundred years.

Readers will be shown that Abbotswood and similar estates can be developed sensitively, and that our historical past can be enriched by so doing. There are many who have an involvement in local history in general, or that of Guildford in particular, or in the Arts and Crafts Movement and social history. For these readers this book may be of interest, as it should be for like-minded types who wish to find out how to investigate their own locality.

I hope that this book will encourage others to work together to protect this type of development for future generations.

MWD, 2008

One

The Edwardian Dream

At birth, Abbotswood was the creation of a modern environment ahead of its time, born out of Edwardian ideals. Indeed for many it was just a dream.

Almost a century ago the idea for the Abbotswood estate was conceived in quite a different world from that in which we live today. King Edward VII was on the throne, and the achievements of the Victorians were still benefiting a country that was economically the third most powerful in the world, after the United States and Germany. It was still very much a society that was evolving socially, politically, economically and technically.

Our story started when one of Surrey's aristocratic families, the Onslows, were doing their best to resist the pressures caused by a period of poor management of their assets, the effects of the agricultural depression of the late 1800s, and growing competition from imported food. William Hillier, the 4th Earl of Onslow, had been selling off parts of his estates since the 1870s. In contrast, a surveyor, and to all intent and purposes an entrepreneur, Alfred G. Taylor, seized the opportunity to create a garden suburb for the wealthy middle class of Guildford, some way out of town, on a farm to be sold by the Earl.

It is not difficult to imagine how this may have come about. One Saturday, probably at Christmas 1908, Alfred Taylor was visiting his good friend W.H. Brown who lived at St Mildred's, a large Victorian house on the London Road to the north of Guildford. Taylor had become the senior surveyor for London and Manchester Industrial Assurance Company, a London firm, and Brown was a Director of that same company.

Taylor had made a great deal of money in and around Sutton, also in Surrey, where he had purchased hundreds of acres of farm land. Having obtained planning permission for housing, he put down roads and services, and sold the plots to builders and prospective home owners.

The conversation might have gone something like this:

Taylor: I really need to find some more land.

Brown: By chance, I heard that old man Onslow is shortly putting Stoke Park Farm up for sale. Have you thought of that?

Taylor: It is a bit far from Sutton for me, but it could work. Whilst it is a fair way out of Guildford, I expect that if the plots are big enough, they should sell to the right sort who can afford the transport. In fact, instead of selling off plots, why don't I give young Claude Burlingham his head? He has recently started work for me, having just qualified. He has some brilliant ideas, and once he has cut his teeth in Sutton, I am certain that this would bring him out. He has so much potential.

Brown: That sounds a good idea. If you decide to sell the houses, rather than just rent them, I know that I can arrange mortgages through London and Manchester for the buyers.

And so the idea was born …

To put the development of Abbotswood into context it is relevant to consider briefly what life was like at the time.

The Edwardian period was one of great social contrasts. For many there were the benefits from the growth of the middle classes that started in the reign of Queen Victoria – a period that created a need for more teachers, medics, accountants, bankers, and technicians. For these people there was a better standard of living, improved housing, and a new place in society. Even so, this was still a relatively small group, and only 15 per cent of the population could be described as middle class. For those in the lower echelons of society life was still a struggle. They lived in squalid accommodation, with poorly paid jobs, often working long hours in dangerous conditions with the threat of unemployment and the workhouse always on the horizon.

The days of the social security payment were still far off and 10 per cent of the population could be described as impoverished, with only a quarter just being able to make ends meet, and put food on the table. For many, red meat was a rarity. In rural areas, the agricultural depression meant that nearly 50 per cent of the workers were in a state of poverty – a privy in the garden, oil lamps, and water from a well, were the norm. In the towns many still lived in dark and dingy terraced houses providing cramped and basic accommodation, with outside toilets, no electricity or even gas. However, clean drinking water piped to many urban houses had reduced illness considerably by the turn of the century.

This rather dismal picture continued up until the First World War, when it became clear that many army volunteers and conscripts were unfit for active duty because of a poor diet, the low quality of many food products, and congested and unsanitary housing. This confirmed a similar situation at the time of the Boer War and was partly the reason why, in the 1920s, the government sought to encourage council housing.

For many, a career in service working for the middle and upper classes was still a way out of the squalor. The 'lucky' ones might have been up at 5 a.m. to clean grates and polish before their employers were out of bed, but at least they could be certain of regular meals and reasonable accommodation.

The accession of the sometimes outrageous Edward, Prince of Wales, replacing the austere and revered Queen Victoria, led to a release for the upper classes. They now entered a period when the dark clothes of Victoria's era could be shed to reflect the exuberant life style of her son. In turn, the evolving middle classes, espying the changes and the revitalised extravagance of the wealthy industrialists, sought to share in the new riches. Entrepreneurs bringing wealth and prosperity, were much admired and encouraged.

Even political balances were changing. For the first time the Prime Minister, Herbert H. Asquith, held an urban seat, rather than one in the country. The power was shifting from the landowners to a professional, political élite.

The plight of the landed gentry was exaggerated by the introduction of increased taxes on the very rich, and most importantly, death duties. They struggled to maintain their assets following years of agricultural depression affecting the land they owned and on which they relied for income. Not all did badly, however. Despite growing concerns about the colonies, industry was still expanding, and the financial services sector was growing fast. There was still money to be made and, with a more stable existence for some, it was time to take stock and plan for a secure future – this was often in property, either as an investment, or as a home.

The Governments were becoming more interventionist, and the previous laissez-faire attitudes were waning. Acts covering public health, artisan dwellings, education and Food and Drugs were evidence of this. When the Liberals came to power in 1906, the introduction of social benefits derived from their higher taxes were an extension of growing government involvement. Lloyd George introduced the first pension and national insurance schemes in his 1909 budget. This step was much abhorred by those in the House of Lords, and only succeeded by the use of the Parliament Act.

Elsewhere, all was not well for the Government. The rising power of Germany, Home Rule for Ireland, and the Feminist Movement, were all to stretch the minds of the politicians. The upper classes were all too aware of the spread of socialism and the problems that it might bring.

Women were now the majority of the population. Around seventy-five per cent in the 15-34 age group were in work, albeit mostly menial, with only a few in professional occupations. The suffragette movement was growing through the likes of Emily Pankhurst, and women were demanding not only the vote but a better lot in life.

Technical advances were forging the lives of many, and travel was considerably improved with the development of the railways. The horse remained the main form of local transport and the car was not to be a real alternative until after the First World War. Telephones and the wireless were to become important, but above all, the age of electricity had dawned. The timing of the Abbotswood development could not have been better, for in Guildford the Electricity Works building for increased electricity generation was completed in 1913. Apart from clean light, it was soon to be in common use for cooking, heating and later for labour-saving devices for the more wealthy.

Electric street lights were still unusual and gas lights were to be around for at least the next 20 years. In the villages outside Guildford street lights were slower to come. Milford, on the London to Portsmouth Road, saw its first gas light in 1884. However, lighting did not come to nearby Witley until 1914, and electric lights not before 1932.

In 1914, with two houses occupied and four others under construction, the architect Burlingham applied for three street lights at Stoke Park Farm Estate, as Abbotswood was then known. Guildford's Lighting Committee declined, but did agree to re-site the gas lights in London Road, so that they would shine into the two new entrance roads!

As the story unfolds, it will become clear how these changes related to Abbotswood.

The regimented housing improvements in Victorian times were not always welcomed; some people did not like change and there was a strongly supported fashion for the handmade crafts of yesteryear. There was a yearning for the ways of the countryside, away from the noise and dirt of town and city. The likes of Helen Allingham, Henry John Sylvester Stannard and Myles Birket Foster became famous for painting and idealising the rustic country cottage, when in fact they were popularising rural poverty. The image of a tumbledown cottage with climbing roses on the outside, with children playing under the watchful eyes of devoted parents drew many an urban professional to want such a property, but within the confines of an urban area. Thus, the popularisation of the 'Garden Suburb' came to the fore, and the demand for estates such as Abbotswood became no longer just a dream, but a reality for the more fortunate few.

Two

The Location of Abbotswood

Abbotswood is situated on the London Road to the north of Guildford, approximately one mile from the town centre. The nearby milestone at the AA Roundabout indicates that Hyde Park Corner is 26 miles away, Guildford one mile and Portsmouth 43 miles. It is marked 'Stoke', denoting the parish in which the stone is located.

Parish boundary stones on each side of the road outside Abbotswood were marked on most maps until 1965. The stone outside Upmeads (49)* can still be found in the undergrowth.

The London Road was once a turnpike road that, subject to tolls, took all manner of horse-drawn traffic between London and Portsmouth, which was the major naval base from which the Royal Navy sailed to 'rule the waves'. The toll road, under the control of the 1748 Turnpike Trust, continued until 1870. The last of the regular horse-drawn coaches from London ran in 1849, just four years after the London to Guildford railway line opened. The Guildford to Portsmouth railway line opened in 1859; the less direct line to London via Effingham had opened in 1855. From the start of the 20th century the car began to challenge the 50-year supremacy of the railways.

Early maps can tell an interesting story of the area.

In 1690 John Seller produced a Surrey map, showing Granghill Farm, now demolished, and New Inn Farm. Stoke Park Farm was shown, but not named. At Burpham cross roads, Burpham Cross is shown, but not the extant *Green Man* inn. Burpham, as a settlement, is not in evidence, but Burpham Farm by the River Wey is shown. A less detailed map by H. Moll, dated 1724, shows Grangehill Farm.

The John Senex map of 1729 shows Watford House along the Stoke Road, and, where Stoke Park Mansion was to be, the words 'Esq. Turner', referring to

2 *The London milestone marked 'Stoke'.*

3 *The parish boundary stone outside Abbotswood.*

---

*   When specific houses are identified, the original name is used with the current road number. In some later chapters the numbers are omitted.

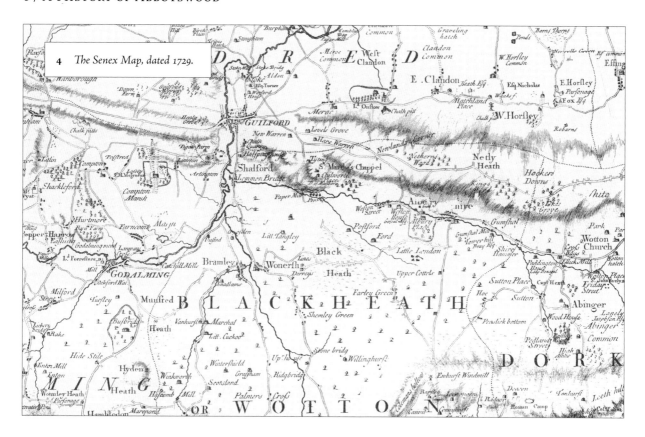

4 The Senex Map, dated 1729.

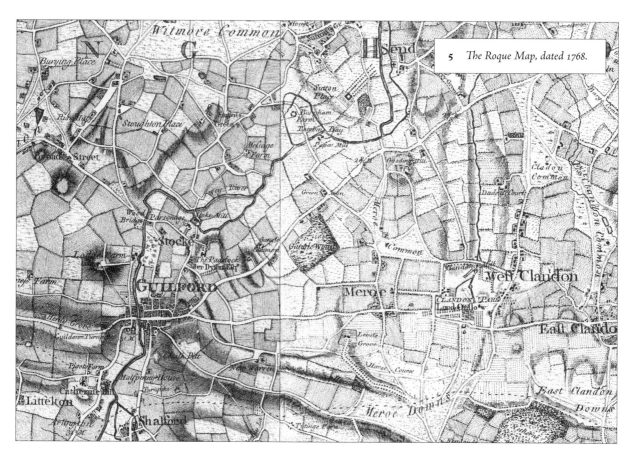

5 The Roque Map, dated 1768.

the owner of the house, Nicholas Turner who had bought it in 1718. Granghill Farm was shown, but not named; instead Alden Farm was shown and named. This was an early name for Stoke Park Farm, on which Abbotswood was to be built. Stoke Church is marked with the road on the opposite side of Stoke Road from that seen today.

The Roque map, dated 1768, was sufficiently detailed to show the fields and the layout of the Guildford town roads. There are two spellings for Stoke: Stocke for the village, and Stoke for the mill by the river. The house on Stoke Park is now referred to as The Paddock, and owned by Jer. Dyson Esq. Burchatt's farm is also shown. Rather than naming Stoke Park Farm, that side of the road is referred to as Gangle Common, and the woodland on the other side as Gangle Wood. The *Green Man* inn appears, and again Burpham Farm represents Burpham.

A map from the Estate Book for Stoke Park Mansion dated 1812 shows the extent of the new woodland that had been planted at the turn of the century. This evidences that Thorneycrofts, Gangle Wood, and the woodland forming part of what is now Abbotswood all belonged to the estate.

In 1816, the name 'Gang Hill Farm' appears on the Headley Brothers' Map.

By 1896 mapping had come of age. The quality was much improved, and can be compared with features present today.

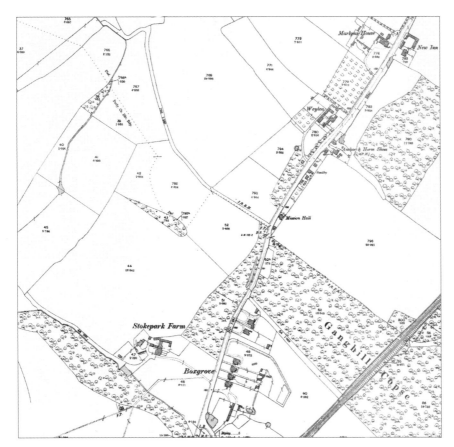

6 *Ordnance Survey Map 1896.*

- In addition to the Victorian mansions two further large houses appear where the Eaton Court development now stands.

- 'Stokepark' Farm is shown to have its entrance where the current lane emerges from the Stoke Farm Cottages. The farm workers' cottages on the park are shown for the first time.

- Gang Hill Wood has now become Ganghill Copse, and comprises 15 acres on the west side of the railway line, which dissected the woodland.

- Stoke Park Farm comprises fields, save for 5 acres of wood abutting the London Road and a small copse at the centre.

- A farm track runs along the north boundary of the farm, which is also the municipal boundary, towards the river.

- There is a long pond in the woodland adjacent to the road, and an artificial pond by the farm.

- There is still no centre to Burpham, which is a collection of farms and workers cottages.

Despite the skill and detailed maps of the Ordnance Survey researchers, a map produced in 1920 showed no signs of developments at Abbotswood, despite 14 houses having been built prior to 1916!

In early times, Stoke Park Farm was then not entirely within the Parish of Stoke. The conveyance dated 29 September 1909, by which the land was sold by the 4th Earl of Onslow to A.G. Taylor, correctly refers to Stoke Park Farm as being within the parishes of Worplesdon and Stoke. There was an indentation from a line between houses numbered 30 and 36, Abbotswood. All the houses north of that line were in Worplesdon. The boundary went north along the small copse and the stream that still runs at the rear of the gardens at 30, 31, and 32, Abbotswood.

The 1934 Ordnance Survey map is relevant to the history of Abbotswood because it shows the completed estate.

- Following boundary changes, for the first time the whole of Abbotswood appears within the Parish of Stoke-next-Guildford.

- It is interesting to compare the configuration of the houses at the time with those of today. For example, in-filling has meant that at Upmeads (49) and Oakdene (44) the main door was approached from quite a different direction.

- By the roundabout, the AA Fanum House building had been erected.

- The Ganghill estate is nearing completion. Ganghill Copse remains on the east side of the railway line.

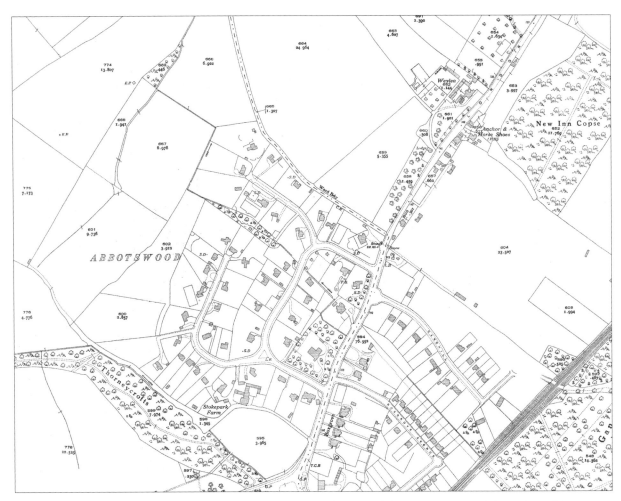

7   *Ordnance Survey Map 1934.*

Transport has been, and always will be, a significant feature of the area. Sometimes the local road traffic has been problematic; as early as the late 1920s, queues through Guildford town centre were getting bad and in order to aid traffic flow a by-pass for the A3 was planned. For the traffic to use this scheme, a roundabout was built one hundred yards south of Abbotswood in 1933, at what is still colloquially known as the AA Roundabout. It gave access onto a new by-pass, now called Parkway, which came into use in 1934 and joined the existing 'New Road' at Ladymead. Leslie Hore-Belisha, then Minister of Transport, opened the extended Guildford by-pass in 1936. This took traffic away from the town and up past the Dennis factory, and under the road leading to the Hogs Back. A further road, skirting Compton and Eashing, by-passed Godalming and led to Milford.

Before this by-pass was built there was little alternative for traffic using the A3 but to go into the centre of Guildford, and cross the River Wey at the town bridge, and then wend its way up along the Old Portsmouth Road towards Godalming for Milford, and eventually Portsmouth.

Today, at the AA Roundabout, a building named The Clock House is situated on the site of the regional office for the Automobile Association. This

8 *Fanum House and The Clock House. Both have the Braby clock.*

building now houses the offices of a well known firm of accountants, Baker Tilly. The original building was called Fanum House, as were all such offices. It was built in 1934, and replaced in the mid-1980s. The distinctive clock tower, made by Braby, a leading zinc manufacturer in London, was once a feature at the top of this Fanum House building and has been retained on the new structure.

During the Second World War, Fanum House was used for the safe storage of the AA records for the London area, which were housed in a special reinforced air-raid shelter at the rear of the building. In the cellar of the nearby Victorian house, now used by Merrow Interiors, there is shelving marked with the names of AA districts. Either the cellar was used for additional storage, or the shelving was moved after the war.

It could have been very different. In November 1932 the town planners approved the building of a house on part of the site for His Serene Highness

Prince George Imeretinsky. This was also to be used as a restaurant. The private accommodation comprised of five bedrooms on the first floor, with the ground floor being largely a dining room measuring 35ft x 15ft. The house was uninspiring in appearance. Y.J. Lovell & Son of Gerrards Cross were the architects.

Whilst the planning application describes the property as 'restaurant and dwelling house', there was no allowance for a sitting room; indeed, a dressing room attached to a bedroom was marked so that it could alternatively be a sixth bedroom. Had it been completed, it could have become a very early type of motel.

The new by-pass traversing Stoke Park, whilst adequate for 30 years, was not enough to satisfy the growing volume of traffic. This became more and more intrusive until 1981, when the new by-pass from Burpham to the Hogs Back was completed. Only then did the traffic reduce to the currently more acceptable levels on the London Road.

Author's Recollection: I can recall living in digs at Rose Cottage, 178, London Road between 1965 and 1970, not far from the *Anchor and Horseshoe* pub. The traffic noise was continuous. I could tell the time on waking in the morning, be it 7 a.m., 7.30 a.m. or 8 a.m., by the amount of traffic droning past the house. During my stay, vehicle and pedestrian accidents occurred numerous times between that house and the AA Roundabout. On one occasion I arrived home to find a bus in the front garden; the driver had tried to avoid a car in which that driver had suffered a heart attack and died.

On the first weekend home to my parents' house in Sussex, I awoke in the morning to the frightening thought that I must be deaf, for I could hear no sound. Only with the song of a thrush did deliverance come.

9 *The proposed restaurant for H.S.H. Prince George Imeretinsky.*

10   *Stoke Mill.*

The early maps above show the River Wey running north through Guildford, a 'gap town' in the North Downs, and then through Stoke where it starts to meander towards the side of Stoke Park and Stoke Park Farm. Abbotswood was built on the higher ground 60 to 80 feet above the river. Where Stoke Road leads into Woking Road, there has always been a propensity to flood, causing much disruption to travellers. In more recent times, the floods of 1968 saw the river overflow its banks at Woodbridge and Stoke Mill. The more elevated London Road remained clear of this problem.

Three

Historical Foundations

O ne of the delightful aspects of life in any particular spot in the British Isles is that, wherever you are, the visible history around you goes back hundreds of years, and often much more. Abbotswood is no exception. The surrounding history is reflective of a relatively poor rural community. Inevitably this history will be linked to traces of settlements before Christ, but since medieval times the history has been centred on the Parish of Stoke.

It is appropriate to start not at the beginning, but at the turn of the 20th century, when the farm was about to go on the market. The place would have been vastly different from that we see today. The early maps reveal that a bicycle ride from Guildford in 1900, along the London Road towards Abbotswood, would have been enlightening.

Passing the Guildford High School for Girls, a singular and very modern building, the vista of the imposing Stoke Park would have opened on the left. It stretched as far as the river, with the mansion in the far corner where the Guildford College of Further and Higher Education now stands. In the middle of the parkland would have been the mature Peacocks Wood, much as it is today. On the road abutting the park was Glebe Farm and a number of houses, some quite large, including St Margaret's, St Mildred's, and Oak Lodge. These properties would have been considered to have a prime location, overlooking the Stoke Park Mansion and the park.

On the right, surrounding the houses, were fields belonging to Burchatt's Farm. After Boxgrove Road on the right stood the now demolished Gang Hill Farm. At the end of the park on the left were Burchatt's Farm buildings, dating from the 18th century, looking rather more ramshackle than they do today. Two workers' cottages stood against Thorneycrofts wood. Mature trees would be seen at Thorneycrofts and to the north, along each side of the London Road. Stoke Park Farm appeared beyond, on a small hillock on

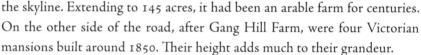

11   *The Victorian mansions along London Road.*

the skyline. Extending to 145 acres, it had been an arable farm for centuries. On the other side of the road, after Gang Hill Farm, were four Victorian mansions built around 1850. Their height adds much to their grandeur.

A little further on were two large detached houses, long since demolished and replaced by flats, followed by Ganghill Copse. At the time the road was not as wide. When Lorraine (39) was built in 1915, abutting the London Road, on the road-side of the boundary fence was a border to the road, 15 feet wide. It was planted with large trees and had an admittedly narrow pathway by the side of the road. Today, the 200-year-old trees stand in the middle of the pavement, indicating that the road has been widened by 12 feet. It remains a single carriageway road, just wide enough for today's lorries, and a cycle lane travelling in each direction. In 1909 it was a mere 15-19 feet wide, rather than the 30 feet of today, and was unlikely to have had a tarmacadam surface.

At the end of this stretch, the fields of New Inn Farm would appear, followed by a smithy, and then an ale house called the *Anchor and Horseshoes*. This name has changed over time, and is thought to reflect the link between the farming community and the river craft. This 17th-century building was not a pub until the mid-1800s. On the left is Weylea Farm, once called Shagden Farm, and then adjacent to this is then Marlyns Farm. On the right would have appeared New Inn Farmhouse, currently the Burpham Surgery. These were not big farms; Weylea Farm comprised 48 acres, and New Inn Farm 106 acres.

12   *The trees win outside Abbotswood.*

13 *New Inn Farm.*

Some two hundred yards further on, the traveller would have arrived at a cross roads where the *Green Man* inn is situated on the left. This site for a pub dates back to 1593, but the present building is mainly Victorian. The right lane went towards Merrow, and the left to Worplesdon, and Burpham Court Farm. Further farms appear on the London Road after the cross roads, with Bowers Farm on the left, and Winterhill and Gosden Hill Farms on the right.

There would have been no shops and no school, just St Luke's chapel and a few cottages around the area. Burpham was but a hamlet; it was a poor rural community with labour-intensive farming, and no obvious signs of wealth. It was not yet a village in the truest sense of the word.

An 1896 map places the local blacksmith's forge where the office of Guildford Signs now stands. Examination of the existing floor reveals where the anvil once stood. During the replacement of a drive at Rose Cottage next door, the rings by which the horses were tethered were uncovered.

The 18th century had brought danger to those voyaging far from their homes. Not only did Hindhead have its highwaymen hanged by the roadside, but so did Abbotswood.

On 26 August 1776 James Potter, highwayman, met his end, along with two other felons, Christopher Ellis, a burglar, and Frederick William Gregg, convicted of robbery with violence. Potter had been a coachman who lived at the *White Hart Inn*, and was convicted of robbing William Calvet of 11 guineas and his watch. It was reported that 'They were conveyed in a cart to

Ganghill Common from a jail at 11 o'clock where they continued to pray for half an hour. They all behaved penetant and were turned off'.

Some believe that the word 'Ganghill' originated from this villainous trio, but it was around long before. Other theories include the possibility that 'gang' referred to villains who generally troubled travellers on the road, or gangs that would push carriages out of the mud at the incline at this point. The real meaning has been lost over time.

STOKE PARISH

Any English community would have had a life centred on the church. Near the church the house of the gentry would normally be found, in this case Stoke Park Mansion. Life centred around these two elements of the village for hundreds of years. A community such as this would have seen the vast majority working in the fields for six days a week, and most would attend church on Sunday, paying due reverence to God and their masters.

The name Stoke derives from the word 'stoc' meaning place, and it is thought that this could relate to a defensive place. The parish was split in two by the River Wey; hence it ended up with two manors, Stoke and Stoughton. It is thought possible that Stoke was an early Christian centre, and the Stoke church stood on a royal manor, and predates the first Guildford parish church of St Mary's, the tower of which was built around 1050. However, the experts at Guildford museum believe that there might have been a wooden church as early as A.D. 700 on the site of St Mary's.

Domesday Book confirms the existence of the parish of Stoke and its being of Saxon origin, noting that Stoke once belonged to Edward the Confessor. However, there is no evidence of a Saxon building, and the church, St John the Evangelist, is of 14th-century origin. King William later held the whole

14 *St John the Evangelist, Stoke-next-Guildford.*

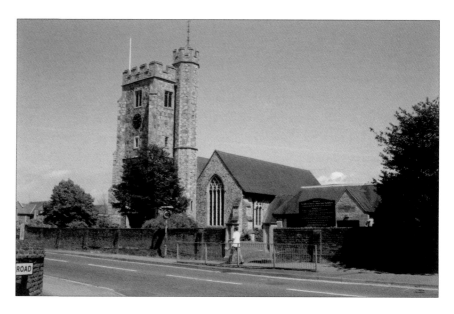

of Stoke, at a value of £15, including the church and the mills. These early records show that most of Stoke parish was arable land, and it stayed that way until the end of the 19th century. From 1615, the manorial courts were held at Court Close adjoining the church parsonage.

The parish stretched from Warren Farm in the south, on a line to Ganghill in the east, to Slyfield and Stringer's Common in the north, and across Stoughton to Chitt's Common in the west. Before 1835, the boundaries went into Guildford centre, almost reaching the Royal Grammar School. After the Municipal Corporations Act in 1835, that part of Stoke parish nearest the town became Stoke-within-Guildford. It was known as that until the Guildford borough Extension Order of 1904, when Stoke-within-Guildford became Christchurch Ward.

In theory at least, the Extension Order saw the end of the references to Stoke-next-Guildford, as Stoke was brought within the Borough of Guildford. Nevertheless, house deeds and other official documents contained references to Stoke-next-Guildford for many years thereafter. Even as late as the conveyance dated 16 April 1935 for The Croft (4), the property was described as being 'situate in the Parish of Stoke-next-Guildford'.

Stoke parish benefited greatly from the work of the Paynter family. The first of the family to hold the title of rector was Samuel Paynter, from 1831. The living had been purchased for him by his father, Francis, a wealthy London merchant.

Samuel's son, also named Francis, was ordained in 1861 and took over from his father to become rector of Stoke in 1862. At that time there were 3,797 parishioners, up from only 788 when his father began as rector 30 years before. The parish population continued to expand rapidly and in 1987 had reached fourteen thousand. Francis Paynter decided that the best way to take the strain off his church was to build a chapel in Waterden Road, now Christ Church. The foundation stone was laid in 1868, and it was consecrated as a chapel of ease. The church was not fully completed until Francis Paynter retired in 1896 and donated £600 for the tower to be constructed.

Church-building in the parish continued. In 1876 a temporary iron church was built in Woodbridge Road, called St Saviours, and in 1881 Emmanuel was constructed in Stoughton, also as an iron structure. In 1899 St Saviours was consecrated, and Mrs Paynter laid the foundation stone of the permanent church in 1902. Francis was also involved in education, and in 1887 requested Mrs Morton to start what is now the Girls High School. This was initially in the Parish Hall at Haydon Place, and soon moved to the London Road, where it still stands, much enlarged, today.

Long before Christianity, much worked flint from the Stone Age was deposited around the area where the Guildford fire station is at Ladymead. There is yet further evidence of very early history on Weylea Farm. The River Wey was very slow running and the land beside it in the valley was marshy and susceptible to frequent flooding. This will have meant that the nearest dry land was on the higher slopes at the western edge of the recently built Weylea Estate where it is closest to the A3 – at this point there was a settlement for early Britons where they made pottery from the local clay.

Later came the Romans. Their burial ground was also nearby, approximately where Pimms Row stands today. In 1897 Romano-British pottery and other artefacts were discovered on the slopes overlooking the river to the west of Pimm's Close, just 400 yards from the boundary at Abbotswood. In writing the history of Burpham, Roger Marjoribanks comments that: 'It is likely that the remains of a small villa lie buried in the soil not far away'. He further comments that: 'It was probably defensible, for when the Saxons arrived in the 6th century A.D., they called the place Burh-ham (m), which means either "Fortification Hamlet" or "Fort in the Water Meadow."'

> *Author's Recollection*: Despite the disadvantages of the busy London Road, when in digs at Rose Cottage in 1965, I well remember that Abbotswood lay between the open space of Stoke Park, and the fields of Weylea Farm where the combine-harvesters would cut the corn in the summer with their lights blazing across the fields, lighting up the trees around them.

Towards the end of the 19th century, brick-making started as a small industry using local clay. Brickfields were to be found in the grounds of New Inn Farm along New Inn Lane, and Winterhill Farm, as well as Slyfield, a short distance away across the river. Little wonder that the deeds of the houses in Abbotswood include a covenant stating that: 'No bricks or tiles shall at any time be burnt or made nor any clay or lime burnt on the land …' These covenants were introduced by Taylor, and were carried through to the other deeds of subsequent purchasers, reflecting his wish that the estate should not be turned into a brickworks.

Before leaving this associated history of Burpham, it is worth noting that until St Luke's church was built in 1859, the villagers had to travel to Worplesdon for worship each Sunday. During the winter, flooding at Jacobs Well caused problems and eventually the time came for the folk of Burpham to have their own church and graveyard. Initially it was a chapel of ease attached to Worplesdon. In 1920 a new parish combining Burpham and Sutton Green was created, and St Luke's became the parish church in 1954.

The Wey Navigation

From the houses in Abbotswood, the River Wey can be seen next to the Navigation – both are important historical features of the area. The term 'navigation' refers to a combination of locks and cuttings to make a river more navigable, rather than a canal which is the creation of a new waterway between two places. The Navigation was built by Sir Richard Weston who lived in Sutton Place, possibly the greatest Tudor house in Surrey, situated but a mile from Abbotswood. It was built on the site of an earlier house in the 1520s by his great-grandfather, also called Sir Richard Weston, and a favourite courtier of Henry VIII. The king was a frequent visitor and some claim that it was there that he first met Anne Boleyn. Importantly, Sutton Place was, and indeed is, one of the finest early brick houses in England.

The equally famous 'running river' was built a few years before the Navigation. Because the River Wey was slow and meandering through marshland north of Stoke, this resulted in an abundance of nourishing alluvial mud. Conversely, down river, Sir Richard's land at Sutton Place was of fairly poor soil, comprising mainly of Bagshot sand. He decided to cut the 'running river' through to his land and thus irrigate his estate bringing both added water plus increased sustenance. In 1618 he obtained a 1,000-year lease of lands at Stoke from Sir George Stoughton for the purpose.

To create the running river, between 1618 and 1620 Weston constructed a channel eight feet wide and 4½ feet deep, and three miles long between Stoke Mills and Sutton Place. This was a great success. In the winter months, water was allowed to overflow and flood water meadows on the Sutton Estate, which meant that he could now grow annually an additional 200 loads of hay in meadows watered by the 'new' river. The course of this great ditch has been lost but it crossed the valley where Slyfield Estate stands today. This was the first step towards the 'Navigation'.

In the 17th century, the roads were poor, and badly affected by adverse weather. The local clay and sand made travel very difficult, if not impossible. At the time, London was expanding rapidly and Richard Weston, who had

15 *Sutton Place and Stoke Lock.*

inherited Sutton Place in 1613, recognised that matters must improve if Guildford and the surrounding area were to get goods up to the City to meet the growing demand.

The second great project was underway by 1635 when Sir Richard created a lock on the river at Stoke with the intention of making the river navigable all the way to the Thames. After a delay caused by the Civil War he persuaded his influential contacts to pass an Act of Parliament on 26 June 1651 '… for Making Navigable the River of Wye'. Parliament agreed to this partly because of a need to get gunpowder from the Chilworth Mills to the Thames arsenals – it would prove to be quicker, cheaper, and safer than by road. The only similar structure to precede it was the Exeter canal, built in 1552. However, the Surrey canal was the larger with 12 locks over 10 miles, costing over £15,000, and achieved at great speed. It took only 2½ years to complete and was a major influence on the building of the great industrial canals.

Sir Richard died before the completion of the canal in 1653. Despite the enormous debt created by the cost of the venture, which his son George had the dubious privilege of clearing, his legacy immediately helped the locality join in the new found prosperity of the suppliers to the London markets. Its usefulness as a trade link was only overtaken by the coming of the railways in the mid-19th century but, until the 1930s, goods were still a feature on the Navigation. The 'Wey Navigation' is still used today by many pleasure craft.

Thus was the history of the area up to the point that Alfred Taylor purchased Stoke Park Farm. It had largely been a quiet and uncomplicated rural environment, little altered for centuries. That way of life was soon to disappear.

Between 1909 and 1925, the time Abbotswood was designed and built, there was to be a period of immeasurable change for the British Isles. It covered the end of the Edwardian period, the butchery of the First World War and the uncertainties of the post-war years. The car, and motorised transport generally, were to become more and more important. So, too, was the development of the social state, and the more complex way that people ran their lives. The deference that servants had towards their employers, and that which women had towards men, would fast disappear.

In 1913, when the first residents moved to Abbotswood, Guildford would have been described as a significant market town, indeed, a county town with a court of justice known as the assizes, which were held at the Guildhall in the High Street. It generated more industry through the Dennis Brothers factory than most such rural towns. John and Raymond Dennis started to build bicycles in 1895, progressing to motorised tricycles. In 1901 they built the world's first car factory at Onslow Street. The business expanded with the construction of buses from 1903 and, from 1908, fire engines.

The town had its fair share of both Tudor and Jacobean properties as well as Victorian terraced houses, although on nothing like the scale seen in the industrial north of England. The need for most people to walk to and from work had largely kept the building of houses within the town boundaries.

Economic growth and more sophisticated needs created a demand for houses of a standard to reflect the status of the emerging middle classes. The houses needed to be big enough for the family and servants, with modern conveniences, and be near enough to places of work, allowing for the improved transport services available.

Where there was room to build houses in the town, these were invariably on a small plot, restricting architectural flair. Abbotswood, however, and the houses to come later in Fairway, Trodds Lane and Ganghill would reflect a countryside ideal. The theory was that a middle-class man saw himself as someone who was unfortunate not to have his own seat in the countryside, and as a substitute wished for something to reflect a small Tudor yeoman's house – this thinking was also reflected in the houses of the Arts and Crafts Movement; an organisation promoted by William Morris which sought to bring back the ideals of the countryside, and is described in Chapter 8. Houses would reflect the past, using the methods of craftsmen rather than machine-made features. Some of the architects following this idiom used the Surrey style of house in order to augment this process; Taylor and Burlingham were to provide houses that more or less satisfied those ideals.

The Abbotswood houses built before the First World War would be built to the highest standards and be large and imposing, exclaiming the wealth of their new owners. They would have all the modern conveniences of running water, mains sewerage, gas and electricity. Even telephones would be available. In contrast, Clandon House, in West Clandon, the home of the Lords Onslow, had neither a bath for servants nor electricity until 1913. Some smaller houses were still being built with the assumption that the inhabitants would fill a metal hip bath in the kitchen in front of the fire for the weekly bath-time. In most towns there were public baths and wash rooms available for those who wished to use them.

War and economics would affect the development of Abbotswood; as the First World War progressed, building work slowed and finally ceased in 1916 and no new planning applications were made until 1920. Afterwards, there followed economic uncertainties, and this can be detected in the size of the properties, and the materials used. The plots of land used were smaller, and for the first time a number of bungalows were built. This was partly because the government was to stimulate the building of houses by offering very generous grants after this period of great uncertainty.

From the early 1920s, encouraged by the government, the building of the urban sprawl was to commence and continue up until the Second World War. Many council houses were built by local governments for renting to the masses, supported by central government grants. The rate of house-building grew to such an extent that house prices for owner-occupiers began to fall.

The economy started to recover slowly, but soon headed downhill towards the great depression. The positive images of playing tennis and dancing, so commonly seen in the 1920 movies, was a short-term illusion. Fortunately, the Abbotswood created by Burlingham was completed before the growing economic problems with the General Strike of 1926, building up to the 1929 Wall Street crash. By this time he had turned his attention to other areas of Guildford, including Orchard Road, Merrow Downs Estate, Ganghill, and finally Boxgrove Estate. The glory days of the large houses designed by Burlingham and built by Taylor in Abbotswood were, by then, long over.

During the 1920s Burlingham's designs continued to reflect the need for servants, and additionally, the use of cars. Many motor houses were built for the early owners of the houses, and from 1923 some were integral to the design, when the properties were still of four or five bedrooms, but less grand than pre-war. The houses still reflected the Arts and Crafts style with the use of the craftsman's skills in constructing handmade front doors, the heart shaped window catches in leaded casements, pegged woodwork, tile cladding and Tudor-style half-timbered overhangs.

The Abbotswood houses always reflected an era when the woman of the house entertained frequently, using the drawing room and the dining room. The kitchen was primarily for the staff. Today, houses are built for the family to live mostly in the kitchen and television rooms.

In 1909, few middle-class women went to work. They were not expected to be in business, go to university, or even have the vote – they were there to look after their men folk and control the household, and above all bear children. Fortunately, the Victorian era was now over, when, due to the high child mortality rates, women could expect to be in the throes of childbirth for most of their adult lives. The average number of children in a family fell from 5.8 in 1871 to 2.2 in 1930 – the health of the new born was improving with better diets, healthcare and living conditions.

Had a woman wanted to work, or been forced to do so in order to put food on the table, she would normally have been in service, or had a menial job in a business but infrequently in banking or insurance. As an example, Midland Bank Limited, the fourth largest bank in the world at the time, employed its first woman in 1907, as an interpreter. Others were employed from 1912, mainly as typists. The First World War was to change all that.

In August 1914 the ration strength of the army was just 164,000, later rising to a staggering peak of 5,363,352. Because so many men were at war, from around 1916 women became key workers in factories making equipment and munitions and their appetite to earn good money grew. The roles of women in the professions such as teaching and medicine were also to accelerate from this point. Sadly, women were the long-term replacement for a generation of young men lost on the battlefields of Europe.

This irreversible liberalisation of women had started, but its progress would be slow. For example, the deeds seen for the houses in Abbotswood invariably describe the ladies as 'wife of …', even when acting not as a principal but as a signature to a witness. Conversely, a significant number of houses were owned solely by the wife.

Most houses in Abbotswood had one servant's bedroom, some had more. Bell pushes were available to call staff, and there was invariably a tradesman's entrance gate. For the gardener and the servant, usually a living-in maid, there was a toilet accessed from the outside. In the bungalows the servant's bedroom would be reached through the scullery, whilst those for the householder were accessed from the hallway. Status was everything.

Even in lesser houses, where a lowly clerk earned little more than an artisan at perhaps £200 p.a., his aspirations to status were such that he endeavoured to afford to maintain a servant for cleaning and cooking at £20-5 p.a. The higher paid would demand more, and had servants living in at perhaps £50 p.a. The expectation that servants would live below stairs was disappearing by the turn of the century, and more often than not larger houses were designed with specific rooms for servants on the ground and upper floors.

From the 1920s fewer houses had a living-in servant and the role of the daily help emerged – houses were to be built to be more manageable and needing less help from servants. Household appliances such as the vacuum cleaner, along with the refrigerator and washing machine, were coming to the aid of the housewife.

In 1909 house ownership was far less common than it is today; only 10 per cent owned their own homes. Mortgages were obtainable, and had been for years. Often developers would rent out the properties they constructed, and finance the houses long term themselves or sell them to others for renting. A problem was the freezing of the level of interest that lenders could charge, and more importantly, the level of rents landlords could charge under the 1915 Rents Act which kept levels to pre-war figures.

Examination of the deeds of the 14 houses built in Abbotswood before hostilities forced curtailment reveals that initially few were sold and instead many were rented out. This was most likely due to a lack of interest by prospective buyers, rather than Taylor wishing to remain the landlord. Only three houses were sold as complete, and four were sold as a plot and built-out on a commission basis. Seven were rented until buyers could be found.

House Name	Date of Planning Consent	Date of Sale
Churston (5)	December 1912	January 1913 – as a plot, for £100
Aoetearoa (7)	December 1912	July 1913
Hazlewood (2)	September 1913	April 1914
Gate House (1)*	September 1913	March 1919
Lorraine (39)*	December 1913	April 1915
Friars Oak (40)*	December 1913	December 1918
The Hurst (146)*	December 1913	July 1925
Hestercombe (47)*	March 1914	July 1924
Upmeads (49)*	March 1914	September 1923
The Cottage (6)	November 1914	January 1913 – as a plot, for £100
The Croft (4)	March 1915	February 1915 – as a plot
Littlefield (9)	June 1915	June 1915 – as a plot
Sunnymead (22)	January 1916	November 1916
The Lair (26)*	January 1916	May 1918

* Rented

There seems little doubt that this stock of houses would have put an immense strain on Taylor's finances, leading to a reluctance to build more before the post-war government grants became available. Building lower priced bungalows would seem the sensible thing to do in an uncertain market. His capital expenditure would be reduced, and the ability to move into a prestigious area at less cost would certainly attract buyers. This seemed to be the correct solution, because following the first planning application for bungalows sanctioned in April 1920, all seven Abbotswood bungalows had been built and sold by July 1921. He then returned to the building of prestigious houses.

Subsequently, most houses were sold directly to purchasers, or as plots, with the purchaser building out either using Burlingham and Stanley, or, as happened at Eaglehurst (31) and the three 1930s properties, with someone else carrying out the design and building work.

Travelling to and from town, for work or pleasure, would get much easier. With improved motorised transport and trains that were efficient and plentiful, a home in the country while working in London was a reality. The Abbotswood houses were to meet the needs of a variety of people, the wealthy retired, the local professional and city types.

As the first residents arrived in Abbotswood in 1913, the car was still in its infancy, but its importance would grow quickly. Ten years previously, not many wanted to live a mile from town, indeed in the countryside, with the inconvenience of having to use a horse-drawn bus service, or cab. The motorised versions were to change all that; so, too, would the use of the telephone to call for a taxi.

The new owners would be expected to be of a standing that meant that they were soon likely to be able to afford a car. Cars were very expensive, costing around £200 for an ordinary car to over £1,000 for a superior make. Most cars cost more than a medium-sized house in town; therefore Burlingham normally did not include a garage in his earliest plans.

The demand for the motor car was about to take off. In 1909 there were just 45,000 cars on the roads, which then comprised of a compound of stones, dirt and manure. In dry weather, dust was a major factor. By 1913, this figure had rapidly risen to 140,000. August 1913 saw the last horse-drawn bus through the City of London, thanks to firms such as Dennis Motors.

Figures from the Automobile Association indicate that there are approximately 26 million cars in 2008; this equates to about 185 cars for every one in 1914. Assuming that there are 3,000 cars parking spaces in central Guildford today, this equates to only 16 parking spaces being required at that time.

As more traffic came, so the problems began. There were 1,328 fatal car accidents in 1914 which meant that on average one in every 100 cars was involved in such an accident!

Author's Recollection: Perhaps this amazing statistic is not that far out. A group family wedding photograph taken on 15 September 1909, showing my grandparents as bride and groom, is inscribed on the reverse 'The reason that they look glum is that one of the party when driving to the wedding in a car, hit and killed a pedestrian'. Two weeks later the Earl of Onslow sold Stoke Park Farm to A.G. Taylor.

16 *The Edwardian wedding.*

Reflective of this period, there was formed the Abbotswood Sketching Club. The club was founded in 1923 by Mr and Mrs Elliott Kitchener, who lived at Iomhar (32), Iris Savage, and General A.A. Garstin, C.M.G.

Mr Kitchener, a first cousin of Lord Kitchener, was the first hon. secretary. The club held its first exhibition at the Stoke Institute in 1925, which was opened by a great supporter of the Arts and Crafts Movement, Mary Watts, the widow of the painter G.F. Watts.

The members developed the idea of forming an art society in the town. Consequently, they asked two well-known local artists, Max Ludby R.I. and Victor Barnard A.R.C.A., who was an instructor at the Technical College, if they would like to join. Thus the first meeting of the self-constituted committee was held on 11 June 1926; thenceforth it became known as the Guildford Art Society. Exhibitions were often held in the same building as the Assizes, and on one occasion the venue for the Assizes was re-arranged to make way for the exhibition. During November 2007 the Society held its 75th annual exhibition in Guildford House.

The membership lists in the exhibition catalogues of the 1920s name Elliott Kitchener as the hon. secretary, and Mrs Kitchener as a committee member. This continued until 1929, when Elliott died. Mrs Kitchener, joined by Miss Madge Kitchener, remained a member into the 1930s. They were in good company, for the list of members included two local architects – Annesley Brownrigg and a certain Sir Edwin Lutyens, both of whom exhibited.

Finally, an advertisement in the *Guildford Street Directory* of 1916, for the King Edward VI's Royal Grammar School, lists the fees:

> Entrance fee 5/-, Sports fee 2/6, Term fees £3 6s 8d for Boys under 12, and £4 for Boys over 12.

How times have changed.

Four

A Garden Suburb

Should you take a walk around Guildford today, the familiar pattern of most long established towns will soon emerge. At the centre is the all-important river, in this case the River Wey, which was the foundation for early defence and used for the transport of goods. At the foot of the Downs, above the river, is the Saxon church, and a Norman castle. As you move up the High Street, laid with 19th-century granite setts, you will find evidence of medieval dwellings, and also Tudor, Jacobean, and Queen Anne houses. Moving out from the centre you will come across several rows of Victorian houses. Edwardian houses are found as infillings and sometimes extending to whole roads. A visit to York Road reveals fine examples of late Victorian and Edwardian buildings.

Sadly, the structure of Guildford, like that of many similar towns, has succumbed to the demands for more and more accommodation, until now, when there is a featureless blur with just the odd aspiration to good taste, such as Onslow Village. What will our children's children think of the many large estates around the town and the general over-crowding?

There are some better-structured developments known as the Garden Suburbs of Guildford, including Guildown, Warwicks Bench, Abbotswood (including Ganghill), Fairway and Trodds Lane. These are fully described in a work commissioned by Guildford Borough Council in 2006 entitled *Guildford Landscape Character Assessment*. The purpose of this was to identify different areas around the town and to address issues with regard to the environment and landscape. This document highlights the importance of the Arts and Crafts style of architecture for Guildford and also provides a link to those suburbs around London, and in particular Hampstead Garden Suburb.

The garden suburb movement is an important part of the urban scene for British architecture in late Victorian times and well into the 20th century. It took two overriding forms. Firstly, it was a reaction of the owners of great

17   The Abbotswood
entrance, 1920s.

businesses to the need to house employees in better accommodation so that they were fit for work. They were finding that the squalid living conditions of the workers led to illness which in turn led to poor output. Also, employees often had to work miles away from their homes, and nearby accommodation helped towards better performance at work. Sometimes, Victorian philanthropists simply sought better accommodation for the poor. Secondly, there were those who recognised the demand from the more wealthy for housing some way out of town, if not quite in the countryside then away from the Victorian squalor. These were the entrepreneurs wishing to satisfy the needs of the middle classes.

The most famous of the workers' housing schemes was that created by Cadbury, the Quaker family, famous for chocolate product manufacture in the West Midlands. They started to build Bournville Village on 140 acres of land near their factory in 1895. The early houses had drainage and running water but did not feature bathrooms.

Before the construction of Bournville Village in 1888, Lord Leverhulme had built Port Sunlight for the workers of his soap factory. This site was also of 140 acres, and over a 20-year period tree lined roads were established with formal gardens. Houses were built in various styles, including those of Queen Anne, Neo-Georgian and Domestic Revival. All had front and rear gardens and bathrooms. Joseph Rowntree, a confectioner and philanthropist established New Earswick, just north of York, in 1902 on a 150-acre site, building mainly three-bedroom houses.

Many other employers built properties for their employees and in Guildford we can also see housing of this ilk. In 1915, Dennis Motors created Dennisville, south of the factory on the present A3 by-pass. It comprised mainly Raymond Crescent and St Johns Road. In 1936 a further 50 houses were built on Bannister's Farm.

In a more altruistic vein, in 1862, Dr Thomas Sells commissioned Henry Peak to lay out Charlotteville, named after his wife, which was a mixed development of artisan cottages and comfortable detached buildings. This is to be found in Guildford, comprising the roads off the lower end of Harvey Road. Some of these are named after medical pioneers such as Jenner, Bright, Addison and Harvey. The Charlotteville Board School, opened in 1886, is now used as an adult education centre.

The first of Guildford's council houses were be built in Charlotteville at Cline Road, in 1906. Rents for each of the 18 homes was six shillings and three pence a week, or 31p in today's terms. In 1912, a further 20 homes were added.

After the First World War the need for more housing was intense. With the recognition that houses were needed for rent, and eventual ownership by the residents, Lord Onslow sold 646 acres to create what is now Onslow Village. The sale price of the land was just 25 per cent of the true value, at £57 an acre, and building started in 1920 and continued into the 1930s – eventually 450 dwellings were built on the estate, largely in an informal vernacular style which emanated from the Arts and Crafts Movement.

It is the second reason for development, the need to provide homes for the middle classes, that was to be of significance for Abbotswood. This involved the creation of the Garden Cities and Garden Suburbs. The Cities were intended to become self supporting, but the Suburbs were normally an adjunct to larger towns, where, in times of improved transport, people could use the area as a dormitory and travel to work, returning each evening to their own piece of countryside, away from the smells and noise of the city.

Whilst there are many such developments, the most famous are Bedford Park, Letchworth, and Hampstead.

Bedford Park was started in the 1870s by Jonathan Carr, who purchased 24 acres on the edge of Bedford. His intention was to create an ideal for both artisans and professionals. Richard Norman Shaw (1831-1912), hereafter referred to as Norman Shaw or just Shaw, was the principal architect for the 500 houses, many reflecting a Queen Anne style. The density of housing, at 20 houses to the acre, meant that it was a change from the rows of normal Victorian terraced houses directly abutting the road in city centres where 40 to the acre was accepted. Thus it was far from the plans of later spacious garden suburbs.

Letchworth, in Hertfordshire, was built on a much larger scale on a site purchased by the Garden City Association in 1903. Under the direction of Raymond Unwin, houses were built in a vernacular old English style with wide tree-lined roads and their own community buildings. This very much reflected the ideas of Ebenezer Howard who envisaged a reversal of the exodus of people from the countryside to the town following the 1870s agricultural depression. He wanted to see developments in the countryside of around six thousand acres and inhabitants of up to 32,000 people. He envisaged towns designed with small industry, and workers living in good accommodation nearby, with the wealthy occupying larger houses at the periphery, all supported by schools and shops.

Hampstead Garden Suburb was the brainchild of the philanthropist Dame Henrietta Barnett, the wife of Canon Samuel Barnett of Toynbee Hall. The development is situated to the north of London, on the edge of Hampstead Heath. Dame Henrietta envisaged that the artisans would live alongside the more prosperous middle-class householders, and that housing would be laid out with generous gardens and wide spaced avenues, and would cluster around the community's centre of churches and educational institutes.

Raymond Unwin was appointed as the town planner and Edwin Lutyens the consulting architect. Unwin indeed gave Hampstead wide and winding tree lined roads, which were designed to present a series of street pictures. Existing trees and field landscapes were carefully preserved within the plan. Housing density was to be no more than eight to the acre and the houses were to be surrounded by hedge-lined gardens. These Arts and Crafts style properties were constructed from 1906 to the 1930s. The house designers also included Philip Webb and Charles Voysey.

Some houses were grand and imposing, and others were roughcast semi-detached properties. The Lutyens Trust records that Sir Edwin Lutyens was responsible for the design of 54 listed houses in the period 1910-12 of which 12 are in North Square and of the Queen Anne style. He also designed the two churches, and a number of the public buildings. Lutyens emphasised that the roads should be laid down in such a way that the churches were a distant focal point for those travelling along them. Another legacy is his design for the houses of working-class tenants, in that he made them look much bigger than they actually were, either by concealing doors at the sides, or having a central porch for two houses.

Many more such suburbs were planned and constructed around the country in the early part of the 20th century. It can be argued that this desire to build for both the artisans and the middle classes, and to encompass the rustic charms of the countryside through both the estate planning and the houses designs, created a reality closer to the dreams of the Arts and Crafts originators than the over-priced single houses of the likes of Lutyens, which are so often presented as epitomising the Movement.

The document produced for the Guildford Borough Council describes the key characteristics of Guildford's garden suburbs in some detail:

 ❧ Spacious suburbs developed during the late 19th century and the first half of the 20th century.

 ❧ Individual houses on large garden plots are set along gently winding streets and private roads with wide grass verges.

- The houses within each area are largely consistent in scale, materials and spacing with minor variations to style layout and detailing.

- The influence of the Arts and Crafts Movement is visible in outstanding individual houses and gardens but also in design principles of individualism and handcrafted local materials.

- Buildings are of brick, and render. Tile, timber frame and occasionally stone are used to reflect a vernacular style.

- Plots are enclosed predominantly by hedges and mature trees creating a secluded rural character; grassed verges and mature street trees reinforce this.

- Entrances to the areas are clearly signified by the transition to private, unmarked roads, and occasionally by purpose-built gateways.

- A private landscape with a general lack of public open spaces, landmarks and focal points.

- Some areas are based on dramatic topography exploiting rural views over the North Downs or greensand hills, while the more level areas have corridor views down roads that are framed by hedges and trees.

- Front gardens form the main visual element in the landscape with some enclosed by well kept hedges while others provide a setting for the street with open lawns and decorative planting.

Referring specifically to the Guildford area, Guildown and Warwicks Bench are cited as two of the earlier areas and are noted as featuring the Surrey style created by outstanding designers working around Guildford at the time such as Mackay Hugh Baillie Scott (hereafter referred to as Baillie Scott), Edwin Lutyens, Roger Fry, and a garden by Gertrude Jekyll.

18 *The Abbotswood Entrance today.*

19   *Raised flower beds.*

20   *The Ganghill entrance with turrets and piers.*

21   *The ivy covered entrance at Fairway (above and below).*

Abbotswood is singled out as having a distinctive purpose-built gateway, designed by the architect to the estate, Claude Burlingham.

Whilst it is not readily apparent today, the archways in Abbotswood led not only to a tree-lined avenue, planted mainly by the developers, but also to raised flower beds along the side of the road. These were full of shrubs, creating a true garden effect. The demise of gardeners with time to spare has left the edges with low cut grass, and broken pieces of York stone along the pavement edges. At least the raised bed at 'the triangle', where the post box is to be found, still merits the occasional titivation, and has recently been enhanced by the planting of Spring bulbs.

The entrance at Abbotswood is built largely of brick, with stone bases and plinths; that at Ganghill includes Bargate stone, similar to that at the renowned Tigbourne Court, on the Petworth Road at Warmley. This house was designed by Lutyens and built around 1900, long before the Ganghill archways were constructed in 1929. The general construction and the use of horizontal roof tiles in the walls, leads one to suspect that Tigbourne might have inspired Burlingham.

The entrance to the third estate, Fairway, at first sight appears less attractive. Currently it is covered in ivy, and the knapped flint construction is difficult to see. It has been said that, in exchange for allowing the Guildford Council to take some of his land to widen the road, Burlingham persuaded them to build an entrance to his design. The story went that he submitted drawings, which the council let through 'on the nod', but without studying them and fully appreciating that the entrance extended some distance along the road, making walls for the houses all along their roadside perimeters.

The removal of the ivy and bushes would restore the structure to that envisaged by Burlingham back in 1929.

For Abbotswood, the planning consent for the first roads was given in early 1913, and it is likely that the archway's construction was incorporated within that consent, and that they were built soon after. As early as 1915 the semicircular walls appear on the deeds to various properties.

The construction features a brick asymmetrical semi-circular ornamental wall, dissected by the road. Two arches straddle the pavements either side of the road. The central columns have plinths of Bath stone with acorn shaped toppings carved with leaves. The word 'Abbotswood' is carved in stone on each pillar, surrounded by a wreath not dissimilar to that found on a gable at The Hurst (46). The corners are made up of plain red bricks, in the same manner as the Hestercombe (47) and Upmeads (49).

By 1992 repairs were required to remedy damage due to weathering and vibration from passing traffic. The archways had developed cracks at the spandrels, the caps on the pillars had been badly corroded by frost damage and cracks in

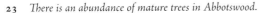

23 *There is an abundance of mature trees in Abbotswood.*

22 *The Abbotswood name in a garland of fruit and flowers.*

the side walls necessitated replacement of broken bricks, and re-pointing. Guildford Borough Council donated £1,000 towards the overall cost of £5,800. The balance was paid for by the owners of 71 out of the 107 properties on the estate.

The foot of the town-side pillar was cosmetically repaired with paste where the stone had started to fall away – this proved to be unsatisfactory, and the Bath stone was replaced at a cost of £3,038 in 2004, financed by contributions from 68 households.

The Name 'Abbotswood'

Having established that the estate is a garden suburb, one can but wonder how the name Abbotswood came about.

One would like to think that the name 'Abbotswood' dated back to ownership by the famous son of Guildford, George Abbot (1562-1633), who was the Archbishop of Canterbury from 1611-33. He was a former pupil at the Edward VI Grammar School, and one of the translators of the King James Authorised version of the Bible, which is still used today, and founded The Hospital of the Blessed Trinity, also known as the Abbot's Hospital in 1619. However, the Abbotswood name was a 20th-century creation.

The first planning application for the estate was submitted in December 1912, and referred to Stoke Park Farm, London Road. Later applications refer to 'Stoke Park Farm Estate'.

The earliest recording of the name Abbotswood appears in 1914 on the planning application for The Cottage (6).

The maps described above do not evidence woodland prior to 1812 – the part of Abbotswood fronting the London Road was known as Gangle Common, and was doubtlessly used by villagers for grazing livestock until the 1789 and 1791 Enclosure Acts.

The Court Book refers to the Act of Parliament commenting that this was 'an Act for enclosing by the mutual consent of the Lord and tenants part of any commons for the purpose of planting and preserving trees for Timber and Underwood and for the more effectually preventing the unlawful destruction of trees'. As a result, the owner of Stoke Park, William Aldersley, was able to progress his ambition to create a park with trees that would grow to maturity. To this end he planted the large clump of trees still at the centre of Stoke Park today, and extended the planting at Thorneycrofts, and to the east at Boxgrove, and north along each side of the London Road towards Ganghill Copse.

It must have impressed visitors from London who had to drive through this swathe of woodland, belonging to Aldersley, on the way to Stoke Park Mansion. His good work was carried on by his successor, Nathaniel Hillier.

An early plan of Lorraine (39) shows a hedge cutting through the middle of the plot. Comparing this with the maps of 1896 and 1914 would indicate

that this was the edge of the strip of woodland. The Hurst (46), Hestercombe (47), and Lorraine (39) were all built in the original wood, which amounted to an area of 5.08 acres.

For the remainder of the original estate, there is no doubt that, save for a small strip at the back of 17, 18, and 19 Abbotswood, the land was entirely arable when building work commenced. The rusting pieces of horse harness and horseshoes sometimes found when digging in the gardens support this comment.

Most of the larger trees in the older gardens are at a maximum age of 90 years. The gardens of the Westward Ho properties and those of Abbotswood Close, have few trees of great age. Many of these houses were built on the site of orchards in private gardens, which were part of the horticultural scene in the 1920s. As further evidence, the sales literature for Red Cottage (37), detailed later, has a photograph of the property which features newly planted eight-foot-tall pine trees. Those trees are now mature and are today protected by a tree preservation order.

Taking matters in another direction, we know that Burlingham came from Evesham, and there in the 1920s he designed eight houses on a small estate, also called Abbotswood. This was long after the 'Surrey' Abbotswood was started. Not far from Evesham there is a junction on the Oxford, Worcester and Wolverhampton railway line, constructed in 1850 and called Abbotswood Junction. Noting that Burlingham was a train enthusiast, it would painful to think that this fine estate in Guildford was named after a railway junction.

Instead, the name 'Abbotswood' was doubtlessly created in order to encompass both a reference to a popular Guildford figure, and the fact that part of the estate was indeed a wood, and that the developers were intending to encourage the woodland image for following generations.

Five

Stoke Park Farm and Stoke Park Mansion

Perhaps the most endearing features about Abbotswood, and the Merrow Downs Estate, as Fairway, Downsway, and Trodds Lane were originally named, are the existence of the original farm houses. Stoke Park Farm dates back, in parts to medieval times, and Hall Place Farm to the Jacobean era. Both are rich with original features. This book is primarily about Abbotswood, and therefore Stoke Park Farm deserves close examination. After all, the registered deeds of every Abbotswood house relate back to this one property.

The name of the farm has changed over the years. In 1729 it was Alden Farm; 1812, Aldham Farm; 1840, Oldhams Farm; and latterly Stoke Park Farm.

The Farmhouse and Buildings

The farm and the farmhouse are integral to the history of the estate. Maps at the end of the 19th century show that most of the farm buildings present at that time have remained in situ. They have been restored and maintained as appropriate.

The original entrance was not that for the current Abbotswood, rather the lane, recently shingled, abutting the Stoke Park picnic area.

A survey of the farm house and associated buildings was undertaken in 1988/9 by the Domestic Building Research Group, which is affiliated to the Surrey Archaeological Society. They concluded that:

> This house contains one reconstructed bay and short remnants of two other bays of a medieval hall. A large chimney (late 16th/early 17th century) stands on the site of one demolished bay linking it to a timber-framed cross wing which was probably contemporary with the chimney. A late Georgian extension stands beyond the cross wing and a modern (Victorian) extension replaces the other demolished bay of the hall.

25 *Stoke Park Farm.*

The report confirms that:

> The joists of the floor in the timber-framed section of the house … rest upon the girth beams and are therefore inserted, not original. This is consistent with the presence of smoke-blackened rafters in the roof above it indicating that this was one bay of a medieval hall. The wall plates continue in both directions from this bay and have scarf joints showing that the medieval house continued in both directions.

> The rafters contain mortices for the collars of a crown-post roof, or perhaps a paired rafter roof, but the roof has clearly been reconstructed and is now a queen-post roof with clasped purlins and wind braces. One pair of rafters also has mortices for a gablet through which smoke would have emerged above a hip at the end of the house. Smoked rafters on both sides of this gablet and a scarf joint in the wall plate beyond the bay post indicate that they are probably not be in their original position. The framing of the hall contains straight braces and a downward tension brace which are not medieval features. This suggests that the entire hall has been rebuilt.

26 *Stoke Park Farm.*

27 *The granary at the farm.*

At the northern end of the hall there is a brick chimney (late 16th or early 17th century) standing in place of one of the missing bays linking the hall to a timber-framed cross wing, which is probably contemporary with the chimney. Since the cross wing is framed with a curved upward braces, which are earlier than the straight downward braces, it appears that the cross wing was built before the reconstruction of the hall took place. It seems probable that the chimney and wing were added to a hall house that was later rebuilt although it is also possible that the wing was built independently as a house with a chimney at the back and that timbers from a demolished hall were used to build an addition.

It appears that this could be a medieval hall that was reconstructed on the site with Tudor additions, or a Tudor house was constructed on the site and extended using the frame pieces from a medieval hall.

The granary to the right of the present driveway to the house has staggered butt purlins and stands on brick staddles. The small scantling of the timber suggests a late 18th-century construction. The light red bricks are of typical Georgian appearance and it is thought that the granary and the Georgian extension to the house were built at about the same time.

What better example is there of the 'Surrey style'? The exterior presents evidence of a farmhouse that has stood the test of time. The first floor is almost entirely covered with tile cladding to protect the timber frame, perhaps added when the Georgian extension was built, along with the brick cladding on the ground. The chimneys are simple and not overlarge, with a stone capped square top, rather than a chimney pot. The windows are of varying shapes and sizes, reflecting the fact that the house has not been over-restored. Finally, as one would expect, there is a large front door, constructed with vertical planks,

28 *The excellent front door at the farm.*

held in place by bolts and supported by wrought iron hinges. It was surely an ideal example for Burlingham to follow.

This farmhouse, had no value save as a dwelling for the tenant farmer, and it would have been repaired or added to only when necessary just to meet the requirements of the farm and the farmer. Thankfully, the freeholders were not tempted to pull down an existing house and start afresh, leaving no trace of the medieval dwelling, which was the fate of many old buildings.

Ownership of Stoke Park

The ownership of the farm is interwoven with that of the Stoke Park Estate but prior to 1781 is unclear, save that it is known that it was previously owned by the Lords Onslow.

The kings and bishops were the early lords of the manor of Stoke. Between 1589 and 1697 the Stoughton family were the lords of the manors of Stoughton and Stoke, and the manor house was Stoughton Place. In 1697 Edward Hubbald bought the estate and pulled down Stoughton Place. His son William inherited the estate in 1707, but died within three years and the assets were sold over a period of time.

The property was bought in 1718 by Nicholas Turner who died in 1722. His wife, Margaret, kept the estate going for their eldest son, Jonathan. It was around this time that Clandon House was being built. A young Jonathan Turner, aged just 20, took over Stoke in 1734, but died aged thirty-three. His younger brother, Nicholas, took on the estate, eventually selling it to Jeremiah Dyson in 1761, but retaining some land at Woodbridge.

Dyson was a friend of Arthur Onslow at Clandon, which probably led him to buy this property nearby. Dyson became a Member of Parliament, firstly for Yarmouth, then Weymouth, and finally Horsham in 1774. In the same year he became Lord of the Treasury and Cofferer of the Royal Household. He had a stroke and died at Stoke in 1776. His son, also Jeremiah, still a minor, inherited the estate and his guardians let the property in 1777 to Wm. and Robt. Gemmell on a five-year lease.

In 1780 it was sold to George Vansittart who almost immediately put it up for sale. William Aldersley purchased the property after returning from India in 1781. He did much to improve the estate, including re-routing the often flooded Stoke Road from the east side of the church to where it is now; hence the graveyard, appears split from the church. He commenced the plantations already described above, and importantly built the Stoke Park Mansion, on the site of the previous house.

At this point Stoke Park Farm, under a different name, became part of the Stoke Park Estate. For William Aldersley had purchased Oldham Farm from Lord Onslow, paying £3,920 with timber at £87 3s. He purchased Gang Hill Farm at the same time.

29 *Stoke Park Mansion,*
c.1865.

Aldersley died in 1800, and, having no children to whom the estate could be left, his wife sold the Stoke Park property, along with the lordship of the manor of Stoke, to Nathaniel Hillier. He continued Aldersley's work of tree planting in the Park, and enforced the enclosure rights on the common.

Nathaniel Hillier died in 1810 aged seventy. Having had two children, both daughters, the estate was settled on his eldest daughter Harriett, the wife of Col. James Bogle Delap. She lived there with her husband for 50 years. In the event that she had no heirs, the estate was to pass to her younger sister, Susannah Elizabeth Hillier, a competent artist.

It was at this point that the connection with the Onslow family was re-started, for in 1812 Susannah married the younger brother of the 3rd Earl of Onslow, Thomas Cranley Onslow. They had a son, George Augustus Cranley Onslow. George came of age on 14 May 1834 and inherited an interest in the estate including consolidated bank annuities amounting to £4,585 19s. 9d.; a very large sum in those days.

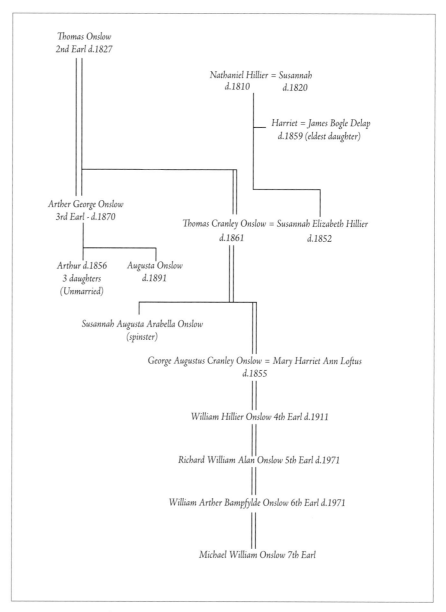

30 *Onslow family tree.*

Thomas Onslow
2nd Earl d.1827

Nathaniel Hillier = Susannah
d.1810   d.1820

Harriet = James Bogle Delap
d.1859 (eldest daughter)

Arther George Onslow
3rd Earl - d.1870

Thomas Cranley Onslow = Susannah Elizabeth Hillier
d.1861   d.1852

Arthur d.1856   Augusta Onslow
3 daughters   d.1891
(Unmarried)

Susannah Augusta Arabella Onslow
(spinster)

George Augustus Cranley Onslow = Mary Harriet Ann Loftus
d.1855

William Hillier Onslow 4th Earl d.1911

Richard William Alan Onslow 5th Earl d.1971

William Arther Bampfylde Onslow 6th Earl d.1971

Michael William Onslow 7th Earl

George married Mary Harriet Ann Loftus and they had a son, William Hillier Onslow. George died in 1855, at the age of 44, leaving William as his heir.

The house and the park were rented from 1862-9 to Charles Hulse, although another source states this to be to Ross Donnelly Mangles.

When the 3rd Earl died in 1870 without a living heir, William Hillier succeeded to the title because both Thomas his grandfather, and George his father, had pre-deceased him. At the age of 17 he became the 4th Earl of Onslow. On 6 March 1874 Stoke Park and Stoke Park Mansion passed to William on his reaching the age of majority.

The 4th Earl was a man of great energy; his busy political life culminated in four years as Governor of New Zealand. Unfortunately, his accession to the title coincided with the period of agricultural depression. His great uncle had not lived in Clandon Park for a number of years and he found the estate to be in disrepair and the house dilapidated. William had little alternative but to sell part of the vast estate.

William firstly decided to sell Stoke Park to help with the restoration costs. Sale Particulars of 15 July 1879 reveal the following lots:

Lot 1 – Stoke Park Mansion, with stabling, pleasure gardens, and park, Stoughton private chapel and Stoke Manor.

Lot 2 – Stoke Park Farm with farm buildings and homestead.

The mansion, with the title, lord of the manor, together with 109 acres was sold to James Smith Budgett, of Ealing Park, for £24,000, but Stoke Park Farm remained unsold. Budgett added 83 acres to Stoke Park in the Burchatt's Farm and Thorneycrofts areas before his death in 1906 at the age of 82, and his widow continued to live at Stoke Park Mansion until 1912, when she died. The place was vacant until their son returned to live there from 1916-19 until he, too, died. From 1922, his successor, Herbert Maitland Budgett, leased it to C.E. Lewis who used it as a boarding school.

In 1925, Herbert Budgett agreed to sell the park with the mansion to Guildford Corporation. When the school closed in 1935, the Corporation leased the property to Surrey County Council, who used the buildings as a technical college from 1939.

31 *Clandon House.*

Stoke Park Mansion House, to give it its full name, was never a building of great virtue, but there was much opposition before the council eventually pulled it down. It was replaced by new buildings at the college in 1977.

> *Author's Recollection*: Whilst not a great success at examinations, I was perhaps fortunate enough to be able to take some of my banking examinations in the old house around 1966, and admire the woodwork and fireplaces when waiting between questions for inspiration for the answers, which seldom arrived.

Following the acquisition of the parkland and the house, Guildford Borough Council created the by-pass which was opened in July 1934. Concurrently, the Surrey County Council Act of 1931 was enacted, which protected the parkland for use by the people of Guildford for recreational purposes. The Act not only limited access but also limited house building so avoiding ribbon development.

Stoke Park Farm was again put up for sale by auction in July 1909 as one of 22 lots, which included a farm in Pyrford, Woking Park Farm, Papercourt Farm, Winterhill Farm, Park Barn Farm and Manor Farm, Artington. The Right Honourable William Hillier, 4th Earl of Onslow, sold Stoke Park Farm on 29 September 1909 to Alfred George Taylor.

The cottages at Stoke Park Farm were part of this sale, having been built prior to 1860; initially they were two attached workers' cottages, which have now been converted into one house.

There was clearly an ongoing sale of the Onslow estates. In 1905 the Earl had sold building land north and east of Guildford together with land in Burpham, including Marlyns Farm, 32 acres, New Inn Farm, Pimms Row with a brick field and sand pit behind, and Burpham Court Farm with 114 acres. He also sold the lordship of the manor.

Further information about the ownership of Stoke Park and how it evolved, can be determined from the Abstract of Title, which was made available to all original purchasers of the Abbotswood properties. This amounted to 16 pages of print and detailed the sale of the property between the Earl of Onslow, and A.G. Taylor. Prior to the days of computerised land registration the abstract was used to list the dates of previous sales, the names of those involved, and the conditions of sale. This *inter alia* verified previous ownership going back at least 25 years. Without this, proof ownership of the land could be questioned by future purchasers, who feared not getting a good title to the property. These abstracts were often typed on very flimsy paper; a few have survived and are an invaluable source of information for researchers.

The basis for all the house sales in Abbotswood is the original conveyance of Stoke Park Farm comprising the farm house, two cottages and about 145 acres of land, all for £7,890, which is copied opposite:

An Indenture of Conveyance

dated 29 September 1909

BY INDENTURE so dated between the Right Honourable William Hillier Earl of Onslow G.C.M.G. (thereinafter called "the Vendor") of the one part and Alfred George Taylor of 16, Southwark Street in the City of London, Surveyor (Hereinafter called "the Purchaser") of the other part.

Rectg seising of the vendor in fee simple in possession free of incumbrances of the hereditiments (thereinafter described and expressed) to be thereby conveyed and agreement for sale to purchase for the sum of seven thousand eight hundred and ninety pounds.

IT WAS WITNESSED that in (pursuit) of the said agreement and in consideration of the said seven thousand eight hundred and ninety pounds to the vendor pd. Etc (the rec. etc) the Vendor as beneficial owner thereby conveys to the Purchaser:

All THAT farm with the messuage (tenements) or farmhouse and two cottages bldgs close and parcels of land belonging thereto called Stoke Park farm situate in the Parishes of Worplesdon and Stoke next Guildford in the County of Surrey containing together by admeasurement One hundred and forty five acres and thirty eight perches (little more or less) now in the occupation of Frederick Blake (with the exception of the enclosure 51 in the schedule which is in hand) all the messauages farms tenements and heredits are more particularly described in the first schedule hereunder written and are also delineated in the map or plan drawn hereon and edged red and referred to in the said schedule but in respect of so much of the said herediments as adjoin the navigable parts of the River Wey only to the extent of such rights as the Vendor has in and over the said River and the banks thereof and the adjoining towing path.

TO HOLD the same unto and to the use of the Purchaser in fee simple subject to and with the benefit of an Indenture of Lease dated the twenty-ninth day of September 1888 and made between the vendor of the one part and the said Frederick Blake of the other part and subject to and with the benefit of an agreement dated the twentieth September 1906 and made between the Vendor on the one part and the Major, Aldermen and Burgesses of the Borough of Guildford of the other part.

ACKNOWLEDGEMENT right to production and delivery of copies of the documents set forth in the 2nd schedule thereunder written undertaking for the safe custody thereof.

'The First Schedule Hereinbefore Referred to' was a schedule listing the areas of land at the farm together with a map. The areas are numbered and are divided between the parishes of Worplesdon and Stoke-next-Guildford.

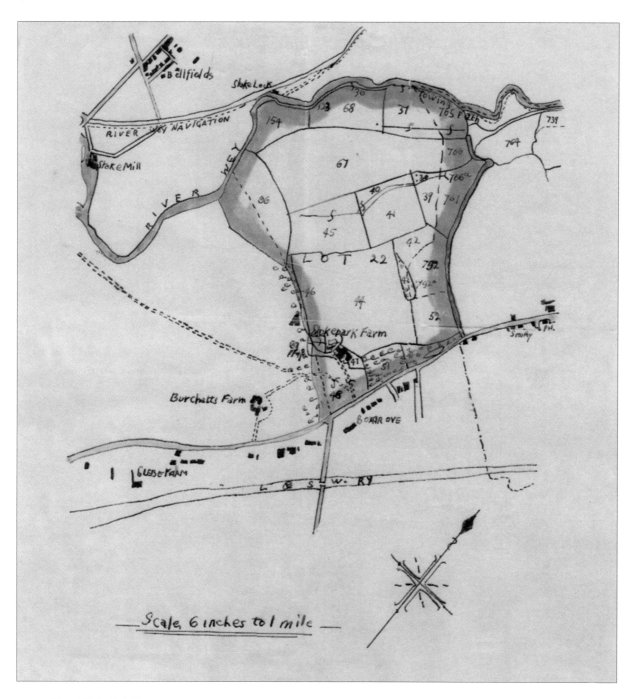

32 *Plan of Stoke Park Farm, 1909.*

Worplesdon Parish

765	pasture	3.697 acres
766	arable	2.132 acres
766a	osiers*	0.030 acres
767	pastures	4.938 acres
792	arable	4.524 acres
792a	wood	0.037 acres

STOKE-NEXT-GUILDFORD

36	towing path	0.038 acres
37	pastures	6.089 acres
38	osiers	0.465 acres
39	pasture	1.935 acres
40	pasture	2.026 acres
41	pasture	6.893 acres
42	arable	2.634 acres
43	wood	0.785 acres
44	arable	26.942 acres
45	pasture	9.736 acres
46	lane	0.836 acres
47	house, buildings etc.	2.320 acres
48	pasture	6.111 acres
51	wood	5.081 acres
52	arable	5.408 acres
63	pond	0.128 acres
66	arable	13.438 acres
67	arable	26.133 acres
68	pasture	7.820 acres
123	towing path	0.340 acres
154	pasture	4.725 acres
	Total	145.241 acres

*An osier was a willow tree cut for basket work, indicating that such trees abutted the river, as they do today.

The Second Schedule hereinbefore referred to:

30 June 1879   Indenture made between Susanna* Augusta Arabella Onslow of the one part and the Vendor of the other part.

* More often spelled as Susannah.

Various events and documents are recited and summarised. These include the marriage settlement dated May 1809, made between Nathaniel Hillier, Harriet Hillier, James Bogle Delap and other documents referred to properties in the possession of Nathaniel Hillier by way of indentures dated July 1801. These gave a life interest to Susannah Hillier, Nathaniel's wife, upon his death. Thereafter, Harriet has benefit as part of her settlement on her marriage with James Bogle Delap, which later passed to Susannah Onslow, as previously described.

24 June 1879   Declaration of George Sowton Newman and the Vendor.

George S. Newman, a Land Agent from Fareham, confirmed that he and his firm had been land agents since 1859 and, at 1876 when they retired, had an expert knowledge of all the relevant land and property under their control. It confirmed how the rents and other income had been disbursed to Messrs Herries Farquhar & Co., bankers, St James Street, London, on behalf of Mary Harriet Anne Onslow, mother of the 4th Earl.

17 November 1881   Indenture made between the vendor of the one part and Frederick Edward Beauclerk, John Philip Martineau and Henry B. Mayne of the other part.

By this indenture the 4th Earl borrowed £10,000 from Beauclerk, Martineau and Mayne. The security was Stoke Park Farm. There is reference to a rent charge to Lady K.A. Cranley. The rent for Stoke Park Farm was £200 per annum, and was let together with part of Winterhill Farm, at £80 p.a., for a term of eight years from 29 September 1880 to a Mr Walder.

4 August 1887   Indenture (endorsed on last Indenture) made between the said Frederick Edward Beauclerk and John Philip Martineau and H. Blairmayne of the one part and the Vendor on the other part.

This indenture recites the above loan agreement, and in reference to the rent to Katherine Anne, Dowager Lady Cranley, notes her death on 18 October 1885, commenting that all rent charges of £1,000, and £200 were made, and that annuities of £1,000 and £200 had ceased. By this indenture the mortgage was duly noted as repaid, and the lands re-conveyed to the Earl of Onslow.

The Ownership of Stoke Park Farm continued to change after 1909:

A portion of the farm was conveyed by A.G. Taylor to Allen Ansell on 26 November 1917, and on 11 November 1918 Taylor together with Ansell sold the farm and farmhouse to Samuel Bartlett Jerrard Symes. Concurrently Symes mortgaged the farm to Margaret Mary Messenger.

In October 1919, a further piece of land between the farmhouse and the new lane was sold by Taylor to Symes for £1,350, together with the field abutting Thorneycrofts wood. There was a restrictive covenant to the effect that should Symes wish to use farm vehicles on the Abbotswood Road, he could only do so from his entrance onto the new lane, and then left past Sunnymead for the meadowland beyond.

In June 1921 Taylor sold the remaining building land comprising 24½ acres to the Onyx Property Investment Company Limited (hereafter called

Onyx Property Investments). This company, together with A.C. Burlingham, sold the then remaining building land to Onyx Country Estates Limited on 15 February 1926 for £6,598 in cash plus 2,398 shares.

The farmhouse and the worked fields remained intact and were sold off by B.J. Symes on 18 September 1950 to Wilfred Henry James Long for £12,000. It included the farmhouse, two dairy cottages and land, being 97 acres 2 roods and 26 perches. Robert William Marlow was the tenant farmer. A rood is a quarter of an acre and a perch is five and a half yards.

Mr Long sold to Archibald Hunter Elwell for the sum of £7,500 on 21 January 1954 land amounting to 91.658 acres, including the cottages, barn and dairy buildings. He kept the paddock abutting the London Road, the farmhouse and some other buildings. On 18 May 1956, by a deed of grant, Long gave right of access over Farm Road, skirting the southern end of Abbotswood to Thomas Walter Saint of 2, Abbotsford (*sic*), Guildford.

In September 1966 Mr Long conveyed the property to his wife. He died in 1971.

On 31 July 1975 the present owners, Bernard Roy Suttill and Ruth Suttill purchased the farmhouse. They were offered the five-acre paddock, but in the knowledge that the Council were intent on buying it, probably by way of compulsory purchase, they declined. Mr Suttill had considered the possibility of turning the barn into a squash court, and the five acres into a mini golf course and creating a private club, but this was not to be. At the time of the purchase there was planning permission for a bungalow on land next to the farmhouse. This would have meant that the driveway would have become shared, which was unacceptable as a condition of purchase. In order to avoid the problem the Suttills purchased the plot and, because they were very keen on tennis, thereon built a hard tennis court, which remains to this day.

Around 1976, Guildford Borough Council purchased the five acres from the Longs for the use of the community, adding picnic benches for those inclined to use them. This gives a useful addition to Stoke Park, and above all prevents the area from becoming victim to a developer. Across it, there is a pathway giving the public access to Thorneycrofts wood.

Abbotswood House Deeds

The deeds of the houses often provide a treasure of information which is quite lost in this era of electronic records.

The following copy of a conveyance is in respect of Lorrain (36) sold by Taylor to Mrs Dufort on 30 April 1915, and contains covenants standard for Abbotswood houses. These seldom changed, save for the prescribed cost of the houses to be built, which increased over the years. This document links the purchaser not only to the covenants, but also, the original sale document between Taylor and the Earl of Onslow. In turn this document would have formed an important part of the title deeds for the next purchaser, until the Land Registry centralised and 'dematerialised' the process.

Alfred. G. Taylor – to – Anna Caroline Dufort

Conveyance

of freehold land in the Parish of Stoke-next-Guildford in the County of Surrey

This Indenture made thirtieth day of April One thousand nine hundred and fifteen between Alfred George Taylor of 'Stowford', Brighton Road, Sutton in the County of Surrey, Esquire (hereinafter called the Vendor) of the one part and Anna Caroline Dufort of 3 Cadogan Court Gardens Cadogan Place in the County of London Widow (hereafter called the Purchaser) of the other part whereas the vendor is seised in fee simple in possession free from incumbrances of the hereditaments hereinafter described and expressed to be hereby conveyed and whereas the Vendor has agreed with the Purchaser for the sale to her of the said hereditaments and premises for the sum of one thousand nine hundred pounds but subject to the restrictions and stipulations set forth in the first schedule hereto and whereas the document expressed in the second schedule hereto which is in the possession of the Vendor relates as well to the herditaments hereby conveyed as to other heriditaments belonging to the Vendor and it has been agreed that the Vendor shall retain the said document and give such acknowledgement and undertaking in relation thereto as is hereinafter contained now this indenture witnesseth that in pursuance of the said agreement and in consideration of the sum of one thousand nine hundred pounds to the vendor now paid by the purchaser (the receipt of which the vendor doth hereby acknowledge) the Vendor as Beneficial Owner hereby conveys unto the Purchaser ALL that piece of land lately and forming part of Stoke Park Farm situate in the parish of Stoke-next-Guildford in the County of Surrey and delineated on the plan hereby annexed and thereon coloured pink and which said piece of land forms part of the land comprised in an Indenture of Conveyance dated the twenty ninth day of September one thousand nine hundred and nine between The Right Honourable William Hillier Earl of Onslow on the one part and the Vendor on the other part together with the messuage or dwellinghouse erected thereon or on some part thereof and known as 'Lorraine' and together with the full and free liberty for the purchaser her heirs or assigns owner or owners for the time being of the piece of land hereinbefore described or any part or parts thereof and her and their servants and all other persons authorised in that behalf by her or them for all purposes from time to time and at all times hereafter at her and their will and pleasure to pass and re-pass with or without horses carts wagons carriages and motor cars in along and over the road constructed by the Vendor on the north side of the said piece of land leading from the London Road to the said piece of land and over the extension thereof that the Vendor may hereafter make to hold the same unto and to use of the Purchaser her heirs or assigns absolutely subject nevertheless to the restrictions set forth in the first schedule hereto and the Purchaser for herself her heirs executors and assigns to the intent and so that such covenant shall be binding on the said premises so hereby assured into whosoever hand the same may come but not so as to render the Purchaser personally liable in damages for any breach thereof after she shall have parted with all the interest in the said premises that the Purchaser her heirs and assigns shall duly observe and perform the restrictions and stipulations contained in the first schedule hereto and the Vendor doth hereby acknowledge the right of the Purchaser to the production of the document specified in the Second Schedule hereto (the possession of which is retained by the Vendor) and to deliver of copies thereof and undertakes for the safe custody thereof in witness whereof the said parties to these presents have hereunder set their hands and seals the day and year first above written

The First Schedule above referred to:

1. The purchaser shall forever maintain a good and sufficient thick set hedge or fence on the sides of the land hereby conveyed marked 'T' within the boundary and on the plan drawn when the same have been erected by the Vendor. No hedge or fence shall be less than 4 feet and no more than six feet in height

2. Not more than one dwelling with the usual outbuildings stables or motor houses shall at any time stand on the land hereby conveyed The cost of such house shall not be less than £1,200 and for the purpose of this stipulation such cost shall be taken to be the net first cost thereof in labour and materials alone and shall be exclusive of any stabling and outbuildings No house or other building shall be erected on the land unless the plans drawings and elevations thereof shall have previously submitted and approved of in writing by the Vendor

3. No building now or hereafter to be erected on the land shall at any time be used for any other purpose than as a private dwellinghouse or as stabling and outbuildings belonging thereto and no trade manufacture or business of any kind except that of a solicitor surgeon or physician shall at any time be set up or carried on upon the land without the consent of the Vendor his heirs and assigns No hut shed or caravan or house on wheels shall be allowed to stand on the land and no chalk clay gravel marlstone or sand shall at any time be excavated or dug out of the land except for the purpose of preparing for buildings thereon No bricks or tiles shall at any time be burnt or made nor any clay be burnt on the land nor shall anything be done on the land that may be or grow to be a nuisance or annoyance to the Vendor his heirs or assigns or her or their tenants or the neighbourhood

4. The Purchaser shall at all time hereafter when required by the Vendor his heirs or assigns pay for him or them or contribute a fair share not exceeding the sum of two pounds in any year towards the expenses of repairing cleansing and maintaining the road on which the land hereby conveyed now abuts or may hereafter abut and the sewers and drains under the same respectively until the same respectively shall be adopted by and taken into the charge of the Local Authority such share in case of dispute to be settled by the Surveyor for the time being of the Vendor his heirs or assigns

5. The Purchaser shall pay on demand the proper apportionment of tithe rent charge in respect of land hereby conveyed calculated according to acreage until such time as the tithe rent charge shall be legally apportioned or redeemed.

The Second Schedule above referred to:

29th September 1909 – The hereinbefore mentioned Indenture of this date made between The Right Honourable William Hillier, Earl of Onslow GCMG of the one part and the Vendor of the other part.

Indentures

There is reference to the word indenture, which is used to describe the document for undertaking a conveyance, or making other agreements.

When a document was drawn up in the 18th and 19th centuries, often it was necessary to make a copy. In order to stop forgeries, the script was written twice on a single parchment. The centre line between the two copies was cut in an undulating manner. Thus, when there was a need to check authenticity, the two portions were married up. If there was not an exact fit, it could not be the original copy.

The wavy line was described as an indentation, hence indenture. A similar method was used when an agreement was drawn up between master and apprentice.

Covenants

There were no covenants contained in the deed between the Earl of Onslow and A.G. Taylor in 1909. Taylor decided to impose a number of covenants

33   *An indenture.*

which fed through to subsequent sales and applied standards for the estate that would be maintained as it expanded. Effectively, he imposed a building control that only he and his successors could apply. When part of Stoke Park Farm was sold to build The Croft (4), the covenants appeared on the deeds for that property. These were repeated in the new deeds in 1962 when a bungalow was built in the garden of The Croft.

When Donald Bennett wanted to run his chiropractor business from The Gate House (1), he had to obtain the permission of Alfred Taylor, despite the building being constructed 40 years previously.

Tithe Rent Charges

The deeds invariably contain reference to tithe rent charges and these could be levied by the church authorities.

This ancient system was initially three separate tithes. The praedial tithes which were calculated on income from produce such as corn, oats and wood; mixed tithes based on income from a combination of stock and labour such as wood, pigs and milk production; and personal tithes which were derived solely from income. The tithes, which were theoretically a tenth of the income, went towards the upkeep of the incumbent of the parish church. Under the Tithe Commutation Act 1836, tithes could be commuted to a rent charge, and Commissioners were appointed to negotiate fair land deals with the inhabitants. The Tithe Act 1925 transferred the income to the Queen Anne's Bounty Fund. In 1948 this fund, together with the Ecclesiastical Commission, were combined to form the Church Commission.

In practice, during the early part of the 20th century, tithes or rents were not always collected from house owners, but just in case there was such a call on the property owner, the vendor ensured that any obligation was passed on to the purchaser. The accounts of Orchard Estate, detailed in Fig. 41 show that they were still active, and could be bought out. The reference is to 'Tithe 10/- dtd. 18th March 1927', and another per 'Tithe Lfd £2.3.2d dtd 22 March 1926'.

Both a council rate and a poor rate were levied on the Abbotswood houses from the time that they were built.

Six

The Developers of Abbotswood

Guildford was an area of growing importance and, as communications were improving, people wanted better houses out of town. Alfred Taylor needed to set out his stall, and began planning for three houses along a yet to be built lane, leading to the back of Stoke Park Farm. When they sold, he would invest more and build even larger and more imposing houses next to the busy London Road; one of these would be The Hurst (46). This displayed significant features copied from the Arts and Crafts Movement as would many other houses around Abbotswood. It was considered so architecturally important that 85 years later, in 1998, it was listed by English Heritage.

Taylor would have considered whether or not to finance the houses and lease, or sell outright. Also, whether he should build to order, or build speculatively, hoping that a buyer would come along who liked the completed house. Alternatively he may wish to sell a plot of land, and let the buyer employ a builder, as he had done in Sutton, which meant less risk, but also less profit. He had to consider the state of the economy, for these houses were very expensive compared with other houses in Guildford, and whether the emerging problems in Europe would affect sales.

It turned out that all these considerations would impact on the new estate. It would be successfully completed over a 12-year period, resulting in one of the premier estates in Guildford, and indeed Surrey as a whole. In all, 45 dwellings would be built on plots of half an acre upwards. The first planning applications were presented to the Guildford Council on 16 December 1912, and the first property sale took place on 25 January 1913 – land was purchased by Mrs E.D. Falkus and Mr R.U. Falkus respectively for building Churston (5) and The Cottage (6). The first house sale, on 29 July 1913, was for Aoetearoa (7). Taylor's address was given either as the Estate Office, Devonshire Avenue, Sutton, or his home address at Stowford, Brighton Road, Sutton.

London and Manchester Connection

From the beginning there was a connection with the London and Manchester Industrial Assurance Company Limited, later to become London and Manchester Assurance Company Limited (hereafter referred to as London and Manchester).

The fact that the sales until 1921 were in Alfred Taylor's own name would appear to dispel any theory that London and Manchester were behind the early funding of Abbotswood, although Alfred was the company surveyor.

As a vehicle to develop the later stages of Abbotswood, in June 1921 Onyx Property Investments Limited was formed. At that time, the company purchased from Taylor 24½ acres in Abbotswood plus two freeholds. Because it now owned the land, one would have thought that the company name would have appeared on the deeds. This was not the case. In December 1923, Onyx Property Investments was named as the proposer on a planning application, but not the vendor on the deeds. There was still no evidence in the deeds that London and Manchester was involved, save as a prime source for the provision of mortgages.

Onyx Country Estates Limited was formed in 1926 and immediately purchased assets from Onyx Property Investments. The two companies became the property companies of London and Manchester. By the time that Hall Place Farm was developed in 1927, all the planning applications by Burlingham were submitted on behalf of a new company: Onyx Country Estates. The farm was purchased by Burlingham and Ernest Taylor from The Blessed Holy Trinity Church, and the purchase documents had no reference to Onyx. Subsequently, the names of Burlingham and a Taylor appeared on the house sale documents. There is little doubt that they were acting on behalf of Onyx, but the name does not appear except on the planning applications. All very confusing, if not a little odd.

Details of a contract between Burlingham and Onyx Country Estates, dated 15 February 1926, appear in the next chapter.

A grandson of Alfred Taylor, Peter Kirwan-Taylor, kindly provided clarification. He confirmed that from February 1926 the two companies became part of the property arm of London and Manchester. By far the larger was Onyx Property Investments. Using this company, London and Manchester was involved with the management of a property portfolio, and in particular the purchase of the freeholds of tenanted homes in London, and the selling of the freeholds to the sitting tenants. Tenants were told to use the companies insurance products and doubtless, were they to purchase the freehold, the company would have been pleased to provide a mortgage, too.

35 *Imperial House, designed by A. Claude Burlingham in 1932.*

The second company, Onyx Country Estates, having purchased the remaining assets in the estates from the sister company in 1926, was used mainly for the development of domestic housing. These arrangements remained until London and Manchester moved head office from London to Exeter, in the 1980s, when the Onyx companies reverted to Taylor ownership. The large office block, Imperial House, in South Street (now Dominion Street), London EC2, designed by Burlingham, would have formed a substantial part of the property investment portfolio.

An insight into the company dealings is given through the company records that exist for the formation of the first Onyx company, which was the vehicle used by Taylor after he chose not to trade in his own name. The following are extracts:

Minutes of a Statutory General Meeting of Onyx Property Investment Company Limited, held at Central House, Finsbury Square on 21 June 1921:

The minutes noted that the company had been duly incorporated and the registered office duly filed. The certificate of incorporation was produced. It was resolved that the company should enter into an agreement with A.G. Taylor. The solicitors present were told to prepare a conveyance. This Agreement, of the same date, is detailed below.

It was further resolved that Mr A.J. Suenson-Taylor and Mr Ernest Taylor be appointed directors of the company at a salary of £500 per annum.

The minutes were signed by Alfred G. Taylor, Chairman.

By an agreement dated 21 June 1921 between Taylor and Onyx Property Investments, the terms of the developer were set out.

These can be summarised as follows:

1. The company had a nominal capital of £10,000. This was made up of 9,500 ordinary shares at £1, and 10,000 deferred shares of 1/-.
2. Taylor sold the freehold land for £6,000. He received £1,000 in cash and 10,000 deferred shares, and 4,500 ordinary shares.
3. Completion to take place on 14 July 1921.
4. The land purchased comprised of:

   > All that Freehold Land situate at Abbotswood, Guildford in the County of Surrey of about twenty four and half acres in extent and more particularly shown and coloured on the plan attached hereto. The Freehold houses known as 'Upmeads' and 'Ardenholme' and coloured green, subject to, and with the benefit of present existing tenancies and the plots adjoining each of them as shown and coloured blue on attached plan.

5. The seal of Onyx is witnessed by A.J. Suenson-Taylor.

Minutes of the Directors' Meeting of the Onyx Property Investment Company Limited, held at Central House, Finsbury Square on 2 August 1921:

1. The purpose of the meeting was to discuss the scheme for the development of the company's estate at Guildford.
2. It was noted that the New Road had been completed and planning consent had been obtained for four houses which should be commenced immediately, in order to receive government subsidies.
3. It was agreed that the architect Mr A.C. Burlingham, and the builder, Mr A.E. Stanley be allowed to participate in the profits of the scheme. This was enabled by them contributing ¼ of the cost of building. Burlingham should find a minimum of £750 in cash, and Stanley £500, the remainder could be by way of a loan at seven per cent from the company.
4. The price of the plots were to be £550, £375, £375 and £375.
5. Payment to each shall be ¼ of net profit.
6. In the event of the scheme not being completed by December 1922, the participants would have to take a property each.

There is no indication that Burlingham owned part of the Abbotswood estate with Onyx, but see agreement of 1926 below.

Minutes of Directors' Meeting, held on 5 April 1923:

Burlingham mentioned that having sold Red Cottage, he had to vacate on 10 May next and that his new house would not be ready in time. He asked if he could purchase a house referred to as 'F'. A detailed arrangement was made for purchase and resale.

Burlingham's ownership of various plots is identified in deeds and at the Land Registry, including The Hazard (33), Waysend (34), and Red Cottage (37). The dates of the planning applications for The Hazard and Waysend, the likely build dates, and the eventual dates of sale, would indicate that Burlingham did not live at either The Hazard or Waysend.

Mention was made of land that Mr Burlingham was buying at Merrow. It was noted that his agreement with the company precluded him from personally developing this land, and should he decide to sell it, it must be sold as plots, and not a development. Should he be asked by the new owners of a plot of land to build a property, this could only be done with the agreement of the Company. Whilst not identified in the agreement, the land was doubtlessly that on which Greys and Newlands Cottage were both built in Trodds Lane.

Selling the Houses

The Red Cottage, initially owned by Burlingham, featured in a general advertisement for the estate in the early 1920s, which included a picture of

the house. The description is enlightening. The advertisement was placed by The Onyx Property Investments and commences by stating that Abbotswood is 'On the right of London Road nearing Guildford'. This implies that anyone coming to view the houses will be from London rather than coming from Guildford and Portsmouth.

The advertisement notes that sites are of half an acre upwards, pre-built house are available, as too are plots for the purchaser to build on. In fact, some of the earlier houses had plots of 1¾ acres and at the other end of the scale some plots were just 70ft wide with a depth of 100ft. Houses could be constructed in six months for an inclusive sum or a percentage of costs, and mortgages are available (no doubt from London and Manchester).

The photograph shows that Red Cottage has changed little externally over 80 years. It also shows young pine trees, about eight feet in height, which became mature specimens – several still stand today. Clearly the trees on the estate had not yet grown enough to present an attractive picture, and for some unknown reason the advertisement encompasses a large photograph of a very leafy Shalford Road, found to the south of Guildford.

Mr A.E. Stanley was the builder first used by Taylor for Abbotswood after the First World War, erecting six bungalows in March 1920. Previously, up to 1916, Taylor had described himself as the builder, presumably bringing in contracted craftsmen and workers. Stanley's address was given as Down Road, Merrow. He also gave a site address, which was The Office, Abbotswood. On one of the site plans this was shown to be in the front garden of The Orchard (38).

36 *The 1920s advertisement for Abbotswood houses.*

Stanley remained in business with Burlingham after the completion of Abbotswood, and worked to develop the Orchard Estate in Burpham, and later assisted with the Merrow Downs Estate and Ganghill. Some of the Orchard houses were not only built by Stanley, but he submitted the plans to the council, some of which he prepared. Furthermore, he was very much involved with the Boxgrove Estate, where he built the majority of houses, and again put his name to some of the designs. His work from 1934 onwards in creating the estate comprising Meads Road and Green Lane led him to describe himself an 'estate builder'. By the late 1930s, Burlingham had started to use other builders for his houses in Fairway.

The Taylor Family

The Taylor family played a large part in the development of Guildford and there is no better way of explaining this than introducing Alfred Taylor, and detailing the impressive careers of his sons.

Alfred George Taylor

In 1872, Alfred G. Taylor was born. He married Mary, the daughter of Andrew V. Kirwan, an Irish barrister, in 1892, and from as early as 1905 was the Surveyor for London and Manchester Assurance. Alfred was a staunch follower of the Plymouth Brethren, and would lead Sunday prayers at home before going to church, and returning for lunch and more prayers.

Alfred and Mary had a large family of nine children in just 17 years; six boys and three girls. Mary died in 1951.

Stowford was the family home for a long time, from the early part of the century until Alfred died in 1959 – it is a large early Victorian house set in five acres and is now Stowford College, a private school. The family photograph opposite was taken outside Stowford; it is thought this was about 1914, possibly just before Alfred and Harold went off to war, in anticipation that one or both of them might be killed.

The eldest daughter, Grace, married a man called Smith, a surveyor with the Onyx companies, but she died in childbirth. The middle sister, born in 1904 and known to the family as Girlie, died of a brain tumour in childhood aged about ten. The third, Joyce, was born in 1908, and went on to marry John Turnbull, who followed Alfred and later John Taylor as senior surveyor to London and Manchester. Joyce and John had five children: Stuart, Anthony, Mary, Sarah and Amanda. Anthony has related much of the family history.

It was Joyce who used to recall that Alfred made a fortune for himself as a property developer. He started life with but modest means, working as a booking clerk for the railway. He identified opportunities for a career in property and set about being trained as a surveyor. His hard work bore early fruits as he identified development opportunities south of London in the Sutton area. He became the

37   Alfred Taylor, with his family. Back row: Ernest, Grace, Alfred, Girlie, Harold. Lower row: Jesse, John, Joyce, Charles, Gordon and Mary.

surveyor for London and Manchester Industrial Assurance Company Ltd, and in time made a great deal of money for them and with them.

Success must have come quickly, for from the early 1900s onwards he was able to send all his sons to public school, and soon purchased Stowford. Joyce said that Alfred made so much money for London and Manchester, and in turn had so much invested in it, that he was invited to become a director, but declined because of his Plymouth Brethren beliefs. His eldest son Jesse became a director and later chairman and was well able to look after the considerable Taylor family interests.

Alfred was a very strong-willed paterfamilias and it is understood that he and his sons operated a legal partnership right up to the beginning of the Second World War. By this time all his sons were independently successful but they still put all their earnings into the partnership. This patriarch, who put in much more than anyone else, then decided who should get what. Since the boys each got back much more than they put in, they seemed prepared to accept this rather authoritarian approach.

ALFRED JESSE TAYLOR
(LATER CHANGED TO A.J. SUENSON-TAYLOR, AND AFTERWARDS, LORD GRANTCHESTER), 1893-1995

Alfred Jesse Taylor, known as Jesse, married Mara Henrietta Suenson in 1920, changing his name accordingly. Her father was the Danish Admiral Albert Suenson, whose statue still stands in Copenhagen.

Alfred was educated at Epsom College, and King's College, Cambridge, where he attained a double first. He was decorated in the First World War, receiving a Military O.B.E., and was mentioned in despatches twice whilst serving in Gallipoli and France, rising to the rank of Major. After the war he became a barrister in Middle Temple. He had wanted to become a priest, but his father would hear nothing of it. He failed to become an MP although he was the Joint Hon. Treasurer of the Liberal Party, and the President of the London Liberal Party. In 1935, he was knighted.

He joined the board of Cow & Gate in 1928, became Chairman in 1929 and resigned in 1936 to follow his other interests. In June 1953 he was created Baron Grantchester of Knightsbridge, in the City of Westminster.

Alfred was associated with the insurance industry holding various eminent positions. He became a director of the London and Manchester in 1934 and between 1953 and 1961 was its Chairman. His Chairmanship ended when Nigel Birch and Enoch Powell connived to remove him after he discussed a possible merger with Eagle Star without mentioning it to the rest of the board. He always claimed that this was not a serious discussion, but only a 'cockshy'.

His other business and political interests included County Fire Office Limited, Close Brothers (merchant bankers), Brightstone Estates and Property Trust, the British Society for International Understanding, and the United Nations Association. He was a director of the Onyx Companies.

The 2nd Baron Grantchester, Kenneth Bent Suenson-Taylor, was born in 1921, and succeeded his father in 1976. In 1947 he married Betty, the daughter of Sir John Moores, who was the driving force behind the postal shopping and football pools empires. Lord Grantchester became Speaker of the House of Lords from 1990 to 1995 when he died.

In 1951 the 3rd and present Lord Grantchester, Christopher John Suenson-Taylor, was born. He is a director of Everton Football Club and one of the few remaining hereditary peers in the House of Lords.

Harold George Taylor, F.R.C.S.
(Later changed to H.G. Kirwan-Taylor), 1895-1981

Harold was educated at Epsom College and Trinity College, Cambridge. He served in the R.N.V.R. in the First World War with the Grand Fleet as a Surgeon Lieutenant. Whilst not recorded in Burke's, there is a family understanding that Harold might have been promoted to Surgeon Commander when, in action at the Battle of Jutland, he was mentioned in despatches. In the Second World War he served with the Middle East Force as Lieut. Colonel when he was again mentioned in despatches. Serving with the British North Africa Force he had responsibilities for hospitals in the Western Desert. After further service in Italy, according to *Burke's Peerage*, he retired with the rank of Hon. Colonel, Army Medical Service. However, his brother Charles recorded that he retired as Brigadier, and his red lapels were remembered by others in the family.

He was an eminent consultant obstetrician, and the senior gynaecological surgeon at St George's Hospital, London, where he was also a lecturer. During the 1930s he was one of the most fashionable gynaecologists in London, working from the same house in Cadogan Square as his brother Gordon. Harold had the reputation of being able to determine the sex of children. When Anthony Turnbull, shortly after he was married, asked him how one went about having a baby boy child, he put his hand on his knee and said 'My dear boy, I couldn't possibly tell you. It's far too disgusting'. Despite not wishing to give guidance to his kin, he was happy to help the Shah of Iran and King Farouk of Egypt, not always successfully.

Harold was a man precise in every way. As he did his rounds, the ward sisters would scurry before him, removing flowers from in front of mirrors. For as Harold approached his patients, he would invariably turn to the mirrors to check that his appearance was just so, before talking to them.

He married in 1926, and had four children, Timothy, Jane, Shirley and Caroline.

ERNEST EDWARD TAYLOR C.B.E.

Ernest was born in 1897 and educated at Epsom. He married in 1920. Whilst he may not have had the academic prowess of his brothers, with the support of his father his career with Cow & Gate was exemplary. At the age of 28 he was a director of Wincanton Transport and Engineering Company Limited. His career progressed through this business to include being Managing Director of Cow & Gate and ultimately Chairman of Unigate. He was also a director of the Onyx Companies and Master of the Fruiterers' Company.

At various times he was the Chairman of the British Sailors' Association, the Royal National Throat Nose and Ear Hospital, and the Laryngology and Otology London Institute – Ernest was awarded the C.B.E. for his hospital work. He had five children, Alfred, Margaret, Dorothea, Eileen and Elizabeth. Sadly, the youngest, Elizabeth, died at sea at the age of 25, when she was lost off an ocean liner in mysterious circumstances.

GORDON KIRWAN TAYLOR (LATER CHANGED TO G.K. KIRWAN-TAYLOR), 1901-75

Gordon was educated at Epsom and Trinity College, Cambridge, and married firstly in 1934 and had two children, Roy and Deidre. In 1956 he married again.

He became a successful general practitioner in Cadogan Square, London, and served in the R.A.M.C. as a Major during the Second World War. He was also involved with the family business, for the records of Cheam state that he purchased the freehold of the Windsor Castle public house in Myrtle Road, Sutton in 1922, and sold it to the brewers, Charringtons, in 1949. Indeed, he was, at one time, the Chairman of Onyx Property Investments.

LT. COL. WILLIAM JOHN TAYLOR O.B.E., F.R.I.C.S. (LATER CHANGED TO W.J. KIRWAN-TAYLOR), 1905-94

John, as he was known, was educated at Epsom and Trinity College, Cambridge. He became a Lt Colonel in the Rifle Brigade, and GSO (1), Airborne Forces.

38 *John, in Rugby kit.*

He landed with the Airborne H.Q. across the Rhine in a glider. For his war service he received a Military O.B.E.

During his business career he became a director of many companies including Brightstone Estates, London and Yorkshire Trust, Bowater Paper, Cow & Gate, and Unigate. He was also a director of the Onyx Companies.

He firstly married in 1929, and had two children, Peter and Hélène Fleur. Having divorced in 1941, his first wife then married Charles L. Hill. In 1938 Hill had become a director of L.G. Motors Ltd, the manufacturer of Lagonda cars. Peter recalls discussions between his step-father and the great W.O. Bentley who had joined Lagonda in 1935 after the Le Mans win. Duly inspired, Peter went on to head the design team which, from 1957, produced Colin Chapman's Lotus Elite.

John remarried in 1944, and had a second daughter, Tessa, and in 1970 he married for a third time.

All the Taylor boys, with the exception of Ernest, went up to Cambridge and excelled in sport and academia – between them they earned several blues and half-blues. John went further and for his prowess at rugby was called to play for England when a member of the Blackheath Club in the 1927/8 season. He played against Australia: England won 18-11; Wales: England won 10-8; Ireland: England won, 7-6; France: England won, 18-8 and Scotland: England won 6-0. What a season, the Grand Slam and the beating of Australia!

Sir Charles Stuart Taylor T.D., D.L. (Sussex), 1910-89

Charles was educated at Epsom College and Trinity College, Cambridge. He married Constance Shotter, an actress, in 1936, and had four children, Charles, Alexander, Jonathan and Jasmine. Unlike his brothers he did not change his name and sometimes referred to himself as Charles 'Plain' Taylor.

During the Second World War he was a Captain in the Royal Artillery, and in 1941 rose to T/Major. In 1958 he became the Hon. Col. 3rd (Sussex Bn.) Mobile Defence Corps. He was a keen yachtsman, sailing 6 metre craft for Great Britain after the war.

He became a director of Cow & Gate at the age of 22, and through a by-election became the youngest of MPs at the age of 24 in 1935, representing Eastbourne until 1974. He supported Churchill to be prime minister in 1940 in a revolt of 33 Conservative MPs, against the government of Neville Chamberlain. He was knighted in 1954 and at retirement was deputy father of the House of Commons.

During his career he was President of Grosvenor House (Park Lane) Hotels, and the Residential Hotels Association, vice-president of the Building Societies Association, Chairman of Onyx Country Estates and Managing Director of both Cow & Gate and Unigate. When Grosvenor House was taken over by Forte he immediately fell out with the new owner, Charles Forte – this was because he had given himself a flat in Reeves Mews, which Charles Forte wanted back!

He received the Order of St John, and became an Under Warden for the Worshipful Company of Bakers in 1976 and in 1980 he became Master. A story related by Anthony Turnbull goes back to an occasion when he and his cousin Peter were invited to a banquet at Mansion House with Charles as Master. Charles and his guests imbibed a little in an anteroom before the dinner and Charles became more legless than his guest of honour, Douglas Bader. Anthony confidently expected to be embarrassed when Charles gave his speech, but he delivered it perfectly with no notes, no hesitations and no slurring – the legacy of 45 years in the House of Commons, he supposed.

In 1989 both Charles and Constance died within six weeks of each other.

The Cow & Gate Connection

Many appreciate that there is a connection between the dairy firm of Cow & Gate and Abbotswood, but few know the depth.

The firm of Gates can to traced back to 1771 as a grocery business at a shop in Guildford High Street between the Abbot's Hospital and *The Three Pigeons* public house. By 1881 it stocked beers, wines and spirits. At around this time, Charles Gates handed over the business to his two sons, Leonard and Charles Arthur Gates. They soon decided to concentrate on dairy products and do away with alcohol, and to prove their point it is said that they hauled all their stock up from the cellars and tipped it into the High Street. The family were Plymouth Brethren.

The firm sold cream, buying the milk from local farms. It was trading under the name of West Surrey Central Dairy Company and its original trade mark was a pair of wrought iron gates. A new emblem was devised after the brothers had juggled with pictures of cows and gates, cut out of paper, and in 1891 was registered as the trade mark.

To ensure supplies of the best quality milk, over the years they built their own creameries in the West of England and also in Ireland, where Cow & Gate infant formula milks are still produced.

The success of their cream business gave the Gates brothers a problem: they were left with huge quantities of skimmed milk. In 1900 there was no demand for low fat milks. To use up this milk they purchased the latest drying equipment from America and began selling milk powder to the bakery and catering trades for making puddings. In 1904, they received a bulk order for milk powder from the Medical Officer of Health in Leicester, Dr Killick Millard, for use as a baby food.

The result of this initiative was to encourage doctors and hospitals all over the country to buy this new product from this Guildford firm. Cow & Gate was destined to be a successful and very large company, and from 1908 the Cow & Gate brand name was widely used. Leonard and Charles died in 1915 and 1919 respectively. In the meantime, W.R. 'Bramwell' St John Gates and 'Ernest' Rayer

Gates had joined the board, along with A.H. Mitchell. They were joined in 1911 by Stanley, William and Alfred Gates – truly a family business.

It appeared from the outside that the only connection with Abbotswood was that Bramwell lived at The Gate House (1) from 1915 to 1919, and from 1917 to 1920 Ernest lived at The Croft (4). Ownership details in Chapter 11 show that both purchases were supported financially by Alfred Taylor.

Taylor supported more than just the house purchases, indeed, he supported the business as a whole. Anthony Turnbull recalls that his grandfather, Alfred, told him that he had borrowed for the Gates family 'a mind-bogglingly large sum of money using his contacts in the city to do so'. It could well be that Taylor had recognised that this was not only to be a useful investment for the family, but also a way of putting Ernest's skills to good use.

Ernest had formed a friendship with the Gates family, and later in 1925, at the age of 28, probably at the instigation of his father, helped to form Wincanton Transport and Engineering Company. Any evidence of a direct loan has been lost in the mist of time, but the ensuing scenario, of Alfred's financial assistance linked by the board membership of his sons, was also seen with London and Manchester.

If help was given early on, it had been successful. In 1925 the Gates family was very much in control with seven family members on the board of West Surrey Central Dairy Co. Ltd, the holding company. The issued capital was £97,500 – a substantial sum. The business included the wholesale supply of bottled milk, numerous creameries and dairies in the West Country and Ireland, and of course the dried milk business.

The year 1928 was a year of change for the company. Several directors, including Ernest Gates resigned, leaving only Bramwell Gates and A. St John Gates. Joining the board were Ernest Taylor and Alfred Jesse Suenson-Taylor. In 1929, at the aged of 24, John Taylor joined along with Bramwell's son, Valder Gates. Hence there were now three directors from each family. Jesse became chairman, giving the Taylor family virtual control. This supports the view that Taylor money was, and possibly had been for some time, supporting the business. In 1932 even Charles Taylor, at the tender age of 22, joined the board.

In 1929, the name Cow & Gate Company Limited was adopted. Thereafter the Taylor family figured large and at one time or another Jesse, Ernest, John and Charles held prominent positions. Bramwell Gates, at the age of 83, resigned in July 1958, after 69 years' service to Cow & Gate, for which he was chairman for 21 years. In October 1959, he died. On the merger with United Dairies in 1959, to form Unigate, Leonard Maggs, formerly of United Dairies, was chairman, and Ernest Taylor deputy chairman. When Leonard died in August of that year, Ernest became chairman of Unigate. John and Charles Taylor were also directors. Of the Gates family, only Valder Gates remained a director. Alfred Taylor would have been very proud of Ernest – sadly he had died in May that year, and did not witness his son's ultimate success.

Seven

The Architect:
A. Claude Burlingham (1885-1963)

Alfred Claude Burlingham was the architect, and in the latter stages may be described as the co-developer for the Abbotswood estate. Alfred Taylor once commented to him that it was unusual for such a hard-headed businessman to be so artistic!

A. Claude Burlingham, as he signed his plans, attended Birmingham Municipal School of Art.

The Birmingham Municipal School of Arts and Crafts, as it was known from 1884, was under the headship of Edward R. Taylor from 1877 to 1903, when teaching was strongly influenced by the Arts and Crafts Movement. Burlingham travelled abroad as part of his tutelage. Initially he went to Italy with another student on a sketching and measuring tour, visiting among other places Milan, Venice, and Verona. Later he went by himself to study the chateaux of Normandy and Brittany.

From 1904 to 1908 Burlingham was articled to Mansell and Mansell at 47, Temple Road, Birmingham. Having completed his architect's examinations he applied for membership of the Royal Institute of British Architects and was proposed by A.H. Ryan-Tenison, C.E. Bateman, T.G. Mansell, and J. Slater. At the time of his qualification, Burlingham was living in Evesham.

Moving south, he practised with Alfred Taylor in Sutton from 1909, and in Guildford between from 1912 until war broke out. Burlingham's earliest work, to 1912, was as architect for 24 private houses around Sutton, Purley, Wallington, Redhill and Bexhill. He designed a Memorial Home for Nurses in Evesham. Work was also carried out on Lord Falmouth's estates in Kent and Cornwall.

Working in Guildford, and as a follower of the Arts and Crafts Movement, it seems likely that the young Burlingham visited the houses around the area built by those he much admired. From his designs, as will be shown later, these perhaps included Merrist Wood House by Norman Shaw, the myriad of Arts

39 *Newlands Cottage in 1923.*

and Crafts houses in the outlying villages, as well as those in Warwicks Bench and Guildown, some of which were quite new at the time.

His application for a fellowship, submitted in September 1927, reveals that during his first period in Guildford he designed 18 different houses of values between £1,000 and £5,000, the lay-out of Abbotswood, and a house in Send. From 1919 Burlingham designed 20 houses in and around Guildford, a house and a lodge for Lord Onslow, three houses at Dorking, six houses at Evesham, 12 small houses at Cheam, two houses in Peaslake, a factory premises with offices in Guildford, 12 small houses in Burpham, two blocks of commercial premises in Cheam comprising 26 shops, and seven houses in Merrow at values of between £2,000 and £6,000, of which his own was probably the most expensive. Further single houses were built at Warwicks Bench, Pewley Down, Chilworth, all of which were around Guildford, and one in Fleet, Hampshire. Many of these houses have been identified and are commented on below.

Claude Burlingham was elected a Fellow of the Royal Institute of British Architects on 5 December 1927, by which time he was living at Newlands Cottage.

Burlingham's association with the Onyx companies continued with a revised agreement in 1926. Through the new agreement he would hold new shares in Onyx Country Estates, but yield his interests in the housing estates.

DEED OF COVENANT DATED 15 FEBRUARY 1926: COPY UNSIGNED

This agreement contained terms including the following provisions:

1. It was recorded that under a Contract of Sale also dated 15 February 1926, Onyx Country Estates agreed to purchase from Onyx Property Investments and A.C. Burlingham three estates at Cheam, Surrey; Guildford, Surrey; and Evesham, Worcestershire.

2. The consideration paid to Onyx Property Investments was £4,323 in cash and the issue of 1,998 shares in Onyx Country Estates, and that paid to Burlingham was £2,275 in cash and 400 shares in Onyx Country Estates.

3. The terms of employment and portion of the development of the estates was recited and where required, changed.

4. The revised terms were that Burlingham would cover losses to the extent of ¼ at Cheam and Guildford and ⅓ at Evesham, as before. For any new sites, he would cover ⅙ of losses.

5. Burlingham would continue to fund site purchases and building works in the same proportions.

6. Burlingham would be entitled to ⅙ of dividends declared by Onyx Country Estates.

7. He would receive ⅕ of the profits on the Cheam site, and ¹⁄₁₀ of the profits on the Guildford and Evesham sites.

40 A. Claude Burlingham.

No details are given for his salary, which continued.

By the date of this contract, Burlingham's involvement with Abbotswood was all but finished. The design of the last house, The Odd House (16), was submitted for planning approval in July 1925, and sold in September 1926.

This document refers to the sale of three estates. These can be identified as the Hall Place Farm estate in Merrow, comprising Trodds Lane, Downsway and Fairway; Abbotswood in Evesham, and the Cuddington Golf Estate near Cheam.

Burlingham, in conjunction with the Taylor family, was to devote much of his time in Guildford to the identification of areas for development, the purchase of the land and, having obtained consent for the development of the estate, the selling of plots for other builders, sometimes employing their own architects. This would provide a mixture of styles, reflecting current tastes and the funds available at the time. Orchard Estate was the exception.

41   *Ledgers for Orchard Estate written in Burlingham's hand, headed 'Orchard Estate'.*

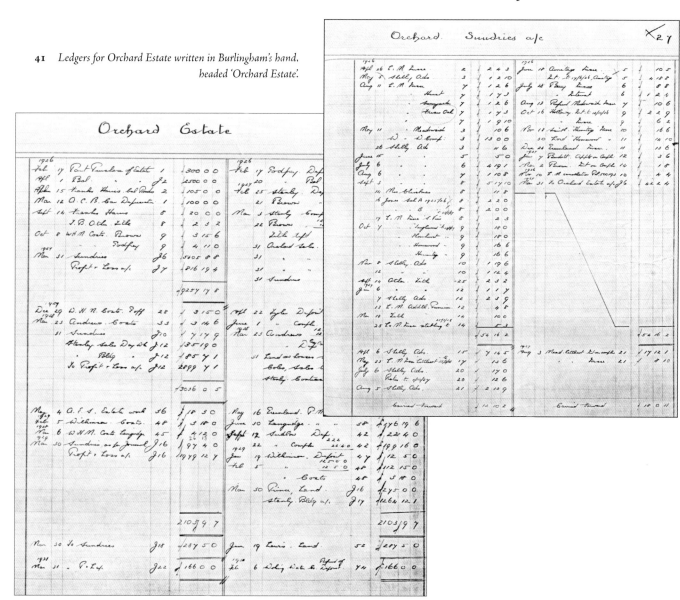

ORCHARD ESTATE – 1926

Away from Abbotswood, Burlingham had his own interests to follow with the builder, A.E. Stanley. In 1925 he started his own development which is now Orchard Road, Burpham, and called it Orchard Estate. No reference to Taylor appears on the planning applications to the Guildford Rural District Council. This estate comprised a number of smaller houses, at least one of which was designed by Stanley, the builder. References to Onyx Country Estates came later and are sparse, but these indicate that London and Manchester might have had an interest at some point.

The accounts show no trading activity for 1930 and 1931. Planning records show that planning applications for the Orchard Estate and construction continued until the Second World War. Many plots were sold off to be developed by third parties.

The minor sundries ledger shows costs for advertising with Shelly Ads, and numerous payments for London and Manchester Insurance for such properties as The Hurst, Sunnymead, and Friars Oak.

THE MERROW DOWNS ESTATE, FORMING FAIRWAY AND DOWNSWAY – 1927

In mid-1926 Burlingham started the ball rolling for the purchase of Hall Place Farm with the Church authorities. He then involved the Taylor family and the Abstracts of Title and the house deeds show that the original plots were sold by both Claude Burlingham and Ernest Taylor as joint vendors. They had purchased the property from The Blessed Holy Trinity Hospital, Guildford, through a somewhat complicated process. The transaction comprised several deeds, required because of the charity nature of the holdings by the Church, and the fact that some of the farm was still tenanted. Onyx Country Estates Limited was described as the owner of the plots on planning applications where houses were designed by Burlingham. Thus there can be little doubt that in the purchase the funds backing the development were those of London and Manchester.

The farm, near St John's church, Merrow, comprised parts of Trodds Lane, and more importantly land abutting Merrow Downs, which was used to form the Downsway and Fairway Estate. The purchase took place on 7 January 1927 where for the grand sum of £13,300 over 63 acres were bought.

Burlingham put forward plans for three roads on the farm in November 1926, and these went

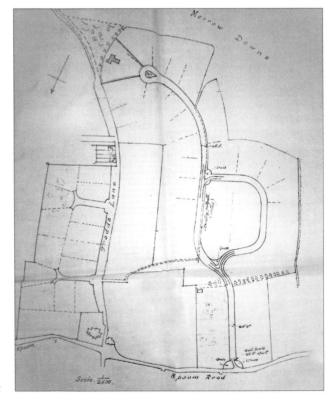

42   *Plans for three new roads, Merrow, 1926.*

43 *Hall Place Farm.*

before the Planning Committee on 4 January next. He also started sending in planning applications for houses in December, until there were seven in all. They were sanctioned at the same time. With this good news under their belts, Burlingham and Ernest Taylor completed the purchase of the farm three days later.

The roads to be constructed were Abbots Way, and Three Pears Road, both of which are off Trodds Lane, and the third was Fairway. Fairway, off Epsom Road, comprised a long road to include what is now Downsway, with a circular adjunct to the south. It was later changed after 1928 to the extent that the furthest portion forming Downsway then led onto Trodds Lane. The circle in Fairway was never completed. The roads were set out with a width of 40ft, and reinforced concrete some 13ft wide, bordered by brick paths 3ft 6ins wide. The brickwork can still be seen at the entrance to Fairway.

Initially this development was called Merrow Downs Estate, and the current names did not appear until some time later. Reference to 'Merrow Downs' continued well into the 1930s although the earliest use of the name 'Fairway' appeared in December 1929 when it was referred to as 'Fairway, Merrow Downs'. Later, it was sometimes referred to as 'The Fairway'. Burlingham's first house in Merrow Downs was Little Court, which is now 32, Trodds Lane. In 1927, the planning application for Little Court had the entrance to the long estate road and was later changed. A reference to the name 'Downsway' first appeared by way of planning applications submitted for other houses in 1934.

A walk along the concrete road that forms the Fairway Estate is an experience. Somehow it differs from Abbotswood; it is more genteel, quieter, but lacks the architectural surprises that one finds in Abbotswood. The houses are more regular, smart, 1930s style; expensive, yet architecturally, from the outside at least, mainly less exciting. Nevertheless, they remain imposing. The estate, comprising just over 50 houses, was developed from 1927 and

44 *The brick pavement at Fairway.*

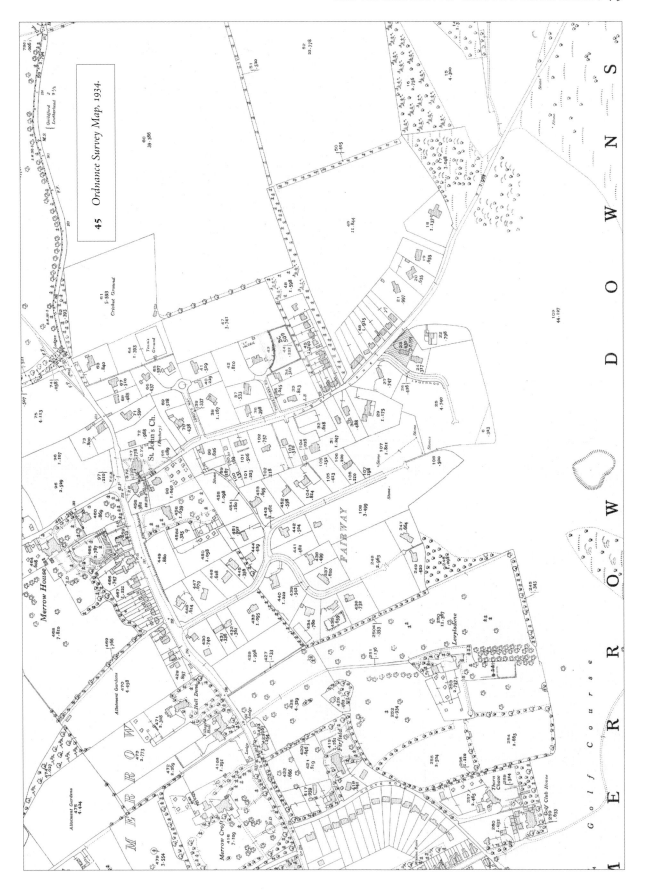

45 *Ordnance Survey Map, 1934.*

throughout the 1930s – depression was still in the mind of everyone as was the possibility of war in Europe.

The first batch of houses were mostly completed in 1928 near the Epsom Road. Thereafter there was slower progress until 1934, when the economy started to revive. Building work then continued apace, and by 1939 most houses had been built.

The Hall Place Farm development comprises mostly of houses in large gardens. Generally, both present and former residents have not yielded to the temptation to take a profit and grow a further house in the garden. In Fairway this was helped by the fact that one resident purchased the frontages, and restricted the building of new entrances on to the road. This land is now collectively owned by the residents.

One of the most impressive houses in Downsway, called Brandlehow, was built in 1936 for C. Faulkner S. Hole, Claude's nephew, and his wife Ursula. Their son was Roderick Hole. Faulkner's brother Dick was responsible for persuading the council to name a road in Merrow called Burlingham Close.

Trodds Lane – 1923

46 *The cover for the article featuring Greys in 1926.*

Trodds Lane was basically a track up to the downs and the Merrow Racecourse, where from 1701 to 1870 races were held regularly. It appears on the Roque map: Fig. 5. It was formed before Epsom, and for many years remained the superior attraction. The better accessibility by rail of both Ascot and Epsom eventually led to falling attendances, and on 26 April 1870 the last 'Queens Plate' was run. The racecourse eventually gave way in 1886 to the Guildford Golf Club.

The road and the topography had not much changed when Burlingham arranged to purchase Hall Place Farm. Before that, in 1923, he purchased plots of land at £675, amounting to over an acre each, from Lord Onslow. In respect of the land for Greys, of the purchase money £500 was paid to the mortgagee in reduction of an outstanding loan of £31,000 secured by land in the area.

Burlingham set about building two of the last houses on the left-hand side, being Greys and Newlands Cottage. From 1923 he was to make the latter his family home. These very special houses are of the highest quality, at a level seen in the best of Abbotswood built before the First World War. For this they deserve particular mention.

Greys was of sufficient importance to be featured in 'Town and Country Homes', in June 1926, with seven photographs, showing the interior and exterior, taking four full pages of the magazine. This was built for his sister, Mrs Hilda Gray Hole, who initially purchased the plot for £416 from Claude, on 20 June 1923, with the proviso that the house should cost not less than £1,200 and be built by him. Hilda was married to Charles Henry Hole from Evesham.

The deeds reveal a strip of land, 40 feet wide between the house next door called Dreva and Newlands Cottage. A condition of the sale of the land for Greys, and presumably Dreva too, was that the purchaser should not have any right over that strip, nor should they be liable for the cost of surfacing it. In other words, it was to be for a road, presumably for future development of the parcel of land on the Downs at the back of these houses, to which Lord Onslow retained ownership. Furthermore, Burlingham had to run a water pipe over the golf course that could be used for further development, which thankfully never took place.

Greys and Newlands Cottage were very similar when they were first built.

Newlands Cottage was built with a stipulation in the deeds that it should cost not less than £2,000. He had become a wealthy man, and Newlands Cottage was a way to show the world. It is perched on the side of the slope on the North Downs with wide views to London. He sought to make the best of this not only by having a verandah overlooking the garden, but also one off the main bedroom on the first floor, with panoramic views across the Thames Valley.

The house is a splendid example of the Surrey vernacular. The grand entrance leads to an oak panelled hallway, with a large fireplace having a carved stone surround, similar to Abbotswood houses. The ceiling is oak beamed, as is the one in the drawing room. The ceiling in the oak panelled dining room is plain and without decorative plaster.

48 *Newlands Cottage: Note the wooden scaffolding used during construction; when completed baby Russell and nanny enjoy the patio.*

The windows have been replaced with a brown painted metal, but the wood frames have been retained and only replaced where there was rot. A kitchen has been built on by a later owner. The designer of this probably took no heed of the fact that he was partly to hide one of the most interesting chimneys designed by Burlingham, which had two steps, and two integral windows, with the inset bricks on the stack.

49 *Newlands cottage today.*

50 *The Baillie Scott-type entrance hall. Note the fireplace tiles, similar to those at Undershaw.*

Burlingham's early changes are clear, but generally adhere to the original design. For his first born, Russell, now three, he decided to add a day nursery, and a night nursery on the first floor, with a kitchen and servants' sitting room beneath. This was to the side of the front door, which some may say slightly off-balanced the house. In January 1927 the plans were submitted.

When comparing the early photographs with the present building, and by looking at the interior walls, it is clear that he extended two gables to enlarge the rooms. Firstly, the study was enlarged by ten feet, and the bedroom above, and secondly the dining room, on the opposite side of the house, was extended by a similar amount. He simply removed the façade, added the extra works, and replaced the gable intact – it is so well done that from simply looking at the brickwork it is hard to detect. One can but wonder why he did this significant work for scant advantage. Perhaps it was done in the times of the depression, and it was a way of keeping his men employed. We shall never know.

The early integral garage was a sign of his love of the motor car. The family car was an early Bullnose Morris Cowley.

The name Newlands Cottage is a little odd; anything less like a cottage is hard to imagine. A family story is that to have given it a pretentious name would have dissuaded local servants from applying for jobs!

51   *Main entrance, and carved mullions for the windows …*

52   *… and the interior impressive dining room panelling, and the beamed ceiling drawing room.*

53 *The modern kitchen hides the original chimney.*

TRODDS LANE: 1927 ONWARDS

The sanction of the plan for the roads, and the purchase of Hall Place Farm, enabled Claude Burlingham and the Taylor family to start building along the left side of Trodds Lane, from Merrow church up to Swaynes Lane, and more particularly Abbots Way and Three Pears Road. Sometimes Burlingham sought permission for houses in different roads on one planning application. At the start of this development he applied to build seven houses, using three different designs.

It is not difficult for the residents of Fairway and the Trodds Lane roads to seek out a house similar to their own, for Burlingham continued to build at

54 *Rita Burlingham at the wheel. Note the artillery wheels held on by just three bolts.*

least in pairs, as he had done in Abbotswood. Chapter 12 identifies and lists the houses designed by Claude Burlingham on Hall Place Farm land.

GANGHILL – 1929

From 1929 onwards, Burlingham, together with Onyx Country Estates, developed Ganghill. Ganghill Copse was purchased from the 5th Earl of Onslow in July 1929, and development started on the London Road side of the railway track that had dissected Ganghill Copse in 1855. Burlingham obtained permission to build a bridge over the line, with a view to extending the road the other side. This extension did not proceed, and only much later, in April 1938, Burlingham applied to build a road to start the Merrow Woods Estate, comprising Merrow Woods and Merrow Copse. This was described as being 'off Horseshoe Lane'. It signalled the end to the centuries-old woodland but, apart from seven houses near the entrance, the principal development was left until the 1960s.

55 *Ordnance Survey Map, 1934.*

Burlingham had a considerable influence on the design of Ganghill, and by 1939 he had built 11 of the early houses for Onyx Country Estates. The orderly layout of the houses, and the simplicity of the designs compared with those in Abbotswood, were indicative of the changes in the social and, most important of all, the economic climate of the time. Nonetheless, Burlingham still managed to design some good quality houses in the road.

Chapter 12 details the planning histories of the Ganghill houses built up to 1939, which are available from contemporary records.

Downside Road, Merrow – 1933

Between Fairway and the *Horse and Groom* public house there is a road called The Paddock. At one time there was a house called 'Downside' abutting Epsom Road with a very large garden, including a walled kitchen garden, a flint cottage and outbuildings.

In early 1933, Burlingham submitted plans for this plot with a view to creating a 'Downside' estate. Surrey County Council had purchased the land, presumably in order to demolish the house for road improvements, and Burlingham bought the remaining land. Having submitted an outline plan for the development with 12 proposed houses, he had difficulty persuading the authorities about the entrance on to Epsom Road. His proposal was disapproved in June 1933. The name 'Downside' was later used for a road at the end of Warren Road in Guildford.

Burlingham and the Taylors sold all or part of the property on 17 August 1933 to Clifford Clare Rattey. They had either received an offer they could not refuse, or had decided to cut their losses.

In July 1934 Mr Rattey applied for permission to build Hunters Moon on the land. This large futuristic house, designed by J.W. Shaft, was rendered

56 *Hunters Moon.*

and is painted white. It stands out in the concrete street, which was much as Burlingham had prescribed, and probably had laid. The road is now filled with neat bungalows and houses built mainly after 1970, save for the flint cottage, which had been standing in the grounds of Downside House for many years. The idea for Burlingham's one and only flint house in the area, at 1, Fairway, was doubtlessly conceived with this cottage in mind.

An application by Mr Rattey, this time for a further house on the land leading onto Fairway, was submitted in March 1937 – it was also approved. However those plans do not reflect the existing house, 8, Fairway, which was completed in July 1938.

Boxgrove Estate – 1933

Another significant development was the Boxgrove Estate. This comprised Meads Road and Green Lane, abutting both Boxgrove Road and Epsom Road. Burlingham submitted the plans for the estate, which surrounded Boxgrove House but these were initially rejected as the frontages for some of the houses were less than 50 feet. The total number of houses allowed was reduced from 70 to 69, and in December 1933 the planning committee passed the application. The sizes of the houses and the plots were generally smaller than those at Abbotswood or Fairway, but the style of house was not dissimilar.

The plots were sold off individually. A.E. Stanley is listed as one of the architects involved in the late 1930s, and he also built many of the houses on this estate for other architects.

Other Guildford Involvements, 1915-20

Burlingham was very much involved with Bramwell Gates, and together with Stanley Ellis, a builder used by Cow & Gate for a large portion of their work, provided a new scullery at Highlands, Harvey Road in 1915. He was again involved with Highlands in July 1920, for the Rev. J. Sharpe, using Bullen and Son, for an 'addition'.

Houses for 5th Earl of Onslow – 1924

Lord Onslow asked Burlingham to design two properties in Clandon and a lodge and a house at Dedswell Manor. Both sets of plans were lodged on 20 October 1924, and sanction was given with some speed eight days later.

The plans reveal a substantial house, along the lines of those in Abbotswood, in the Surrey style, with half-timbering and overhanging rooms. There were two main reception rooms, a verandah off the dining room, and an integral garage. Upstairs there was a maid's bedroom, with a corner fireplace, and three further bedrooms.

The open entrance porch has a beam over the threshold. There are ceiling beams in the hall, and a stone fireplace in the living room with carving so often

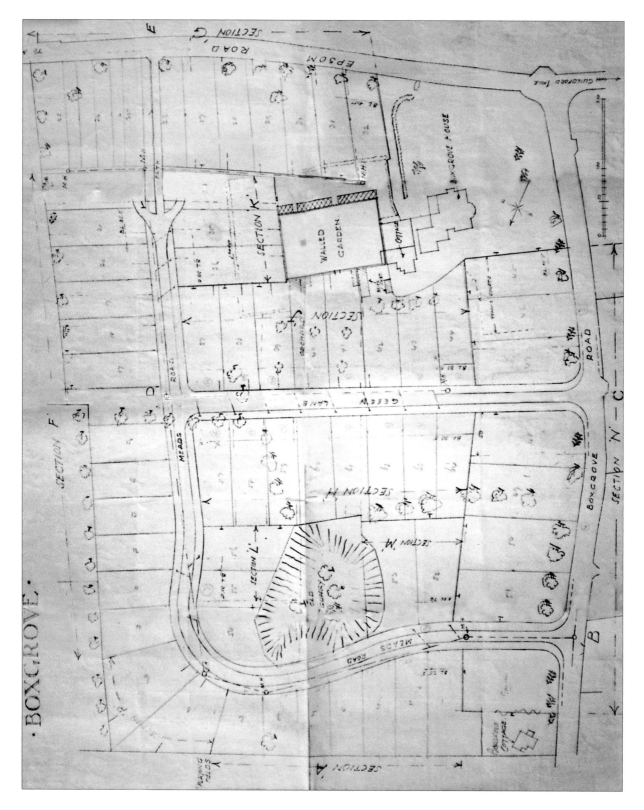

57 *Plan of Boxgrove Estate.*

seen in Abbotswood, all adding to the quality of the whole. The house has the Abbotswood-style window catches and even the balustrade for the stairs is the correct post-war type.

58 A house for the Earl of Onslow in Clandon.

Outside, the end gable is of the highest quality and is enhanced by a well carved bargeboard, square window panes, and a suitable overhang supported by large wooden brackets. There is an imposing chimney at the front of the house, dissecting the roof line.

The planned lodge was much smaller, and had a thatched roof. It had three bedrooms, a hall, scullery, kitchen and parlour. As it was intended for staff, there was no dining area; presumably the staff were to eat all their meals in the kitchen.

WEST SURREY CENTRAL DAIRY COMPANY LIMITED – 1925

Burlingham was the architect for substantial new premises for West Surrey Central Dairies, in Stoke Road, Guildford. This was latterly known as the United Dairies bottling depot and has since been reconstructed to become the offices of Clyde & Co., Solicitors.

Outside Guildford

Imperial House

The largest building designed by Burlingham was undoubtedly Imperial House, an investment property built for the London and Manchester's property portfolio, and is shown in Fig. 35. This was erected in 1932 in Finsbury, and demolished in 1993, despite attempts to have it listed. The address was South Street London, EC2, near the London and Manchester Head Office at 50, Finsbury Square.

Abbotswood Estate, Greenhill, Evesham

Burlingham designed the layout of this estate which, like Ganghill, comprised of a single meandering road. It was situated off Greenhill, which is on the A4148, going north out of Evesham. He designed eight houses, between 1925 and 1926, and infilling over the years has since increased this number to fifteen. Amazingly, not only did he use the name from the Guildford estate, but the house nearest the main road is called The Gate House, and the design is not unfamiliar!

Cuddington Golf Estate

The reference to an estate at Cheam in the 1926 agreement with Onyx Companies is believed to be Cuddington Golf Estate, situated on the edge of the Nonsuch Park Estate. The land was purchased by the Taylor family

59 *The Gate House, Abbotswood, Nr Evesham.*

from Sir Edward Northey. The family decided to build the golf course on the highest 100 acres of the estate, and developed it in the late 1920s. The course was designed by Mr H.S. Holt in conjunction with Mr John Morrison, and built by Messrs Franks Harris Brothers. Mr W.G. Tarrant, who had laid out St George's Hill and Wentworth gave useful advice. The Cuddington Club House was designed by Claude Burlingham; much of the building is in his discernible style. The builder was A.H. Room.

The simultaneous construction of houses abutting the golf course makes this one of the very early golfing estates. The course was opened on 1 January 1929, and the Clubhouse on 6 June that year. The Taylor family continued to support the golf club financially, well into the 1970s.

FARNHAM, MOOR PARK ESTATE

Moor Park House is situated to the south-east of Farnham, and has a history going back to William III. The house is mainly early 19th-century. In recent times it was for sale by auction in 1912 with 500 acres, a little later, by private treaty, with 136 acres, and by auction again in June 1937 with just 67¼ acres. By that time it had been agreed with the Farnham Council that 170 acres of pine woods and brush could be transformed into an high quality housing estate with plots of either ½ acres or two acres plus. Seventy-four houses were envisaged of which Burlingham was to design a number. The selling agent was Eggar & Co. of Farnham.

The developer was Mr Dick Martin, who had obtained outline permission in February 1936 for the building of the estate, and in January 1937 for roads forming Compton Way, Monks' Well, Temple's Close, Swift's Close and Cobbetts Ridge. A visit to the estate reveals that the Burlingham-style designs stand out from the other houses. The setting of mature woodlands, without the crowding of the Guildford estates, must have rejuvenated his ideas, for, whilst the houses have a simplistic 1930s aura about them, the large gardens set off the houses very well indeed. Inevitably, newer houses have been built in many of the gardens, but it remains a glorious woodland setting, with a greater selection of oak and chestnut and fewer pines.

In 1937, John Taylor purchased Moor Park House and he lived there with his family until the Canadian forces took it over for the 'duration'. He stayed for a year at Newlands Cottage in Merrow and sold Moor Park House in 1946. His son, Peter, believes that his uncle Gordon Taylor lived on the Moor Park Estate.

BURLINGHAM: THE FAMILY MAN

Telephone conversations in August 2007 with Russell Burlingham and Patricia Burlingham, the son and daughter of Claude Burlingham, revealed much about their father's family life. Patricia later supplied many early photographs of the family and the properties that her father built.

Claude Burlingham was born in Evesham, in 1885, where his family had a successful agricultural equipment business, trading as H. Burlingham & Co. He was the youngest of four children and went to Channel View Preparatory School, Clevedon, and then to Dulwich College. He attended the Birmingham School of Art, and set his sights on becoming an architect. He favoured the Arts and Crafts styles, and Russell believes that, having come to Guildford shortly after qualifying, he would have been very much aware of the local works of Shaw, Voysey, Baillie Scott and Lutyens. He was an admirer of Sir Edward Guy Dawber (1861-1938), although there is no evidence that he studied under him.

His career was interrupted by the First World War, when he served as a Lieutenant in the Royal Army Service Corp., mainly in Salonika. In 1921, Claude married Margaret Russell (Rita) Rattray, the daughter of Brigadier-General Charles Rattray, C.B., C.S.I., who served all his military career in India.

Russell was born in July 1923, and his sister Patricia is five years his junior. Their parents had left Red Cottage in May 1923 and after temporary accommodation soon moved into Newlands Cottage in Trodds Lane, where the family lived until 1942.

As a young man, Russell was not enamoured with his father's style of architecture, for by the time he was old enough to understand the work the Jacobethan style was all the rage for the growing metropolis and mock Tudor was everywhere. At the time, he failed to appreciate that his father's work was actually started prior to this period, more specifically reflecting the Arts and Crafts style.

Burlingham's intention to leave Merrow was partly because of Rita's deteriorating health and therefore a wish to be nearer his family in Evesham. It was also because he thought that it would be difficult to get servants, as his butler, Dodgson, had been called up. It might also have been because of the bombs dropped by German planes on the nearby golf course whilst aborting a mission to bomb London, or the sight of bombs being dropped over the city. Perhaps it was a combination of all these.

With hostilities well under way, the family left Guildford and moved to The Rectory, in Willersey on the border of Worcestershire and Gloucestershire for about a year, as paying guests. After that, they rented a cottage in Broadway – it was there, in 1943, that Rita died. Russell was 20, and Patricia just fifteen. They returned to Newlands Cottage for a short while, and it was then let for 12 months to John Taylor, and his second wife.

During the early part of the war the house was rented to Lord Broughshane, formerly Sir William Davison, Member of Parliament for South Kensington, and later created Baron Broughshane of Kensington. Therein lies a tenuous link to Abbotswood, for he married Beatrice Roberts, whose parents lived at Henley Park, Guildford, prior to Gordon Vokes buying the house and grounds for his filter business. His son Tony Vokes still lives in Abbotswood.

Having sold Newlands Cottage at the end of the war, Claude and the children moved to Milford-on-Sea.

Russell was educated at Harrow and Oxford. Whilst his mother would have liked him to go into the army, his father was very relaxed about the subject and did not object when he followed his passion of book collecting, and became an antiquarian bookseller. At Harrow he can recall the first time that Winston Churchill returned to the school as a hero, and to a rapturous welcome. He was one of the boys cheering from the front steps in the often shown movie newsreel.

The book collecting started in Newlands Cottage, and ended with a gift of 75,000 volumes to his club, The Reform. Russell's recollection of Newlands Cottage was that it was an enormous house with a large hall where he was allowed to place his books in the bookcases. The view onto the Merrow Downs from the house was sublime. It was from the verandah that he and the family watched the fire when the Crystal Palace burned down on 30 November 1936, and on a fine day the cars racing at the Brooklands Circuit would glint in the sun. Later the bombing of London would be looked at in awe.

Only once, when he was a small child, did he come across Alfred Taylor. He walked up the drive, a tall and austere man, and enquired if he was Mr Burlingham's son and heir. Russell, being just five years old, took fright and ran to the safety of the house.

He knew his father to be a quiet, yet determined and religious man. He recalls that his father, as architect for London and Manchester through Onyx Country Estates, spent much time at Central House, Finsbury Square.

60 *The family enjoying a holiday on the Isle of Wight, during the halcyon days of the 1930s.*

Newlands Cottage was important for Patricia, too. She has fond memories of the large and comfortable house in an idyllic setting, surrounded by the Downs, fields, and with a small copse on one side where they played for hours and hours.

Her memory of the Dodgsons is that they were a marvellous couple, doing much for the family. Dodgson, the butler, used to make smoke come out of his ears, and the cook, Mrs Dodgson, made very fine chocolate rice pudding.

Patricia's recollections of their father are very strong, and she was devoted to him. They had some wonderful expeditions to large empty properties, with magical overgrown gardens – all ripe for redevelopment! She gloried in sharing the making of bonfires with her father. Very often on a Saturday afternoon he took Patricia to the 'pictures' at the Playhouse, in North Street, Guildford when a Ginger Rogers film was being shown. She claims that she was thoroughly bored, and he used to buy her a packet of Rowntrees pastilles as a bribe. Claude was fascinated with trains, and the family had many a picnic by a railway line. He used to get the old copies of Bradshaw out of the public library in Evesham, and plan imaginary journeys all over the country.

As a small girl, she well remembers the children's parties held at The Hurst (46), where she played with Nancy Bullock.

Patricia was friendly with Mary Adams from White Gates (36), and they both went to Tormead, and later Mary followed her to schooling in Malvern, where they both boarded at Clarendon. Girls from both the Taylor and Gates families also attended the school, which was started for children with Plymouth Brethren backgrounds by three Plymouth Brethren sisters. The Burlingham, Taylor and Gates families were all of that ilk, although Claude and his siblings turned to the Church of England.

One of her memories of her father was his objection to the building of Guildford Cathedral by Sir Edward Maufe. He felt strongly that it should not have been built on Stag Hill, where there were all sorts of foundation problems to manage, and would have preferred it to have been built on Stoke Park, closer to the community.

Around 1939, when the road for Merrow Woods had been built, there were only a few houses at the Boxgrove end. The road ran through woodland, and Patricia loved to play along the road, and in the trees. The war prevented further building and the land was left as woodland for many years. She recalled just how cross her father and Taylor were when, having requisitioned the Merrow Woods land during the war, the War Office wanted to give a pittance by way of retribution. This went to court, and much to her father's pleasure the company decided that it should be done in his name, as Burlingham vs. The Crown. It was with great delight that Claude won the case.

Claude retired to Milford-on-Sea. Patricia recalls with some pleasure a visit from Alfred Taylor, or 'old man Taylor', as her father affectionately referred to him, who remonstrated with her father to the effect that, at 61 years of age, he was far too young to retire. Although retired, he was not adverse to a little designing for friends and relations, free gratis. He even helped extend the local school, making it a lot more attractive than it might have been. He designed a cottage in the garden of his house, and eventually moved there to spend a happy retirement by the sea.

BURLINGHAM: THE EMPLOYER

An advertisement in the local press requesting information about the building of both Abbotswood and A. Claude Burlingham drew a very useful reply from Mrs Mamie Grover, who was born in 1914, and for many years lived in Burpham. Mrs Grover kindly provided the following information during an interview.

Mamie first became acquainted with the area when she stayed with an aunt who lived at Collingbourne Cottages, Burpham Lane, Burpham. She personally knew of Burlingham as the architect for the Onyx building company which constructed Abbotswood, Ganghill, and some of Fairway. On his own account he built on parts of New Inn Lane, Burpham, and the small Orchard Road Estate, also in Burpham. This estate abutted Winterhill Farm and originally had two cottages on the land, owned by a Mr Robertson. He used one, and his workman the other.

Mamie and her husband purchased a plot of land on the edge of the Orchard Estate in New Inn Lane. The estate had almost been completed. They had a problem in that they wanted a semi, but Burlingham insisted that the house should be detached. Despite this, they prepared plans for a semi and went again to Burlingham. He said that if all the other house owners gave their consent, then he would allow it. Mamie and her husband relented and ended up with a detached house at 19, New Inn Lane.

Next to 19, New Inn Lane was the house in which the original owner lived. When he died, the land was purchased by the Catholic Church with the intention of building a church. As residents, Mamie and her husband joined others objecting to the plans. Burlingham, however, said that he was religious and would not support them. This resulted in a public appeal hearing against the possible nuisance, and they obtained a music restriction. They all paid 10 shillings (50p) to be represented by a Mr Edgley.

Mamie's father-in-law was approached by Burlingham following an incident. As a boy, her husband had constructed a go-kart, without brakes, and ran it from the cross-roads at Newlands Corner, down Trodds Lane, missing walkers by inches. Clearly cars were not an issue on the road, which was then more like a track. Burlingham exclaimed, 'I will have your boy, he nearly killed my father-in-law when he was riding down the lane far too fast on his contraption.'

Mamie's husband started as an apprentice, working at The Fairway. He became a keen motorcyclist, and Mamie recalls the many times that they would go for a ride at the weekend, heading south to either Brighton or Portsmouth. On their return on Sunday night, they would never go through Guildford because of the terrible traffic problems on the Old Portsmouth Road.

61 *Mamie Grover.*

Mamie remembers a kissing gate and a sheep walk; this went from the driveway at Stoke Park Farm, across Stoke Park to Stoke Church. Her grandfather, who used to live at Peace Cottages, Merrow Old Street, walked two miles to his work at Stoke Mill, using the lane that ran along the north side of Abbotswood. She remembers that there was a fairly good bus service to and from Guildford, costing two old pence from the *Green Man* inn to town.

Her father-in-law, a bricklayer for Mr Stanley, moved from his home in Merrow to Burpham in 1922, when he became one of the first tenants of a council house. Because his older children had started at Merrow Church School, it was decided that they would continue. Both the older and younger children, when of school age, walked the mile each way to school in all weathers. During the winter months, the children put their potatoes onto the embers of the fires to cook for lunch.

Mamie worked as a maid for Mrs Leighton of Albury House, Abbotswood. Mr Leighton was a director of Moon's Timber Yard in the centre of Guildford. Her employer used to annoy her by leaving silver to be polished in the house, paying her, and then going to work in the garden, knowing that the work left to be done would take Mamie well over her allotted time!

Her brother-in-law, Eric Glover, was in the Scouts, and he knew Mrs Neville at 3, Abbotswood who did much to help arrange camping holidays. She was keen on carpentry and left a lathe to Eric. Around 1937, her housekeeper was Mrs Quinlan.

Finally, Mamie recalls that her grandfather used to work on a local farm, but he gave that up to become a lengths man, from Burpham up to the Sutton Lodges. A lengths man was a road sweeper with a length to cover – his length started at the boundary stone at the Abbotswood corner of Weylea Farm and ended at Sutton Lodges, then owned by the Duke of Sutherland. When required he would caddy for the Duke of Sutherland's sister, Lady Betty, at the Sutton Place golf course.

Obituary

An obituary for A.C. Burlingham, FRIBA, recorded the death as being the result of an accident while living at Milford Corner Cottage, Milford-on-Sea. On 30 May 1963, at the age of 77, he died.

Eight

The Arts and Crafts Movement

The Arts and Crafts Movement originated with the Art Workers Guild and developed through the Arts and Crafts Exhibition Society, formed in 1888 as a forum for the promotion and display of designs. The houses in Abbotswood, and the other areas developed by Burlingham and Taylor, are described as being of the Arts and Crafts style, rather than being Arts and Crafts houses. In order to appreciate why this is, it is relevant first to consider the Movement. During these deliberations there will be references to the Surrey style or Surrey vernacular; for most houses, the description is synonymous. Abbotswood residents are fortunate in that they have to look no further than at Stoke Park Farm to discover what these descriptions are. After all, this property has all the qualities that the Arts and Crafts masters were trying to copy.

Sir Edwin Lutyens was brought up in Thursley, just 10 miles south-west of Guildford. He was to become the ideal designer of the Arts and Craft house in the Surrey style, which can be seen through his earliest works. Some were not great houses, but simple additions and improvements built when he was learning his trade. Mostly, the houses around Shere, Thursley and Godalming contain the features one would expect to see, including the large chimneys, tile hanging, half-timbering, red tile roofs and, sometimes around Godalming, the use of Bargate stone, where it is mined. Throughout the Surrey countryside there are many Tudor cottages evidencing the red tiles, the occasional Horsham slates, the long roof extending for two storeys, the gable ends, half-timbering and the brick or stone infilling.

Other areas in Britain have their own easily recognisable vernacular styles: in the Cotswolds, the Tudor and Jacobean houses have fine yellow stone, in East Anglia there are to be found coloured washes on plaster over timber frames, and in Cheshire, the extensive and all enveloping black and white timbering. All these features are reflected in local Arts and Crafts houses. When the

Movement was at its peak, the wealth of the nation was growing more strongly in the South East than elsewhere from the late 19th century to the 1910s and, therefore, many notable examples are to be found in Surrey. Hence the Surrey style is recognised as being an important element of the Movement.

Just how does an early Arts and Crafts house differ from any other, and how do you recognise it? It is easier to identify a Queen Anne house, or one from the Art Deco period. The former is to be seen in most towns. The houses are symmetrical, brick built, with large near-square windows. The latter can be seen as products of the 1920s to the 1940s not only in house and office design, but also that of cars, cinemas, department stores and the grand ocean liners of the time. A viewing of a *Poirot* television episode fully exemplifies this unique style. Only a short while ago Guildfordians were able to see two exemplary Art Deco buildings, the Odeon cinema and the *Surrey Advertiser* offices, both of which have now succumbed to the developer.

The Arts and Crafts Movement was less specific and derived from a reaction against the fussiness and mass production of the Victorian era by a group of artists and designers who valued quality over quantity. They believed in honest materials, traditional craftsmanship and good design, and a return to the functional simplicity of a much earlier period.

In most Arts and Crafts style vernacular houses, the medieval or Tudor influence is nearly always present. This is exemplified by such items as leaded lights in casement windows, hand forged window furniture, exterior doors made of planked wood with, again, forged wrought iron handles and large hinges. Internally, ceilings might be beamed or plastered with the ribs, bosses and pendants like those seen in Tudor houses. Floors were often dark wood or flag stones. Tudor-style exterior frames, either real or mock, were often a feature, along with overhanging first-floor rooms.

Of all features, the fireplace was the most significant. Very much the focus of the living room, and sometimes the entrance hall, too, it was built of stone or brick, and might incorporate patterned tiles, a metal hood and shelves. Often, the windows and staircases were stained wood, with the joints pegged in place. Sometimes Tudor-style panelling in the entrance hall and living rooms was a feature, and even a minstrel's gallery may be seen. A feature sometimes seen is the creation of a front door to the side of the house in an attempt to give a reduction in the impact on the entrance, and enhance other external features.

The Arts and Crafts Movement was an idea from the 1850s. Whilst the majority of the six million visitors to the 'Great Exhibition of the Works of Industry of All Nations' held at Crystal Palace in 1851 marvelled at the exhibits, William Morris, then 21 years of age, was aghast. He deplored the cheap mass-produced household objects as a dreadful indictment of the state of British design and thought that there was much to be gained from looking back at the work of craftsmen working before the Victorian Age.

Morris, a man of independent means, was a poet, writer, designer, scholar and socialist, who wished to get back to basics and called for high standards of design and construction using skills that were in danger of being lost to a world driven by machinery. He thought that such products should be available to all levels in society, and at the same time providing employment for the craftsmen and artists of his time. Little did he realise that his wishes were to lead to an élite form and style, largely available only to the wealthy due to the high cost of creation, be it for his own products or the properties that were to evolve over the next few years.

He had been inspired by John Ruskin and Augustus Pugin, designer of the Houses of Parliament. Pugin had called for a Gothic revival whilst Ruskin had attacked contemporary design in his book, *The Stones of Venice*. This was a revisionist survey of Venetian architecture in which he argued that the Gothic had been a high point in the history of Venice, and what came after was a backward step. He compared this with the changes in English architecture and condemned contemporary design.

Morris shared Ruskin's passion for Gothic, but his interests in architecture encompassed the rustic style of old English manor houses, cottages and barns as well as ecclesiastical buildings. His ideals and principles were encompassed within Red House in Upton, near Bexleyheath, South East of London which he asked his friend Philip Speakman Webb (1831-1915) to design and construct. It was built in 1860 using red brick with leanings towards a vernacular style, with more than a hint of the Gothic and thus medieval tones. It has steeply pitched roofing, dormer windows, a deep porch, and gives the informal impression that the house has been around for years and been added to, from time to time. Its gothic-cum-medieval style was short-lived and was soon to be replaced with vernacular designs.

62 *Red House.*

Because he was unable to find a furnisher and furnishings suitable for his ideas, he and his visiting friends created all that was needed for the house, using their imaginations to suit this unique building. This gave Morris an impetus to his crusade.

Soon Morris joined several of his artistic friends in business, and in 1861 formed Morris, Marshall, Faulkner & Co. where he employed 'Fine Art Workmen in Painting, Carving, Furniture and the Metals' in premises in Red Lion Square, London. The products included not only furniture and furnishings, but stained glass, metalwork, jewellery, embroidery, architectural carvings, and wall coverings. These goods reflected a new style, with an emphasis on nature backed by the use of the skills of both craftsmen and artists. This was no cottage industry, and due to an almost instant success much of the work was farmed out, but with quality being paramount.

Morris was most concerned about the destruction of medieval and Tudor buildings, and for that matter the almost wholesale refurbishment of ancient churches by the Victorians. After seeing Tewkesbury Abbey stripped of its patina of age as it underwent a 'restoration' he called for supporters to halt the practice. As a result the Society for the Protection of Ancient Buildings was formed, of which he was the secretary. As a gesture, he forbade the sale of his very profitable and popular stained glass to any church undergoing an unsympathetic restoration. The business continued in several guises over the years and even the death of Morris in 1896 failed to halt production or customer demand. The business eventually ceased in 1940 by which time the likes of Heal & Son and Liberty had begun to produce similar wares at a much lower cost.

The design of houses featuring the Arts and Crafts spirit was no less popular. The pioneer, Philip Webb, was a partner in Morris' firm. Subsequent Arts and Crafts architects appear to emanate from a small number of enthusiast exponents under the encouragement of the architect of the Early English style, Norman Shaw. These included Ernest Newton, William Lethaby, Gerald Horsley, and Edward Prior. They formed the St George's Art society, and later tried to bring architecture closer to art by forming the Art Workers' Guild in 1884.

Other notable architects working in the style included Edward Ould, Charles Voysey, Mackay Hugh Baillie Scott, Thackaray Turner, Guy Dawber and of course Edwin Lutyens. The latter day Arts and Crafts architects included Charles Rennie Makintosh and Norman Jewson. For the early promulgators of the Arts and Crafts Movement, it was a religion; for those following on it could be better described as a style which, together with other styles, followed the wishes of their clients.

Long into the 20th century, disciples of the Movement flourished and the style spread – some fully embraced this, such as artist and craftsman Frank Dickenson, who laboured to build his own modest Arts and Crafts house in Beeches Avenue, Carshalton, Surrey. He was determined to build a house that his mentors, Ruskin and Morris, would admire, and in 1904 it was completed. The point of citing this property is to emphasise that not all Arts and Crafts houses are the enormous properties that shout about their owner's wealth. Accepting this premise, many of the grander Arts and Crafts houses are splendid in the extreme. Such examples include Wightwick Manor by Ould, Hill House by Mackintosh, Standen by Philip Webb, Melsetter House by Lethaby, and Castle Drogo by Lutyens. Often the Arts and Crafts skills were brought to bear on sympathetic additions to existing houses, such as at Owlpen Manor by Norman Jewson.

In the Guildford area there was a ready market for this new Arts and Crafts style, mostly among the wealthy commuters who had businesses in London, but wished to live with their families in the Surrey countryside. The 'Arts and Crafts Movement in Surrey' has published an excellent booklet about such properties in and around Guildford called *Nature and Tradition*. Surrey is indeed fortunate to have so many examples.

The forerunners of the Movement in the Guildford area included Norman Shaw, who designed Merrist Wood House in 1877, now part of the combined Guildford and Merrist Wood College. The photographs show the 'Old English' style, with half-timbering, tile hanging and Bargate stone. On a smaller scale, there are many features in the design of the house which reflect on those in Abbotswood. These include the first-floor external tiles, the six-light window in the entrance gable, the three-storey stepped bays, the dormers on the large roof, the stepped chimney and the open porch.

Just in case it should be thought that Shaw designed only for the grand, the photograph on p.96 shows one of a number of small cottages designed in

63 *Merrist Wood House.*

64 *A cottage in The Valley.*

the 'Old English' style around 1880 in The Valley, off the Portsmouth Road in Guildford. As shall later be revealed, the design of the exterior of this property with its long roof, solid door, treble stepped gable, a gablet, and the carved bargeboard, could easily have come from the hand of Claude Burlingham. Nearby is Shaw's Piccards Rough, a stone-built mansion.

It is not assumed that Burlingham took Merrist Wood as a design to follow, but it is known that other earlier architects found inspiration from it. Burlingham varied external walls with timbering, tiles or roughcast rendering to create interest and non-conformity, and no two of his houses looked the same. Whereas Shaw created imposing, and indeed disproportionate features, Burlingham, with the Surrey style, reflected a vernacular farmhouse effect in many of the properties in Abbotswood. Indeed, with just a little imagination, one could place most of the Abbotswood properties in a plot surrounded just by countryside and a few farm buildings, and easily pass them as a building of yesteryear; perhaps a yeoman's farmhouse. Sunnymead (22) is a case in point.

Shaw is partly responsible for the Victorian trend of promoting the stark black and white 'look', which is modern when compared with the mellow oak tones of old houses. Conversely, Burlingham's

65 *Sunnymead.*

66   *Cranley Cottages, by George and Peto, forming a secondary entrance to Clandon Park.*

houses with oak half-timbering were, until the 1960s, seldom adorned with black and white paint.

Sir Ernest George and Harold Peto designed the very distinctive pair of cottages in the 'Old English' style, called Cranley Cottages in 1884. These are situated along the main road in West Clandon and form a secondary entrance to the Clandon Estate. Ernest George was also responsible for Watts Gallery in Compton, where he built two studios and servants quarters for G.F. Watts, the artist. In 1902 his wife, Mary Watts, founded the Compton Potters Guild there.

The main entrance to Clandon is through the ornate gates with two lodges at the Merrow entrance.

67   *The main entrance to Clandon.*

Following on from Shaw and George, the true Arts and Crafts architects appeared. Whilst there is no example of Philip Webb's work in Guildford town, various houses of his design are to be found nearby in Holmbury St Mary, in Cranleigh and at the foot of the Hogs Back, just south-west of Guildford.

Better known locally, but not always designing in the Arts and Crafts manner, was Edwin Lutyens. His early works were often created in collaboration with the garden design skills of his mentor, Gertrude Jekyll. His early works were very much of the 'Old English' style of Shaw whom he much admired. He had a two-year pupillage in the offices of Ernest George and Harold Peto. One of his first works, in 1889, was to design a cottage at Littleworth Cross in the 'Old English' style. Examples of his work abound and include the tea shop in Shere; the Lodge, also in Shere; Tigbourne Court, at Warmley; Lascombe, Puttenham; and Littlecroft in Guildford.

Between 1888 and 1943 he had over 50 commissions in Surrey.

Charles Francis Annesley Voysey (1857-1941) preferred a different look and frequently applied roughcast over brick. He designed four houses in the Guildford area between 1896 and 1907, Greyfriars in Puttenham; Norney Grange, Shackleford, Prior's Field, near Compton, which was destined to become a girl's school; and finally Littleholme in Guildown. Littleholme featured his familiar roughcast dressing, but, like so many of these larger houses, was subdivided in the 1950s.

Another fine example, by a lesser known architect, T.R. Clements, is *The Three Pigeons* pub, built around 1918, in Guildford High Street. It has recently been renamed *The Farriers*.

68   *Tigbourne Manor.*

Baillie Scott (1865-1945) was a contemporary of Lutyens, Turner and Voysey. He started his career in architecture rather later than the others, but nevertheless came quickly to the fore. Between 1909 and 1913 he designed three local houses in the Arts and Crafts style. The first was Undershaw, constructed of brick with some decorative stone, which had a Tudor-style oak panelled hall, complete with gallery. Garden Court was the second, built in a similar Tudor vein to his first, but with a garden designed by Gertrude Jekyll. Both of these are in Warwicks Bench, Guildford. The third house, Monk's Path, was of a Neo-Georgian style.

The work of Baillie Scott is likely to be that which most influenced the early work of Burlingham. This is explained more fully when The Hurst (46) is described. Copies of drawings from Baillie Scott's designs for a house in Guildford in the 1930s shows the style seen in so many Abbotswood houses. Could it be that the influence occurred both ways?

Immediately prior to the First World War the taste for grand houses built in the Arts and Crafts style was starting to diminish. In real terms, incomes for the patrons of this architecture were starting to fall. The Liberal Government of 1906 introduced Death Duties, a Super-Tax and Land Value duties in an attempt to help the less well off. There would still be supporters, but in a different guise.

69   The Three Pigeons.

70   *Undershaw, Warwicks Bench.*

71 *Undershaw as it is today.*

As we continue the story of Abbotswood, and of the Garden Suburbs in Guildford, readers may judge for themselves the extent that the designs of Claude Burlingham reflect the Arts and Crafts Movement and the Surrey style of architecture. The important features of the Abbotswood houses are revealed in the next chapter.

72 *A Guildford house in the 1930s by Baillie Scott.*

Nine

Style and Design of Houses in Abbotswood

In 1998 English Heritage confirmed that the Burlingham houses in Abbotswood are fine examples of the Arts and Crafts style. Indeed, starting with the early houses in Abbotswood, Burlingham also successfully emulated the Surrey style; the few exceptions were the two Queen Anne houses, the seven bungalows and the last house he designed, aptly namely The Odd House (16). Virtually all the others have elements of the Surrey style to one degree or another.

In pre-1700 Surrey, timber-framed houses were the norm, using local wood from the area; bricks were uncommon until well into the Tudor period. Sutton Place, built between 1521 and 1525, was one of the earliest Surrey houses to use bricks extensively. In age it is on a par with Hampton Court Palace, constructed by Cardinal Wolsey from 1516 to 1521 – houses built of brick prior to that time are indeed rare.

The older houses in the Surrey villages, such as Witley, are mainly timber-framed partly covered with tiles or boarding at the first floor. The timber frames are either still wattle and daub, or filled in with bricks.

In Guildford town, many timber-framed houses were refaced with a complete brick wall, leaving the frames in place. At Lewes in East Sussex, rather than go to the expense of brick, builders famously applied mathematical tiles that look like bricks. On some buildings they can only be identified by the fact that they are too perfect in shape and colour to be bricks.

Burlingham used all manner of materials to create his houses, yet there is an absence of the local Bargate stone in Abbotswood. One would have thought that he would have followed Arts and Crafts masters, and other Guildford architects, who used Bargate stone extensively. Some may question why this is; there can be no doubt that this material was local, and the Arts and Crafts Movement used it as such. The Bargate quarries are around Godalming; it is a deposit found in Bagshot Sands. It is a coarse

73   *The* White Hart, *Witley village.*

stone, difficult to shape, and easily weathered. The size of the pieces used by builders is small, if not brick-like – it was not an ideal building stone. A similar but better quality Surrey stone was called Merstham or Reigate stone, being found in very narrow beds of the Upper Greensand, just south of the chalk escarpment of the North Downs. In the 12th and 13th centuries, the quarries were owned by the Crown and it was restricted to royal or ecclesiastical use, partly because of the quality, and partly because of the limited supply. The Merstham stone quarries were exhausted by the end of the 16th century; thus the use of stone was unusual when the Tudor and Jacobean cottages were first constructed.

Bargate stone can be seen in Victorian and Edwardian Guildford, yet Burlingham refrained from using it while building Abbotswood. One can muse that to have done so would not have reflected the period buildings at Stoke Park Farm. Thus he was probably more correct than others.

He sometimes used York stone for decorative purposes in Merrow, as he had done for a few porchways in Abbotswood, in the manner seen at Merrist Wood House. The only Bargate stone was used on the side 'stepped' chimneys, such as in Fig. 231, and the porches at designs 'A' and 'C' shown in Figs. 215-6. It would be pleasing to note that this reflected Bargate stone found at Hall Place Farm, but it is not present there. This is a timber-framed house with the ground floor faced with Victorian brickwork. He later used Bargate stone for the entrance walls and piers at Ganghill, but not on the houses there.

There is an argument that the houses in Abbotswood are nearer the Surrey style than those large and imposing buildings created by Edwin Lutyens. The reasoning is that there were few large properties locally in Surrey, which in Tudor and Jacobean times was a relatively poor area, save for Sutton Place,

Clandon House and Loseley House. The smaller properties in Abbotswood are much nearer the size of an original Surrey dwelling.

To appreciate the Surrey style, the book of that name by Roderick Gradidge is highly recommended. It provides numerous drawings by the 19th-century architects Curtis Green and Ralph Neville showing buildings of the Surrey style before they were 'disfigured by the hands of the restorer'.

It bears repeating that the founders of the Arts and Crafts Movement decried the apparent loss of the skills of the craftsman. Their concern was driven by the enormous number of uninspiring and soulless buildings going up during the Victorian period which had lent little in the way of craftsmanship.

As each Abbotswood house is described below, the Arts and Crafts style features, together with those denoting the Surrey style, will be detailed. Visits to Undershaw, designed by Baillie Scott, Munstead Wood by Lutyens, Prior's Field by Voysey, Hurland's by Webb or even the earlier Merrist Wood House by Shaw, will reveal their styles. All these houses were built by prominent architects for wealthy individuals. They were very individual designs, and throughout there was a bulk and heaviness expressed with the features and fittings as if to emphasise a point. Nonetheless, Burlingham's style and features are drawn from these buildings and, were the reader to walk around both types, the many similarities would become apparent.

Burlingham was trying to emulate these masters, yet build houses that would be more affordable. He was to join the latter-day Arts and Crafts followers of the 1910s and 1920s who wished to create the aura of the Arts and Crafts Movement, but would do so with the use of more readily available materials and fittings.

There is little doubt that Claude Burlingham, still a newly qualified architect in 1910 when A.G. Taylor was planning his new estate, had arrived with grand ideas. He must have impressed Taylor with his earlier work around Sutton. The first houses designed in 1912 – Churston (5) and Aoetearoa (7) – reflect the work of a perhaps unsure and naïve designer. However, a year later there appeared the designs for The Gate House (1), The Hurst (46), Hazlewood (2), Lorraine (39), Friars Oak (40), Hestercombe (47) and Upmeads (49), all of which come out of his top drawer, marked Arts and Crafts. After that, the houses are no less impressive in skill, but appear to reflect an anticipated demand from prospective purchasers, rather than the reflection of a style created during pupillage.

Throughout this book houses are identified by their original names and the current numbers. This enables the reader more easily to keep track of the property throughout the period in question. Because name changes were quite common, it would not be practical to refer to each contemporary name. Some houses have had up to four names over the years.

There is now little evidence of furniture and fittings such as bookcases and cupboards of an Arts and Crafts nature. Only two kitchen dressers remain although almost every design contained one. Nevertheless, many houses contain original bedroom and airing cupboards, and door and window furniture, which are less susceptible to fashion changes. The majority of the original building plans are still available, but sadly some are not.

Choice and Design of Houses

Taylor, from the very start, both built houses speculatively to Burlingham's design, or sold the plot prior to this. When the latter occurred, the purchaser could either have the design that had been, or was intended to be, put before planning, or request Burlingham to come up with a quite individual design. When a prescribed design is used, and the plot was pre-sold, buyers often had alterations made to suit their own tastes and needs. Almost all the original houses are found to have a sister house of the same design and some have more than one sibling. Once they have been alerted to this fact, new owners who search Abbotswood for a duplicate are seldom without success.

There are even mirror houses, that is to say the same design, but back to front, such as Hillcrest (21) and Westward Ho (14); Oakdene (44) and Red Cottage (37). This enabled the houses facing different directions to have the reception rooms facing a southerly direction. Burlingham referred to these as being 'handed'.

There is only one instance when five houses were built with the same design, and one where there are three. All others were singles or doubles. Even where there are just two of the same design, the external cosmetic changes make each house different.

Conversely, of the seven bungalows which were built at about the same time, five are of the same design, and with the use of roughcast looked externally identical. Only The Orchard (38) and Abbots Trace (42) differ.

Examples of houses that fit into the 'unique' category include The Gate House (1), The Cottage (6), Wey-ne-Shing (13), Albury (24), and The Hurst (46). The few that were purchased before they were built, but to a design used elsewhere, include The Croft (4), Churston (5), and Postlands (23). The Hazard (33), Waysend (34) and Red Cottage (37) were all purchased by Burlingham as building plots and built by himself. All the other houses were built speculatively for subsequent sale by Taylor.

Before the First World War, the developer was minded to build larger houses. The development started with the submission of the plans for the first three houses in December 1912, followed by four plans for seven more houses in 1913, just one in 1914, and four houses in 1915 – the last plan was sanctioned in January 1916, and completed that year.

The deprivations of war took their toll, and building work ceased until 1920. Except for Albury (24), the houses built after this time were smaller than earlier ones.

Six bungalows and five houses were built in 1920, mostly with the benefit of government subsidies. A further five houses and a bungalow were built in 1921, of which four houses were grant aided. This was followed by two houses in 1922 and seven in 1923 with building work completed in 1924. A final plot was built on in 1925 and in 1926 was completed.

Taylor often submitted plans for a number of houses, and for one reason or another these were sometimes changed. For example, very early on in 1913 Hazlewood (2) and an identical house where Craig Cottage (41) is now, were approved on plan number (hereafter referred to as Pn) 3409. Three months later this was changed and Hazlewood was proposed with Lorraine (39) and Friars Oak (40), under Pn 3438.

In Abbotswood, Claude Burlingham was responsible for a total of 35 houses and seven bungalows for which there are 21 individual designs. There were two houses with seven bedrooms, one house with six bedrooms, 19 with five, 12 with four and one house with three bedrooms. The bungalows all had three bedrooms save for one which had just two. Because Burlingham ensured that all houses were externally different, he was then able to record that he had created the greatest possible number of designs for the records at his institute. His application for fellowship submitted in 1927 refers to 38 'different private houses' built in Guildford between 1912 and 1927, which we know to have been those in Abbotswood. This referred to the 35 houses and three types of bungalow. The values were quoted as being between £1,200 and £5,000. Separately, the 12 houses in Burpham are referred to as 'small' houses, with a further seven houses at Merrow.

It is worth noting that some plans were drawn in Burlingham's hand, and some the hand of others. Some are just signed by him, some signed and dated, and others have neither date nor signature. If a date is given, it is shown in brackets after his name in the details below. Throughout the planning procedure his name is attributed as the architect in all houses built up to 1926 with one exception, Eaglehurst (31). Where there is no signature there is no reason to assume that another architect was involved, for the houses have many similar details and a style that can be assumed to belong to just one architect. It is most probable that the drawings not in his hand were created in his office by his juniors copying from his own drawings under supervision. Lutyens adopted the same process.

Three houses were built between 1931 and 1936. Two of these, numbered 3, and 10, were built by the local firm of R. Holford & Co. Ltd, around 1931 and 1933 respectively. No details of the architect are given. Conversely, while also built by Holfords, the architect for 41, Abbotswood was by R.H. Matthews of Burpham. All three kept very much to the style of Burlingham.

Original Plans, and the Early Abbotswood Properties

Planning Applications and Consents

Initially sanctions were given by the General Purposes Committee, until 14 September 1925 – on 17 April 1925 the Town Planning Committee started operations. Most planning applications are available at the Surrey History Centre, Woking. An early example of a planning application can be seen in Appendix One.

Some planning applications are not in respect of a single property and refer to, say, five bungalows or two detached houses. The sanctions have been allocated to the individual house records as appropriate.

The files also show that all three main players, Taylor, Burlingham and Stanley, were submitting applications. Alternatively they were submitted on behalf of the first owners, who had purchased the plots.

Assumptions

A number of assumptions have been made with regard to the identification of planning consents because some files are not available for examination. For example the first file, Pn 3341, is not available. The answers are therefore gleaned by a process of elimination. In this case it appears that the houses in question included Churston (5) and Aoetearoa (7). The third house was not built. We know that the earliest records in the *Guildford Street Directory* identify that people were living in houses numbered 5 and 7, Abbotswood. Therefore it is a fair assumption that in the absence of any other planning applications at the time, these were two of the '3 New Houses' for which sanction was given.

Quite differently, there is no specific sanction for numbers 20 and 34, Abbotswood. In this instance there was an initial rejection for 17 and 19, Abbotswood, but the building was delayed, and a second sanction was given some months later. It has been assumed that the authorities went along with the original sanction, but allowed the developer to build two very similar houses in nearby plots. There may have been a record of this, but it does not appear in the register of sanctions, yet the building plan for the houses at 20 and 34 appears in the sanction wallet with the original sanction reference number written on the plan.

With few exceptions, houses of the same design would have been built at the same time. Thus if two houses, such as those at 15 and 18 Abbotswood, were built under the auspices of Guildford Borough Council, others built at the same time but within the control of Guildford Rural District, would have been agreed concurrently, although the record is not always identified. In this case there is no sanction for The Hazard (33).

The cause of the confusion and misplaced sanctions was that the houses now numbered 30 to 36 were in the parish of Worplesdon, and therefore the planning applications were considered by a quite different committee. Why they are not recorded is a mystery and is perhaps evidence that the planning controls were not correctly managed at the time. There is no trace of the consent for Eaglehurst (31) in the minutes of any committee.

The houses listed below are in the order of the date of sanction for a particular design. If the sanction is not available, the date of the planning application is given. In most cases it can be assumed that the building work started either before of shortly after the planning application was submitted. From that time to completion normally took six months.

As the details of these houses are considered, and the photographs examined, it will become clear that Claude Burlingham had a number of key features that he repeated in many of the houses both in Abbotswood and elsewhere.

Almost every house had the following:

- A large imposing Gable(s)
- Steeply angled roofs of up to 50 degrees
- Roof splash-backs
- Oak front doors
- Covered open porch
- Elizabethan style leaded lights

- Wrought window iron fixings
- Verandah, loggia or patio door
- External W.C.s for staff
- A maid's small bedroom
- Tiled fireplaces pre-war
- Brick fireplaces post-war
- Tile hanging and/or oak half-timbering

Less common, but invariably adding to the style are the following:

- Tudor overhands
- Extreme roof lengths
- Large halls
- Hearth in hall
- External wood-boarding
- Inglenook fireplaces

- Corner fireplaces
- Dormer windows
- Brick mullions
- Oak panelling
- A common window for two rooms
- Stone multi-mullioned windows

Probably most important of all, Burlingham wanted to make the garden and the house a unit and sometimes made the rear aspect of the house far more attractive than the front. Following this theme he enabled the owners to enjoy the garden using first-floor balconies at Aoetearoa (7) and The Hurst (46), the many Loggias or open Verandahs, and sometime just patio doors from the drawing room onto the garden and window seats. The houses that appeal more to the eye when viewed from the rear include The Gate House (1), Lorraine (39), The Croft (4), Churston (5), Upmeads (49) and others. By making these houses look at their best from the garden, rather than the road, he seems to have enveloped the idea that these houses were not show houses but homes, as well as adopting the Arts and Crafts style for houses that blend into their surroundings.

Design 1:
Churston (5) and Aoetearoa (7) – 1912

These were the very first houses to be built in Abbotswood.

A search of the Surrey archives revealed that Pn 3341 was submitted on 16 December 1912 for three 'new houses' and sanctioned shortly thereafter. Unfortunately this has been lost and the details cannot be ascertained. The records of the planning committee confirm that Taylor was the developer and Burlingham the architect.

On the planning notice for The Cottage (6) dated 5 November 1914, R.U. Falkus, or Burlingham on behalf of Falkus, gave an address as 'Churston', Abbotswood, Guildford (pro-tem). Hence, Churston was constructed before November 1914. As there is no earlier planning application than for these two identical houses, and as some of the features are certainly 'Edwardian', it is reasonable to assume that these were indeed the first. The 1915 *Street Directory* shows that the only two houses to be occupied were Churston and Hazlewood (2), and that The Gate House (1), The Hurst (46) and Lorraine (39) were all built but not occupied.

The two houses for Design 1 consisted of five bedrooms and two reception rooms. The entrance to both was on the right of the property and not visible from the front. There was no front view of the door to speak of. It could be said that this was to de-emphasise the entrance, or, as Lutyens did for some houses in Hampstead Garden Suburb, give the appearance that the house is larger than it actually is. Very recently Churston has been reconfigured at the front to provide an entrance with a porch; thus it is possible to compare with Aoetearoa the effectiveness of the original design.

74 *Aoetearoa.*

75   *Churston.*

Both houses had leaded light windows in metal casements and internally a plate shelf, or delft rack around the entrance hall. In the same manner as The Croft (4) and Littlefield (9), there was a corner fireplace in the entrance hall.

Churston had roughcast walls at the front and Aoetearoa had hanging tiles.

Early photographs show that Aoetearoa had a balcony at the rear, overlooking a long garden planted with flowers and vegetables at the bottom. The roughcast was left unpainted.

The window on the staircase, at Churston, contains two round coloured glass feature windows. These no longer exist at Aoetearoa, but from the early black and white photographs they can just be detected.

Perhaps the more adventurous style of the next houses was so inviting that the third house was not built.

76   *The rear of Aoetearoa in the 1930s.*

Design 2:
Hazelwood (2), Lorraine (39), Friars Oak (40) – 1913

> ✤ Pn 3409 dated 9 July 1913, approved 15 September 1913
> ✤ Proposer and builder: A.G. Taylor; Architect: A.C. Burlingham (June 1913)

The original intention was to build two houses as described in Pn 3409 on Stoke Park Farm, London Road. One was Hazlewood and the other was to be where Craig Cottage (41) now stands. The developer changed this and instead, Hazlewood, Lorraine, and Friars Oak were all built to the same basic design. The last two were sanctioned through Pn 3438 on 15 December 1913 – the plan can be seen in Appendix Two.

These houses had a dining room, a large impressive drawing room and a loggia, together with five bedrooms and one bathroom. Each drawing room contains a feature fireplace, and a window seat overlooking the garden. The ceilings still have plaster decorations, with inlaid panels of fruit and flowers.

77 Hazlewood, Lorraine and Friars Oak (anti-clockwise).

At Friars Oak and Hazlewood the drawing rooms are oak panelled. The dining room at Friars Oak has painted panelling of a different style.

The loggia was fully enclosed, with large windows for extra light. Off this room, and down steps is a heating chamber which contained a coal fired boiler from which three radiators received hot water. These were in the loggia, the hall and the drawing room.

There was a porch, and at the front door a small vestibule led visitors into an inner hall with access to the drawing room, the dining room and the loggia. A nice touch in the porch is a boot scraper: a metal bar let into the wall for cleaning the bottom of shoes before entering the houses.

A feature of the design is the long roof at the front of the houses which reached from the ridge to the eaves at ground floor level. On each house the front chimney breast includes a window let in for additional light. There were several casement windows, a jettied gable, and a double gable end at one side.

To the left of the main building was an attached outside yard, for the tradesmen to use as their entrance. Within this yard was the door to the W.C. for the gardener and the maid. The design is such that the elevation shows an entrance from the front with double doors supported by glorious large scrolled hinges; it could well be taken for a garage. When it came to building the properties, the double doors were replaced with a single door, which remains at both Lorraine and Friars Oak.

The Hazlewood exterior is a mixture of brick, tile hanging, and studded half timbers. The plan shows the frontage to be 100ft. This indicates that the land to form the plot for Orchard Neville (3) in 1931 was not initially part of the garden of Hazlewood. However, the conveyance for The Croft in February 1915 gives the frontage of Hazlewood as 198ft. Perhaps it was decided to extend the larger plot after the plans had been submitted. Lorraine and Friars Oak differed externally, with the latter having tile hanging to the rear extending to part of the chimneys.

78   *The fireplace in the panelled drawing room.*

79   *Dining room panelling at Friars Oak.*

80   *A handy boot scraper.*

81   *The Loggia.*

82 *At the rear there is half-timbering at Lorraine …*

83 *… and tile hanging at Friars Oak.*

Design 3:
The Gate House (1) – 1913

∾ Pn 3410 dated 11 July 1913, approved 15 September 1913

∾ Proposer and Builder: A.G. Taylor; Architect:
A.C. Burlingham (July 1913)

The planning application refers to Stoke Park Farm Estate. This property was destined to be one of the larger houses, abutting the London Road, and very much a flagship house in the sight of passers-by. It was situated in a plot quoted in the application as an acre, twice that for Hazlewood (2).

The plans available in Appendix Two evidence four large bedrooms, and three small ones, one of which was for a maid who had her own bathroom, without a W.C. The occupants of the other six bedrooms, while having the luxury of an upstairs W.C., all had to share one bathroom. The maid had her W.C. in the kitchen/scullery area; nearby was an external door for the use of the gardener and chauffeur.

84   *The Gate House.*

85   *The Porch.*

Burlingham's design led visitors through a porch into a small vestibule area, and into a grand hall which contained a large window with a window seat and an impressive fireplace with a stone surround and delft tiles. Off the hall there is the dining room, drawing room and study.

The servants area contained the normal kitchen, scullery, coal store, pantry and larder, and also a 'Boots and Knives' room.

Two small bedrooms were created by a stud wall division, which abuts a mullion in a four-light window. Because there was no fireplace in one room, a ventilator was put in the ceiling. The second floor was not part of the original plans. As the fittings are of the earlier type it is likely that it was constructed soon after the main house was built.

Externally the plans show the typical mix of half-timbering, and tile hanging. The tennis lawn and pergola were features of the extensive garden.

86   *The features of the large hall.*

Design 4:
The Hurst (46) – 1913

- ◊ Pn 3439 dated 13 November 1913, approved 15 December 1913
- ◊ Proposer and Builder: A.G. Taylor; Architect: A.C. Burlingham (October 1913)

The planning application described the property as being situated in the New Road, leading off London Road at Stoke Park Estate.

This is the largest house in Abbotswood, and situated in grounds of over 1¾ acres. In 1925 this was enlarged to about 2½ acres when a plot along the London Road was purchased. The plans are shown in Appendix Two.

For an analysis of this property there is no better way than to refer to the description provided by English Heritage when, on 22 June 1998, a Grade II listing was awarded.

87   *The Hurst, front and sides.*

Designed by Alfred Claude Burlingham in 1913. Arts and Crafts Style. Rendered on brick plinth with some decorative timber framing and tiled roofs with tall brick chimneystacks, some set diagonally. L-shaped plan on two storeys and attics with irregular fenestration of wooden casements with leaded lights.

Entrance front has left side gable with pattern of herringbone decorative bracing and two storey seven-light bay with chimneystack with stacks set diagonally and projecting one storey room to left. Set back gable to right of large front gable has tall staircase window and herringbone brick porch.

Right hand wing of four bays has hipped roof with two hipped dormers and quartrefoil timber-framed pattern to base of floor. Continuous jetty. Return has some vertical studding. Left side elevation has two gables, the right hand one of herringbone brick with timber sleeping platform later glazed in and stone seven light bay to galleried hall. Left hand gable has attic casement with wreath moulding below, five-light first floor window and four-light square bay to ground floor.

Rear elevation has three windows including five-light square bay to drawing room.

Very complete interior includes central galleried staircase hall with crown post-type roof with ogee braces, plank and muntin panelling, with carved stone fireplace with Tudor rose and lined with delft tiles and straight flight staircase with twisted balusters. Dining room has fireplace with wooden surround, tiles and window seat.

Study has tiled fireplace. Drawing room has fireplace with tiles and over mantel, early 18th-century type panelling and plaster ceiling with square motifs with oak leaves and cockatiels and six triangular panels with floral motifs.

The service end is particularly complete with original cast iron range, built-in dresser, scullery with draining boards and cupboards, and original pantries and coal holes and servant's staircase with square banisters. First floor bedrooms retain original fireplaces with tiles surrounds and original doors and bathrooms retaining tiling and some original fittings. Cast iron fireplace to attic. Ceiling ventilation system.

88 *Photographs taken prior to restoration.*

Photographs taken of The Hurst before restoration are evidence that it was little changed over the years and show an intriguing insight for those early days. One photograph shows the protecting hedge masking the servants' kitchen area. The larder, tiled scullery floor, wooden draining boards and the coal store have

89 *Billiard room and gallery.*

all been replaced by a modern kitchen. The original cooker, which has a central fire, and two ovens remain, but is no longer used. It appears in Fig. 197.

This house is substantial. It was designed with seven bedrooms, one for the maid who had her own bath, and one bath for occupants of the remaining six bedrooms. There was an attic floor, but this was not designated as a bedroom area, and was probably used for storage.

Today, the splendour of the house is evident. The entrance vestibule contains decorated leaded windows leading to a dramatic billiard hall, which is an atrium, with light coming from the large stone mullioned window and the upper balcony.

One can link this to the Baillie Scott house, Undershaw, which was built in 1908-9. The entrance hall at Undershaw has a large fireplace and a beamed ceiling at the upper floor. The early plans for The Hurst showed that the billiard room had a lower ceiling, and a bedroom above. The actual building was changed when Burlingham added an exposed decorative frame in one-inch-thick oak, also to the upper floor. Perhaps he visited Baillie Scott's house before making these changes. The result is most impressive. Oak panelled walls add to the effect, and lead to a staircase rising to the first floor. The balusters are of barley-twist design, unique in Abbotswood.

90 *The staircases of The Gate House and The Hurst are identical.*

91 *The balcony, a ceiling, the drawing room fireplace, and the jettied half-timber.*

Of great charm is a first-floor balcony. It is faced with bricks formed in a herring-bone shape. These are matched at the front door. Burlingham used a similar balcony at Newlands Cottage to great effect. Other features include the decorated ceilings, the external jettied half-timbering and original fireplaces.

This was indeed a house well worth saving.

Design 5:

Hestercombe (47) and Upmeads (49) – 1914

    ❧   Pn 3454 dated 14 February 1914, approved 16 March 1914

    ❧   Proposer and Builder: A.G. Taylor: Architect:
            A.C. Burlingham (December 1913)

The application was for two properties, each in about one acre. The houses were designed in the Queen Anne style, and look similar to The Salutation, in Sandwich, Kent, designed by Lutyens in 1911, but on a much smaller scale. Unusually, the plans, shown in Appendix Two, do not give a detailed drawing of the splendid exterior elevations.

    With all the various designs for houses of a similar pattern, Burlingham tried to create an individual look for each house. In the case of this pair, for the rear elevation at Upmeads there is a horizontal brick first floor with a full roof and a continuation of the large plaster cornice. For Hestercombe, there are two gables with herringbone brickwork, and two brick frame windows similar to those seen at Tigbourne Court. Additionally, there were shutters on the first floor, as shown in the painting of the late 1980s which deteriorated and required removal.

92 *Garden views of Hestercombe (left) and Upmeads (right).*

93 *Both houses have decorative hoppers.*

94 *At one time Hestercombe had window shutters.*

Each house has five bedrooms and three reception rooms, with attic space in the roof comprising a box room and three other rooms. Whilst these are not marked as bedrooms, two had a fireplace, and thus it would be reasonable to assume that this was treated as the servants' quarters. There were no toilet facilities on this floor, which made it unsuitable for anyone other than servants.

Unique in Abbotswood, sash windows were used on the ground and first floors. The high quality brickwork is two toned with the second colour at the corners. As befits a Queen Anne house, the external work is symmetrical.

95 *A fully tiled chimney, with dormers each side.*

96 *A window in the chimney breast adds much light inside.*

97 *The stylish front door.*   98 *Sliding doors to the billiard room open up the hall.*

The chimneys are large, with extensive tile hanging on one of them which has windows either side of it to allow light to enter the top floor. Without this unobtrusive arrangement, separate dormer windows would have been required which may possibly have spoiled have the roofline.

The oak front door is set in a stone surround, carved with a leaves and fruit in relief. At Hestercombe, a figured metal light bracket is matched by a door-bell pull.

The main door gives entry to a small vestibule, and this leads to a large hall, part of which can be partitioned off as a 'Billiard Room Hall' at a double archway with panelled sliding doors. In many of Baillie Scott's designs the hall was a focal point for the house. He sought to use the largest possible space and sometimes achieved this by opening rooms onto the hall, and using sliding doors, to look like panelling, to create separate rooms. This is a fine example of this technique.

Recent alterations at Upmeads could have meant that because of planning regulations these magnificent early 20th-century doors would have to be replaced by modern fire-proof ones. Thankfully, common sense has prevailed and, subject to satisfactory fire-proofing, the doors have been saved.

The dining room and the drawing room are quite symmetrical, each with a door leading out on to the verandah, which has a flat roofed porch supported by four large columns.

The entrance hall has a parquet floor, which extends into the other ground-floor rooms. At Hestercombe it was extended to the first-floor landing, including the intermediate landing. In the dining and billiard rooms at Upmeads the centre floor is sunken, allowing for a fitted carpet to be the same height as the surrounding flooring.

99 *Detail of the porch.*

100   *The hall is panelled and the newel post measures over 12 feet.*

101   *This fireplace features delft tiles.*

102   *The door and window fittings were chromed in the 1930s.*

Light painted panelling features in the hall and the billiards room. The skirting boards are larger than seen in most of the other houses, being around 12ins in height. A significant feature is the imposing open staircase to the first floor. The balusters and rails are quite simple and similar to the other houses in Abbotswood, yet here a single corner newel post rising from below the ground floor runs the length of the stair drop, some 12 feet, using a single piece of oak.

The dining room fireplace at Hestercombe has a plain wood and stone surround with inlaid delft tiles – these are of the pre-war type used by Burlingham in his houses. The wood shown is, correctly, due to be painted. An early serving hatch exists.

The drawing room ceilings have inlaid mouldings similar to those seen in Design 2, featuring fruit, flowers, acorns and leaves. These are shown in Fig. 183.

There are window seats for enjoying the gardens when the weather is inclement.

The handles on the interior three panel doors at Hestercombe are of an early chrome, whilst those at Upmeads, of the same design on the sliding doors to the billiard room, are of brass. Even the catches on the sash windows are chromed. As chrome was not introduced in this form until the late 1920s, there is every likelihood that this new material was introduced by an owner who had the brass fittings plated – this could have been to save regular polishing by the maid. Otherwise, the door furniture is similar to that seen elsewhere in Abbotswood.

Regarding ventilation, the houses had high ceilings, reflecting more of a Queen Anne style than Tudor, and thus, to the question about ventilation on the plans, Burlingham was able to answer simply 'windows' on the planning application!

The large landing is a significant feature, leading to a further, but plain staircase to the top floor. Here, the rooms have leaded light windows with the same Arts and Crafts style wrought iron furniture seen on the other houses in Abbotswood. In line with the roof, two slanting windows look out onto each valley. At Hestercombe there is a particularly attractive Arts and Crafts style metal fire surround, and also a brick fireplace.

In the Upmeads kitchen, the original fireplace had blue tile decoration. White tiles were found in the scullery area.

Both houses had bells to attract the servants. At Hestercombe there was installed an additional feature of an intercom system similar to those seen on the bridge of ships of the period. Pipes were connected from the landing to the receiver in the kitchen. It even has a whistle to draw immediate attention.

103 *Upstairs fireplaces are well designed.*

104 *A stylish kitchen fireplace.*

These houses had a garage and, whilst basically of the same design, that at Hestercombe was longer due to a workshop at the far end. There was a partition between the workshop and the car. Planning permission for this garage was given in November 1916. Nearby, attached to the house is a greenhouse with a solid fuel heating system.

105 *Servants were summoned in style.*

Design 6:
The Cottage (6) – 1914

- Pn 3489 dated 5 November 1914, approved 16 November 1914
- Proposer: R.U. Falkus; Architect: A.C. Burlingham; Builder: A.G. Taylor

Nearly two years after the plot was purchased the planning notice was addressed to the Borough Surveyor of Guildford, and headed 'Abbotswood, London Road, Guildford'. It is the first recorded reference to Abbotswood. The applicant, F.V. Falkus, was described as retired, late Admiralty Office.

The Cottage, one of the most attractive properties in Abbotswood, comprises of three bedrooms and two reception rooms. It probably epitomises the Arts and Crafts style more than any other house in Abbotswood.

The doors are made of planked wood, and the window mullions are of brick. The shape of the windows is seen extensively in Lutyens' design for Tigbourne. Externally, the long roof, the dominating chimney and the covered verandah as part of the garden all lend themselves, collectively, to the Arts and Crafts feel for the house. The windows and door furniture with the heart emblem might have been available from a wholesaler at the time rather than a blacksmith, but they are of high quality and give the impression that they were specially sourced for this house alone.

106 *The Cottage.*

Many of these features were to appear in Burlingham's later designs, including the round windows, the brick mullions, and the brick surround to the porch, but they come together no better than here.

The plans, available in Appendix Two, also show two downstairs toilets, one in the kitchen area, presumably for the staff, and one off the hallway for the guests. The kitchen has attached to it a larder, and a sizeable scullery for washing and so forth.

Finally, the 'motor shed', attached by a small wall with a covering roof, was original to the house, and is thought to be the first in Abbotswood. It was planned to have a flat roof but pencil marks on the plans evidence the gable roof that was actually built.

107 *Internal features include planked doors and brick mullions.*

108 *Outside decorative brickwork is used to good effect.*

Design 7:
The Croft (4) and Littlefield (9) – 1915

- Pn 3512 dated 29 March 1915, approved 30 March 1915 (The Croft)
- Pn 3522 dated 9 June 1915, approved 14 June 1915 (Littlefield)
- Proposer and Builder: A.G. Taylor; Architect: A.C. Burlingham (February 1915)

In similar vein to The Cottage (6), these houses were relatively small, with three reasonably sized bedrooms, and a small one for the maid. The planning application was initially submitted for only one house, The Croft, but it was used again for Littlefield. As no house names or numbers had been used, the houses were identified by the plot sizes quoted on the planning applications.

There were just two reception rooms and the normal facilities for the maid. The hallway, approached through a long porch, features a corner fireplace opposite the door to welcome guests. The plans incorporated a design of stonework for the front garden. This was the only such design of any size on the estate.

Although the plans for Littlefield were exactly the same, the building of the front gable differed substantially. The front bedroom was extended to include

109 *The Croft and Littlefield.*

a bay window of the same size as that on the ground floor. Furthermore, the gable of The Croft is entirely brick, while that at Littlefield has a wood facing. The long porch way differs in detail. Both properties have tile and brick curved lintels above most doors and windows.

The planning notice included an early garage for Littlefield. This was at an oblique angle to the house, presumably to provide width, facilitating easy entry from the driveway. This floor was wooden. Later, however, for other motor houses the Borough Surveyor stipulated concrete floors, and even concrete ceilings for integral garages.

110 *The gable end includes a wide bay at The Croft.*

Design 8:

Sunnymead (22) and The Lair (26) – 1915

➣ Pn 3539 dated 31 December 1915, approved 25 January 1916

➣ Proposer and Builder: A.G. Taylor; Architect:
  A.C. Burlingham (1915)

These were the last two properties to be designed and completed before the hostilities with Germany finally brought house building to a halt. They were completed in 1916. Sunnymead was sold in the November, and The Lair was initially rented out, and sold in 1918.

This brought to an end the first period of house building which was curtailed until 1920. The planning application was for three simple but attractive houses, but only two were built, perhaps because of the shortage of men and materials.

There are four medium-sized bedrooms, and a small one. There is an alternative configuration for the kitchen, which was adopted for Sunnymead, which makes for a more compact house. In fact, Sunnymead is handed. The Lair has the same configuration of the mirror image, but the kitchen area is to plan.

111 *Sunnymead.*

The ground floor is approached through a front door situated in a recessed porch, which, on the plans, intrudes some four feet into the hall, much reducing the same. Both houses have a reduced porch and an enlarged hall; clearly the plans were not adhered to. The porch entrance is faced with cut stone, and attached to this are two small walls with a stone ball on each.

The largest room is described as a 'living room or drawing room'. Burlingham seemed unsure of the nomenclature and hedged his bets.

In Sunnymead the kitchen still has an original cupboard for china and glass. The scullery area is approached through the kitchen and opens on to a small enclosed yard which was uncovered and could have been used for hanging out the washing without offending neighbours. Moving up the stairs, the visitor is confronted in both houses by a window with coloured glass in the top three lights depicting a scene across a lake, with sailing boats.

The first owner of Sunnymead, in the month before he purchased the house, applied for planning permission to build a single garage described as a 'Motor House' in October 1916. The plan is annotated to the effect that the floor is 'concrete heated'.

Some while later, the owner of The Lair applied for a garage, but this was initially declined in January 1928, for being in front of building line. It was subsequently approved that April. The construction was more elaborate, having sliding doors on rollers, with a square roof, and room for two cars.

Design 9:

Postland(23), Aysgarth (25), Hutton Ambo (27), Greta (28) – 1920

Design 10:

Abbots Trace (42) – 1920

    ❮ Pn 3969 dated 18 March 1920, approved 27 April 1920
    ❮ Proposer: A.G. Taylor; Architect:
        A.C. Burlingham (1920); Builder: A.E. Stanley

The application was for six bungalows, one a bungalow of a singular design marked E, and the others of a second design and designated A, B, C, D, and F. Only five were built.

Hitherto all reference to a builder has been to A.G. Taylor, who presumably brought in contractors as required. For the first time the builder is named as A.E. Stanley of Down Road, Merrow, Nr. Guildford.

The estate plan shows Postland as A, Aysgarth as B, Hutton Ambo as C, Greta as D and Abbots Trace as E. F is shown where Crossways (45) was eventually built. On this plan a further bungalow of the second design was

113 *Hutton Ambo (left) and Postland (right).*

114   *Aysgarth, Greta and Abbots Trace (clockwise from top left).*

shown where Brookdale (29) was later to stand, but it was marked 'cancelled'. Thus there was a total of seven bungalows on the block plan; for one they did not seek consent, and another they did not build. This is further evidence that the developer was willing to change his plans to meet the will of clients, or perhaps other obligations.

The road layout is shown with the building plans. The intended roadway was to follow round to 19, Abbotswood, as it does now, but then continue through where No. 18 stands, and back to the horseshoe through the north spur. This parallel horseshoe shape proposal was later abandoned.

The bungalows were the first properties in Abbotswood to be designed by Burlingham after the First World War. The rush to build was partly driven by the Government's plan to provide a grant through The Housing (Additional Powers) Act 1919 which was meant to encourage house building after the war. This was paid depending on the size of the floor area. For example, a property of 775 sq. ft. attracted a grant of £160; 805 sq. ft. a grant of £240; and one of over 850 sq. ft. brought £260. This was an enormous sum, equal to nearly 30 per cent of the sale price. This lasted until June 1922 when the Government tried to curtail the payments sooner than they had planned.

115 *The two fireplaces on the left are from Postlands, which can be compared with the solid beam inglenook fireplace from the larger houses of 1922.*

The fact that the bungalows were the quickest to erect, using less than prime materials, was one reason why they appeared. On the other hand, they would have been easier to sell, and quick sales gave funds for further work. It has been mentioned previously that Taylor had trouble selling the pre-war houses. Whatever the reason, the erection of bungalows must have come as a bit of a shock to those already living in Abbotswood. Each plot was about sixty feet wide.

The design for bungalows A-F showed a little snobbery on the part of Burlingham. Gone were the terms 'drawing room' and 'dining room'. Instead were shown the descriptions 'living room' and 'parlour'.

For each bungalow there was a covered entrance porch, with two timber pillars. The front door opened to a hallway which contained a feature archway. From the hall there were two reception rooms, and two bedrooms, the bathroom and the scullery. The third bedroom was approached through the scullery and an external lobby – this was clearly intended for the maid. The maid's W.C. was only reached by going through the lobby, and then outside, and along to the external entrance to the closet. There was no kitchen included in the plan, and the maid doubtless had to eat in the scullery.

The plans showed two distinctive fireplaces, one type for the living room, and a smaller type for the parlour and the two larger bedrooms. These still exist at Postland, which the client was able to purchase prior to construction and stipulate a design other than the exact plan. In the living room the fireplace was constructed at a more central point, and at either side cupboards extended into the room with doors in the second bedroom and the hall. This gave the effect of an inglenook fireplace with small benches each side and a narrow beam at the entrance. The whole room has a wood beam effect on the walls. This was a reflection of the Arts and Crafts style of modest construction in an unusual setting.

For the first time the planning notice contained a requirement for the applicant to stipulate the type of damp proof course to be used.

The plans show shutters for the external windows. For the first plan they were on all but the north and east elevations, but for Abbots Trace they were shown on all but the north elevation. The shutters remain to this day at Hutton Ambo and Abbots Trace. The original windows were complete metal frames, made by Crittal, rather than the more expensive timber frames in the houses. This reflects both the need to complete the buildings quickly, and possibly the shortage of the type of materials used in the larger properties.

At Aysgarth, there were early changes. These started in November 1926 with a planning application for two bedrooms in the roof space for Mrs Hewetson. The architect was Beverly Young, 43, Bridge Street, Guildford, who wrote '… and shall be glad to know when same is passed, as I am anxious to commence the work as soon as possible'. The planning committee and the Borough Surveyor, J.W.H. Wood, duly obliged. In January 1929, plans submitted by A.E. Stanley were approved for an attached garage. Fire precautions were now to the fore and the door to the house from the garage was lined with asbestos.

For Abbots Trace, the difference between this design and that of the other five was that, whilst the number of rooms was the same, instead of the living room and the parlour being on either side of the entrance hall, these were looking onto the garden at the side of the property, and two bedrooms were adjacent to the hall. One bedroom was for the maid and this time opened onto the scullery. Again there was no kitchen. The plan for this specific bungalow was marked in Burlingham's hand, 'NB Windows will be Reliance Steel windows (cottage), as per letter and numbers shown on plan, and not wooden frames as shewn'.

Perhaps the first owner was a keen gardener and cyclist, for not only did the living rooms open on to the garden, but Burlingham provided a design for a patio and also a small room with an external door marked 'cycle/tool shed'. The plan shows a trap door in the hallway 'for boxes'. Plans were submitted in May 1930 by A.E. Stanley for 'additions to bathroom/scullery'.

Design 11:

Homewell (8), Brookdale (29), Red Cottage (37), Oakdene (44) and Crossways (45) – 1920

Design 9:

Rosedene (43) – 1920

    ♀ Pn 4009 dated 28 August 1920, approved 24 September 1920

    ♀ Proposer: A.G. Taylor; Architect:
A.C. Burlingham (1920); Builder: A.E. Stanley

A planning application was submitted initially to include four two-storey houses of the same design and the bungalow, Rosedene. The planning application was altered to add a further house, Homewell.

The Red Cottage outline on the plan is quite different from the other four, matching the final construction. Also, both Brookdale and Red Cottage appear to have a detached garage incorporated on the block plan, but these were not on the planning notice, and both houses were later subject to retrospective applications for the garages.

The design used for the bungalow, Rosedene, was the same as that for Postland and the other bungalows under Design 9. A garage was built for Rosedene in June 1945, by E.J. Hodgson.

116   *Rosedene.*

117 *Homewell (top left), Red Cottage (top right) Brookdale (above), Oakdene (above right), Crossways.*

118   *Rear servants lobby.*

The final sanction was just for a bungalow and four houses, probably because Red Cottage was under the jurisdiction of Guildford Rural District rather than the town. By 28 June 1921 all houses were completed.

The plan described the houses as 'small', having only four bedrooms, and with no particular references to a maid's quarters. This is reproduced in Appendix Two.

The exteriors were partly mock Tudor style, with half timbers and some tile hanging. All benefited from an impressive rear gable. The ground floor was approached through an interior porch, into a medium sized hall, with doors to the living room, dining room and a combined kitchen and scullery. Unusually the larder is also off the hall, albeit through an archway into the kitchen. From the living room, glass doors open out on to a verandah.

The plans clearly show the gap between the bricks in the 11-inch walls. Hitherto plans have shown this as a single coloured line.

At Oakdene, which is handed, the servant's lobby still exists.

The owner of Aoetearoa (7) from 1913, Mr G.H. Jacobs, purchased the land on which Homewell was built for £125 in December 1916. The debenture states that the house should cost no less than £500. Identifying and dating this house was initially a problem due to the significant internal alterations. The delft rail in the drawing room gave an impression of Edwardian design;

119   *Rear Gable, common to each house.*

however, the gable at the rear which has side windows is identical to that at Red Cottage, designed in 1920.

The first planning application for changes to Homewell was in July 1924, for a coal shed, for Mr R.H. Bryant. In July 1934, it was intended that a wood clad timber-framed garage measuring 15ft by 8ft should be built to the right of the house on the border with Littlefield (9). It had a lining of asbestos sheets for fire protection. A letter from E.R. Manley describes the plan which gives three places where the garage could go. He sought the advice of the council as to the best position. Perhaps the council's officials had baulked at his initial suggestions, and he left the matter to them.

The drawing room is dominated by a large fireplace with a carved wood surround. Around the fire there are a number of blue and white delft tiles. These tiles match those found at Albury, which was also constructed in 1920. There are square leaded lights throughout.

For Brookdale, a plan for a garage with a living room and bedroom over it was approved in 1921. It was attached to the house through passageways at both the ground and first floors. A concrete 'carriage wash' area with a drain was provided outside. Whilst the details on the plan are vague, one suspects that this was a garage and rooms for a chauffeur required by the first owner, who, in September 1921, completed the purchase.

Red Cottage has recently been subject to an extensive restoration but the main reception and bedrooms remained unchanged. The layout upstairs is very similar to the original plan, and indeed so, too, is the ground floor, save for the fact that Burlingham extended the drawing room, which has a wealth of oak panelling, into the verandah area, and had the dining room reduced in size. Instead of a single ground-floor window for the dining room, the design incorporated two; one each for the dining room and the drawing

120 *The fireplace and its panelling were unique.*

room in the same wall. In order to facilitate these changes, the chimneys were repositioned.

At the time the house was built Burlingham applied for an extension for a 'Verandah' and a garage attached to the rear of the house. The verandah clearly replaced the one that was lost extending the dining room. The garage is at a lower level because of the slope of the garden. This can be clearly seen in the contemporary advertisement shown in Fig. 36 and Fig. 204. This unique verandah and garage, with pargeting in the form of a floral design, were both demolished in April 2008.

A further application was submitted in December 1924, for additions to Red House (*sic*) by Mrs Butler who wanted a cottage for her chauffeur. It would have been attached to the garage of the main house and have contained a single bedroom, a living room and a kitchen. It was declined.

A further application, this time for a quite separate bungalow in the north side of the garden, was approved in 1925. This showed that A.E. Stanley was the builder. There is no reference to an architect, but the implication is that it was Stanley's design. There is little doubt that this was not the work of Burlingham for the design was plain, and without the style seen in the other bungalows built on the estate. It could be that this was for the chauffeur, and that the objections to the earlier plans had been dealt with by this proposal. There were two bedrooms, a sitting room and a kitchen. In around 2000 the bungalow was converted to a house.

121 *The drawing room fireplace at Red Cottage.*

Oakdene was also subject to change. In May 1930 W.C.H. Tyler applied for additions to the scullery and the upstairs bathroom. The work resulted in a small flat roof extension, and was undertaken by A.E. Stanley.

Crossways has had several additions. An application in September 1926 was submitted by Jno. Anderson & Co. of 4, Clareville Grove, South Kensington, SW1, architects for Phillip Peebles. The work comprised of two additional bathrooms, a bedroom and an extension to the kitchen with a lavatory for the servants. The inspection certificates for the foundations and the soil drains, dated October and December 1926 respectively, still exist to evidence that proper monitoring took place. A single-storey room was added in November 1928. In both cases the building work was carried out by A.E. Stanley.

Design 12:
Albury (24) – 1920

℞ Pn 4011 dated (1) 14 June 1920 and (2) 10 September 1920

℞ Proposer: A.C. Burlingham for T. Leighton of
       Avonmore Avenue, Guildford

℞ Architect: A.C. Burlingham (1920); Builder: A.E. Stanley

The planning application was submitted twice and eventually sanctioned on 24 September 1920. Mr Leighton purchased the property in August 1920, and the next door plot on 18 September that year. Only the final plans submitted on 10 September are on file, indicating that the house plan is the same but the positioning of the house on the plot was changed to suit the enlarged plot size.

This is clearly a house designed and built specifically for the new owner, and it contains many unique features. Most amazing of all is the number of double gables: there are two facing west and north, with a further two single gables on the opposite elevations.

The front door was approached through an open porch with a stone surround, to which doors have since been added. An Abbotswood style

122 *Albury, just three of the six gables.*

123 *The drawing room has a splendid fireplace.*

124 *The unique panelling is seen to its best in the dining room …*

oak-planked door leads to a large, almost square internal hall which is mainly panelled. The relatively small drawing room features a splendid fireplace, and double doors on to the 'Verandah'.

Panelling is found in the dining room, the hall, around the fireplace in the study and on the ground-floor doors. It is unique to Abbotswood, and comprises a walnut carcase with maple inner panels. Along with other panelling in houses in Abbotswood, there is the romantic theory that this came from a demolished hunting lodge on the Sutton Place Estate. It is far more likely in the case of Albury, that it was purchased and installed at the request of the first owner, for he was a director of Moon's Timber in Guildford. This was a fine way of showing to his visitors the type of high quality timber that he could obtain for his customers.

The kitchen area, included the coal store, a larder, and a lobby with a heating cupboard for a boiler at a lower level. The maid's W.C. is only reached from the outside. The planning application notes that there are three modern pattern pans, with flushing apparatus!

The house had six bedrooms, five of which are a good size. The smallest bedroom has a corner fireplace with a balcony. Two bedrooms are joined by a door and could have been the day and night nurseries. The six bedrooms share a single bathroom and lavatory.

A planning application was submitted in July 1929, proposing a garage for Mr Leighton on the additional plot. It has a room in the pitched roof, and hanging tiles on the gable ends. There are two water butts catching the water from the roof, with any excess going to two soakaways. The architects were Hodgson, Dixon & Quick, of 20, High Street, Guildford. The structure, measuring 20ft x 12ft, comprised a garage for a single car, a workshop area, and a large loft over it with windows front and back – this would have been big enough accommodation for a chauffeur.

This garage was some way from the main house, and utilised a new drive and exit on to the roadway, resulting in a main entrance to the front door, a tradesman's entrance, and the garage entrance.

125 *... and the study, also with a servant's bell.*

Design 13:
The Orchard (28) – 1921

> ❧ Pn 4050 dated (1) 28 February 1921 and (2) 14 March 1921
> ❧ Proposer: A.C. Burlingham for Hubert Falkus,
>   an accountant of CarnBrae, Shalford Road, Guildford
> ❧ Architect: A.C. Burlingham;
>   Builder: Mr W. Bullen, Contractor, Guildford

Re-submitted plans were approved on 26 April 1921. The problem was that the plans showed the intended roof as part tile and part thatched. Had it been built, it would have been the only house on the estate to be so clad.

On 28 February 1921, Burlingham wrote to the Borough Surveyor under the heading 'Undertaking' in respect of a new Bungalow at Abbotswood, Guildford, stating that 'I hereby undertake that the form of construction of the above building will be carried out strictly in the form approved by the ministry and that the standard of construction will comply with the conditions in part 2 Schedule 1 as they are applicable'. Quite clearly the planners did not like the idea of a thatched roof.

On 10 October 1921 it was recorded at the General Purposes Committee of the Guildford Borough Council that: 'Thatched Roof, Abbotswood: The Borough Surveyor reported that the thatched roof of the 'Estate Office', Abbotswood, has now been replaced by tiles'. Relief all round.

A gable end to the front of the bungalow has a wooden fascia, similar to that at Littlefield (9). The windows, the handles and catches, and square bay are typical of Abbotswood.

Burlingham used his normal feature of an open porch into a hall, from which there was access to a living room and a bedroom/sitting room. The living room contained an inglenook fireplace with seats at either end, as had Postland. Unusually, one had to go through the living room and a lobby to reach the kitchen, and through that to reach a further sitting room. Perhaps the sitting room contained a bed for the maid? The only dedicated bedroom, together with the bathroom and W.C. was off this lobby. The configuration would lead one to believe that Mr Falkus was a single gentleman.

For a while, Stanley, the Builder, had his site office in the grounds of this property.

126   *The Orchard.*

Design 14:
Erlesdene (30) and Iomar (32) – 1921

Design 15:
Littledene (35) and White Gates (36) – 1921

Burlingham, on behalf of A.G. Taylor, submitted plans for four houses in Abbotswood on 6 August 1921, with a planning reference number G25. The proposer was Taylor, the architect Burlingham and the builder, Stanley. By a process of elimination, and by virtue of the fact that sanction was given by the planning committee for Guildford Rural District Council in the parish of Worplesdon, the above houses have been identified. The plans for these houses have been lost.

The sanction indicated that all had four bedrooms, a bathroom and two reception rooms, a kitchen and a scullery and in all totalled 1,375 sq. ft. Externally the sizes look the same and they all have an exterior porch, and enjoy a single dormer window to the front at the first floor, however design 15 alone has two further windows each side of the dormer. The detailing of finish by way of tile hanging, timber panels, and roughcast makes each look different, reflecting the style of the architect.

Correspondence on file from Burlingham indicates his displeasure that, whilst the houses were submitted under the provisions of the Housing (Additional Powers) Act 1919 and the Housing Act 1921, the Ministry of Health appeared to withdraw the grant scheme earlier than had been envisaged. He assured the council officers that some of the materials were on site and that work would commence on 8 August 1921, in order to attain the new deadline of 25 August. He also pleaded that Taylor would not have gone to the expenditure of extending the road had he been aware of the new condition. Previously he had understood the grant to be available until June 1922 but was not aware of a conditional start date.

The starting certificates were signed off by the council and the houses were completed between February and April 1922. The grant of £260 per house was paid.

127 *Erlesdene, Iomhar, White Gates and Littledene (clockwise from top left).*

In the absence of a plan, there is the comment made to the planning committee which is as follows:

> These plans are submitted for the purpose of grant under the provision of the Housing (Additional Provisions) Act 1919, and 1921.
>
> The buildings will be constructed with 11' brick cavity walls to the first floor and above first floor level in timber framing covered with tiling and plastered inside.
>
> And each will contain 2 living rooms, scullery, 4 bedrooms, and a bathroom.
>
> The floor area is 1,375 sq ft which entitle the owner to a grant of £260.
>
> The outside W.C. should be placed in the outer walls of the building and not between the kitchen and larder as shown.
>
> *Harry Sheasbury*
> 27 September 1921

A further application, for Erlesdene, was submitted in February 1936 for an alteration for Mr Barrett. This enabled an additional first-floor bedroom, and a maid's room with attached bathroom on the ground floor. Both had a gas fire. The block plan also reveals a timber garage to be built in the garden with a wooden frame and elm weatherboarding. Erlesdene currently has window shutters, with cut-out heart motifs, which are probably an original design feature.

Design 16:
Wey-ne-Shing (13) – 1921

- Pn 4102 dated 23 December 1921, approved 31 January 1922
- Proposer: A.C. Burlingham for Col. Noel Smith; Architect: A.C. Burlingham
- Builder: A.G. Taylor

Early in October 1921 the plot had been sold by A.G. Taylor. Hence Burlingham was designing on behalf of the new owner. This was to be a large house, on a ¾-acre plot, with views over the river.

The house is entered through an integral open porch, into a small lobby, and down steps to a sunken hall, which has an opening onto a verandah, overlooking the Wey Valley. The drawing room, with a ceiling decorated with a plaster vine motif, and the dining room are reached through this hall.

128 *Wey-ne-Shing.*

129 *The sunken hall has a brick fireplace.*

The hall has a welcoming hearth, made of brick. Here, and elsewhere, the doors are pine, but there are oak surrounds with carved roundels at the top corners and oak picture rails too. The reception rooms had art deco lights.

The staff facilities include a china pantry, a wine store below the stairs, a kitchen, a scullery with a built in dresser, larder, coal store and heating chamber for the boiler, and finally a W.C. accessible from the outside.

On the first floor there is a 'best' bedroom, with attached dressing room, and bedrooms two and three. For the maids there is a bedroom with a partition to divide it, and a linen cupboard. They have a separate and rather small bathroom with a "housemaids' sink", perhaps like that shown in Fig. 199.

Design 17:

Westward Ho (14) and Hillcrest (21) – 1922

∾ Pn 4192 dated October 1922, approved 28 November 1922
∾ Proposer: A.G. Taylor; Architect: A.C. Burlingham;
    Builder: A.E. Stanley

Westward Ho, Hillcrest and South Stoke (20), were to be of the same basic design, but at this early stage South Stoke was aborted and a different design was later used.

Both Hillcrest and South Stoke had frontages of 150feet, with Westward Ho having 122feet. The block plan shows all three houses at an angle of about forty degrees to the road, but they were built at right angles.

The estate plan shows that, initially, 4in sewer drains were to go along north side of Westward Ho, and across the garden and connect with the town sewer in Farm Lane through a six-inch pipe. The width of the roadway was given as exactly 40feet between Nos. 14 and 21, including the grass verges.

These two houses were handed. Each had an 'L' shaped plan, built in the 'Surrey' style having mock timber front and side, with the rear and the fourth side of roughcast.

The ground-floor plan shows a dining room, drawing room and a kitchen with a fitted dresser and gas cooker. The drawing room has an inglenook recess for the fire. The porch was open, with a curved widow, as one faced the door, to the left.

130 *Hillcrest and Westward Ho.*

131   *The rear elevations have changed somewhat.*

For the maid, there was a scullery with a solid floor, and a rear open entrance lobby to the W.C. The coal store was accessed through the scullery. The larder, which had a slate shelf, was reached through the kitchen.

On the first floor there were five bedrooms, the fifth, for the maid, measuring only 11ft 3in by 6ft. This and three of the other bedrooms had a fitted cupboard. Two bedrooms shared a six-light window – this remains at Hillcrest to this day.

In December 1923, the owner of Westward Ho, D.C. Evill, received approval for 'Additions' to Westward Ho. These included a loggia, an extension to the hall, a large coal store and tool room, a garage with potting shed and boiler room and, on the first floor, two dressing rooms over the loggia, a night nursery over the extended hall, and a bedroom over the garage.

The story passed down through the owners is that Evill had purchased a Rolls Royce motor car and wished to house this and his chauffeur. At the time a new type Twenty Rolls Royce with a touring body would have cost £1,590, increasing to nearly £3,000 for a Silver Ghost. Either motor would have put into the shade the purchase price of £2,190 for the newly built South Stoke in February 1924.

Westward Ho was again substantially altered in 2000 when not only were the alterations by D.C. Evill removed, but the house was extended to three floors with six bedrooms, five bathrooms and four reception rooms.

Design 18:
South Stoke (20) and Waysend (34) – 1923

∽ Pn 4264 dated 29 January 1924 [no planning application]
∽ Proposer: A.G. Taylor; Architect: A.C. Burlingham;
     Builder: A.E. Stanley

There is some confusion about the planning application for these two houses. South Stoke initially formed part of a trio of houses along with Westward Ho (14) and Hillcrest (21). Instead of utilising the third plot at the time, it was later coupled as a two-house project with Waysend.

An application to build West Hill House (17) and The Corner House (19) submitted in April 1923 was delayed due to problems with the drainage; it is thought that, in order not to hold matters up, South Stoke and Waysend were built instead. The planners allocated Pn 4264 for West Hill House and The Corner House to South Stoke and Waysend. In support of this argument the planning application for the extension to Westward Ho, in December 1923, shows South Stoke as built. On 29 January 1924 the actual planning application for South Stoke and Waysend was submitted retrospectively.

132 *South Stoke.*

133 *Waysend.*

The plans show a long sloping roof reaching the ground floor where an integral garage is to be found for South Stoke. At the front a long open stone-floored porch leads to a hall. On the ground floor there is the usual dining room and living room configuration off the hall together with a kitchen entrance. Through the kitchen is the scullery which in turn leads to an open rear and porch off which is found the servants' W.C. and the coal store. Of note is the fireplace in the dining room, which is positioned in the corner of the room.

The first-floor plan detailed five bedrooms, with two measuring only 8ft x 9ft, divided by a stud wall. These could have easily converted to a larger room, particularly as they share the same four-light window. The central five-inch mullion, which is absent from the other four-light window on the first floor, supports the contention that this was always designed as two rooms – this is recognised as a Burlingham feature.

Waysend has a slightly different configuration in the living room, with a large attached verandah rather than a garage. Thus the fireplace and chimney are moved to the rear of the house which allows access to the verandah. In 1929, Dr Billinghurst had rooms for his surgery added on the north side of the house by A.E. Stanley.

Design 19:

Wykeham Lodge (15), Westcott (18) and The Hazard (33) – 1923

- ✲ Pn 4400 dated 7 December 1923, approved 29 January 1924
- ✲ Proposer: Onyx Investment Company; Architect: A.C. Burlingham (1923); Builder: A.E. Stanley

The planning notice covered two houses, Wykeham Lodge and Westcott. The former had a frontage of 120feet, and the latter 60feet. The Hazard fell within the planning controls of Guildford Rural District Council and, whilst it would have been submitted at the same time, does not show on this sanction. However, there is a reference to The Hazard in a letter and plan from Burlingham regarding the lower-floor garage for this house and Wykeham Lodge.

134 *Wykeham Lodge.*

135   *Westcott.*

In a letter from Burlingham to the Council, Wykeham Lodge was described as house 'M' and The Hazard as 'K'. On the block plan for the planning application Wykeham Lodge is described as 'K' and Westcott is annotated as 'M'. On a site plan with Pn 4562 Wykeham Lodge is 'M', Westcott 'N', and The Hazard is 'K'. Confusing for all concerned.

Little wonder that Burlingham commented in another letter to the Council, 'We have no house lettered 'L.' We omitted this letter on representation from some workmen who thought that if the aspirate were accidentally added when directing other workmen to the job it might lead to trouble.' This does show that the myriad of letters used for the new houses before names were applied caused just as much trouble at the time as they have done for this researcher.

The plans for the ground floor and the first floor are identical for all three properties. They present a covered porch leading to a hall with a beamed ceiling, off which are the drawing room, a dining room and the kitchen. The kitchen leads to a scullery with a larder and a sink with a double drainer, and then to a lobby, open to the elements. Off this is a W.C. for the servants and a coal store.

The dining room contains an inglenook fireplace with a large beam across the width, supported by large brackets, similar to those for Design 17. A further beam is to be found in the drawing room, supporting the bay. Residents recall that a previous neighbour told of panelling in the dining room at Wykeham Lodge. At Westcott there is evidence that panelling existed, reaching half way up the wall, and also in the dining room. If one accepts that two sources point to firm evidence, the panelling might have not found favour and has been removed at some time. An example of the type of panelling that this might have been can be seen at The Hurst (46).

Author's Recollection: When living in a Victorian house in Sussex as a child, I recall the half panelling painted to give the appearance of wood grain. The panelling was made up of vertical planks of wood, capped with a 1½ inch lateral strip of moulded wood. The purpose was to hide the evidence of damp, which was ever present because of a lack of a damp-proof course in the wall of single bricks. Perhaps the residents of Abbotswood believed that visitors might think that they had the same problem, and therefore had it removed.

On the first floor there are five bedrooms, one of which is only reached through the master bedroom and was probably intended as a dressing room or nursery. The long roof provides for a box room. Of note are the splendid carved bargeboards on the gables of Wykeham Lodge and Westcott, and the long sloping roof to the first floor on all three houses.

Externally, the houses are differentiated by tile hanging on The Hazard rather than the half timbers of the other two, and because Wykeham Lodge and The Hazard both had a basement garage measuring 16ft x 14ft, with a workshop and store. This was possible because these houses were built on the hillside, resulting in a steep rear entrance for the cars.

The lower garage at Wykeham Lodge lost favour early on. Mr Crosby, as a condition of purchasing the house from the first owner in 1927, submitted an application for a garage measuring 17feet x 15feet, at the side of the house. It was built with 2in x 4in studding and weatherboarding, and still stands today.

136 *The Hazard.*

Design 20:

West Hill House (17) and
The Corner House (19) – 1923

❧ Pn 4264 dated 16 April 1923, and also Pn 4562 dated (1)
18 September 1924, and (2) 13 October 1924, appr 28 October 1924

❧ Proposer and builder: A.G. Taylor; Architect: A.C. Burlingham.

A problem with services delayed the building of these houses. The planners required connection to the mains sewer from the end of the road, at that time at Westward Ho (14). Burlingham wrote to the Borough Surveyor and pleaded with him that, because it would cost around £600, a lot of money in those days, he should be allowed to use cesspits. He submitted plans accordingly. This was sanctioned by Mr Gross, the Borough Surveyor, on behalf of the Guildford

137 *West Hill House.*

138   *The Corner House.*

Urban Sanitary Authority on 29 May 1923, but clearly the conditions were not satisfactorily addressed and building work was delayed. Consequently Wykeham Lodge, Westcott and South Stoke were built first. Thus a plan was resubmitted some 18 months later incorporating a connection with the mains sewer and approved.

The building of The Corner House was started on 28 September 1924 and completed in June 1925. West Hill House is built to plan, but The Corner House is handed. Each house has shaped brick mullions containing metal window frames.

The two houses had a porch leading to a hallway and then the drawing room, dining room and kitchen. Off the kitchen was the scullery. There were five bedrooms, and the one over the garage for the maid had a lower entrance at the first stage of the stairs from the hallway.

The Corner House originally had timber cladding around the first floor, which has recently been replaced with tiles. An additional sitting room was added to the east side of the house in 1935; this resulted in a flat, asphalt roof. A further first-floor bathroom was added together with coal stores on the ground floor, for which approval was given in May 1936. A second flat roof ensued. Tribe and Robinson of Onslow Street Works, Guildford carried out both extensions.

Eaglehurst (31) – 1923

The planning application for Eaglehurst has not been traced despite an extensive search of the planning records.

It is known that Taylor sold the large plot of land measuring approximately 250feet x 200feet to Mrs Alice Wheeler for £490 on 18 October 1922. On 7 May 1925 the house was sold for £3,825 by Mrs Wheeler to Alice Hobbs. It is reasonable to assume that the building of the house was completed in the middle of 1923, and perhaps marketed soon after that. There are two dates at the property: firstly, the date 1922 is found on the drainpipe hoppers, and, secondly, on the pathway down to the woods the date 1923 is inscribed. The earlier date would have referred to the start of the building work, rather than completion. There are a number of reasons for this. Planning consent would usually have been applied for after the land purchase, and completion would have been 9-12 months after that. The *Guildford Street Directory* refers to Eaglehurst only from 1924, also indicating a 1923 completion date.

There is no feature in the house that would lead one to suspect that it was designed by Burlingham. Indeed, the architecture is quite unique to the suburb. All other Abbotswood houses have a link to one or more other houses by way of design features. This has none. Nevertheless, it is a

139 *Eaglehurst.*

noteworthy Edwardian-style house, reflected in 1925 by the exceptionally high price paid for it.

140 *The garden is reached from the side.*

There is half-timbering all the way round the house at the first floor, and the ground floor has hard red engineering bricks closely set. The external woodwork is more fussy and heavy than that used by Burlingham for his 'Surrey' style. The front porch is enclosed, and topped with a double door on to the flat roof.

At the side, there are two unusual features. Firstly, there is an exterior double door in its own small porch with a pitched roof, which leads from the dining room to the side garden. The same wall has three protruding angled windows each supported by a single shaped bracket. The quality of the brickwork can be seen at this point with the shaped corner wall, and the protruding bricks supporting the upper storey. The use of clay air bricks was unknown in the Burlingham houses, where metal vents were invariably used.

The chimneys were part brick and part roughcast. Originally they were unpainted, as can be seen in the early photographs, but a later resident had them painted white, which presents an expensive problem when it comes to redecorating the exterior. In the 1970s the roughcast was replaced by a flat cement finish.

The roof was once topped by a viewing platform, giving a panorama across the Wey Valley, and to Stoughton and the Hogs Back. This has since been removed, but evidence of the posts remains.

The garden stretched down to the stream, once the parish boundary, and the copse. The more formal garden, towards Iomhar, contained a tennis court.

141 *The panorama from the roof, and the garden.*

142 *The entrance led to a hall with a large fireplace.*

Inside there is an impressive entrance with a large fireplace awaiting the visitor. To the left is an oak staircase leading to the first floor, giving a large open atrium. When first built the staircase was central, hiding the fireplace from the view at the door. This was changed to the present position when renovations were carried out in 1969. The doors on the ground floor are of stained oak with pine surrounds, and the ceilings in the hall, drawing room and dining rooms all have wooden slats for decoration rather than the moulded plasterwork used by Burlingham.

In the hall and on the first floor are ceiling-high oak cupboards, matching the one-foot-tall skirting board. A delft rack is present in the ground-floor reception rooms. The doors have finger plates and handles, rather more ornate than those used by Burlingham. The original tiling in the bathroom and the toilet areas is either blue or brown.

The main ground-floor fireplaces have an impressive polished mahogany frame around brown tiles in one room and a marble inlay in the other. The fireplaces in the bedrooms have metal frames, some with a plain tile inlay. One bedroom fireplace with a wooden frame is particularly indicative of the period.

144 *Blue tiles in the bathroom.*

There are four family bedrooms on the first floor with a single bathroom, and two further rooms on the second floor, approached by a spiral staircase. A third staircase, made with deal and painted white, leads to the roof viewing platform. The window frames at all floors are metal, by Crittal, and the window handles and catches are brass at the ground floor and steel on the upper floors.

143 *The drawing room fireplace.*

Design 21:
The Odd House (16) – 1925

- ❧ Pn 4744 dated 2 July 1925
- ❧ Proposer: A.G. Taylor; Architect: A.C. Burlingham;
   Builder: A.E. Stanley

The file is missing for Pn 4744. The sale of the property by A.G. Taylor and the Onyx Property Investment Company took place on 10 September 1926. The house is individual in its design, and has not the half-timbering, roughcast nor the tile-hanging seen on the other Abbotswood houses. Because the brick construction has not been embellished, it resembles more closely the houses designed by Burlingham in Ganghill from 1929 onwards.

Inside, the pine doors are of a design more frequently seen in the 1930s, with a large top panel and two smaller bottom panels. The triple aspect drawing room, facing east/south/west led to a verandah overlooking the valley, which is what one would expect. This has been absorbed into this room to make it larger. The dining room faces west, and the kitchen west/north.

The open porch at the front is within the walls of the house, which has a timber beam, has been enclosed by a small extension. The original furniture to the oak front door has been retained.

145   *The Odd House.*

Ten

Arts and Crafts and
Surrey Style Features

Many of the features that enable Abbotswood houses to be described as of an Arts and Crafts style have already been identified for some of the houses. These warrant closer examination and can be linked with the work of Baillie Scott. Because of the later period of design and build for houses in Ganghill, Fairway and around Trodds Lane, these features do not necessarily exist in those houses, although many will.

In order to understand why Burlingham used the styles that he did, there are added to the descriptions various comments on, and from, the works of Mackay Hugh Baillie Scott. He was an architect who followed the Arts and Crafts Movement and sought to encourage others to do so by writing numerous articles from 1895 to 1914, published in *The Studio*. His major work, *House and Gardens*, published in 1906 was illustrated with drawings and watercolours which defined his vision of the artistic house. There is little doubt that Burlingham was aware of these writings and they could well have influenced him. It is worth repeating that it was around the time when he was designing the first houses for Abbotswood that Baillie Scott was completing two well known Arts and Crafts houses in Warwicks Bench, Guildford, named Undershaw and Garden Court.

Comments about his works include some by Diane Haigh who wrote *Baillie Scott: The Artistic House*; these perhaps give an insight into the work of Burlingham.

A visit to Undershaw revealed that it was a modest house on three floors, which has now been split into two dwellings. The lower ground floor had the servants' area plus the dining room, the ground floor had a splendid hall, a drawing room, two bedrooms and a study, and the upper floor had three further bedrooms and a dressing room. All rooms, save for the hall, were modest in size. Allowing for the splitting of the house, various additions have been made, but the concept of the Arts and Crafts house has been fully maintained. The author is most grateful to Mrs Oonagh Monckton for providing a well informed tour.

146 *Baillie Scott's designs.*

The photographs in Fig. 146, together with those in Fig. 70 show elements of Baillie Scott's work that are reflected in the early Burlingham designs, which would have been created only a short while after Undershaw was completed in 1910.

EXTERNAL FEATURES

Baillie Scott:

> He tended to have houses with an irregular footprint. This was due to the way he added rooms into the whole. Thus there may be stair towers, chimneys and various bays that stopped the design being a simple one. Having thus commented, he advocated 'in economic building it is wise to make the house itself of simple rectangular form, covered in a single space of hipped roof'. This simple roof form could be elaborated with the addition of abutting wings or an open courtyard. His houses are generally of this form with the outside walls being load bearing with roofs pitched at 54½ degrees.
>
> Many of Baillie Scott's houses have long sweeping roofs, coming down to the height of the front door. The chimneys were seldom the enormous size of those used by other Arts and Crafts masters such as Lutyens.
>
> He believed that houses should be as low and as snug as possible, and objected to the proposal that ceiling heights should become a minimum of 8 feet, rather than the 7 feet 6 inches normally used. He was successful in his campaign. His aim was to allow his houses to sit comfortably on the site. Ideally he wanted the house to harmonise with the landscape, such as those in Warwicks Bench, Guildford, where they hug the contours of the North Downs. In the suburbs, he felt that it was necessary to 'make nature harmonise with the house, or make house and nature meet each other half-way'.

Diane Haigh comments:

> Although some details were repeated from house to house, Baillie Scott generally designed the elements in response to each commission. Doors, fireplaces, skirting, architraves, window latches and hinges were usually made afresh for each house, establishing a unique identity. Elaborate in his early years, these elements evolved to an essential simplicity in his mature work.

In so many of his Abbotswood houses, Burlingham appears to follow these ideals. It can be seen that after his early work at The Hurst and The Gate House the designs gradually became less fussy, partly due perhaps to economic constraints. Nevertheless, the best features of the early houses were continued throughout his time at the estate.

BRICKWORK

Baillie Scott:

> A brick is after all, a piece of baked clay, and its beauty consists in its character. It should have the characteristic surface and texture of another

147 *Above are Flemish Bond, below are stretcher bond with a ventilator.*

148 *Brick mullions at Tigbourne Court (left inset) and Abbotswood (right inset and main).*

earth. Then as to colour: a tint which is subtly varied must be more beautiful than a uniform shade, and more in harmony with natural surrounding.

All properties have brickwork using mostly locally available hand-made brick; indeed the originals are far from uniform in shape. The vast majority are mottled, notably Rudgwick multi-colour, which is still available today. These are interspersed with lighter Warnham Reds; both came from clays just a few miles away towards Horsham. How dull they would have been had they all been like those at Eaglehurst, which are uniform in colour, fitting together tightly, without providing an interesting contrast.

The vast majority of brick is laid using stretcher bond and the walls are generally 11 inches thick and hollow. Around the scullery and coal stores, a nine-inch solid wall is used in a Flemish Bond; the bricks are alternatively placed side on and then end on. This locks the double brick together without a cavity. Nine-inch walls were also used on many upper floors where cladding was to be used. For no apparent reason, on some of the earlier houses the latter is used on some main external walls.

A common problem with older houses is that, whilst the original bricks were of an imperial measurement, new ones are metric, which can give a most odd appearance when a new wall is aligned with an old one. Examples exist where the matching is attempted with thicker courses of 'cement', which gives quite the wrong look. Worst comes when single metric bricks are used to replace a decayed old brick, in which case a hunt in a builder's yard selling second-hand bricks is well worth the effort. The use of cement alongside lime mortar is considered a crime by many a purist. Indeed, mortar gives a softer look and weathers quite differently.

The damp proof course comprises a layer of length of hessian strip, dipped in hot tar and applied to the brick course, topped by a layer of slate. At intervals there are metal air vents where the slate can be seen on top of the metal. On the planning notices this was often referred to as 'Trinidad Bitumen and/or a double course of slates in cement'. Until 1920 there was no requirement to state the type of damp proofing on the planning notices checklist.

On many houses bricks were used on the exterior for decorative purposes, including different colours at the corners for a contrast.

In several houses, shaped bricks are used as a feature of the window frames, giving the appearance of those seen at the Lutyens'-designed houses, Tigbourne Court, Wormley, and also at Goddards, in Abinger Hammer. These include Hestercombe, The Cottage, West Hill House, and The Corner House.

Internally bricks were extensively used for fireplaces and also as a decorative archway inside the bungalows.

149 *Bungalow arch.*

HALF-TIMBERING

Baillie Scott:

> He believed that timber was to bear its origin as a tree, and be left roughly finished from the adze when used as beams or joists. Panelling, on the other hand should be planed to be smooth to the touch.

One of the endearing features of Abbotswood houses is the half-timber effect covering many of the upper storeys in an attempt to recreate the Tudor element of the Surrey style.

The garish black and white of painted timber, with a plaster in-fill, is a Victorian ideal, promulgated by the Early Romantic Movement, and later by Norman Shaw. Not far from Abbotswood, Shaw created Merrist Wood House. Many would consider his style to be pre-Arts and Crafts, but many of the features were carried into the work of this Movement and it is believed that both Voysey and Lutyens were much influenced by this house. The photographs in Fig. 63 can be used to identify similar features in Abbotswood, although on a smaller scale. Were you to visit Merrist Wood House, the external timbering appears plainer and less attractive than that at Abbotswood where it is more weathered and less 'perfect' in appearance.

The timber on most old Surrey houses was covered by tile or an elevation of plaster in order to protect the timber from the elements. Covering with plaster was even more common in East Anglia where most older timber-framed houses have an attractive coloured plaster facing.

The removal of this was rife in Victorian times. The well known half-timbered pub at Shere called the *White Horse* is a case in point. It was once plastered over, and this was removed when the village became popular with walkers and tourists. A photograph in the bar area confirms this.

150 *The adze marks show on the timber 'frames' and the internal beams.*

Above all, original timber was not painted black. The oak was allowed to weather to a silver grey colour, and the plaster either left a natural buff or mixed with ochre to complement the oak grey. Examine any Victorian cottage painting by Helen Allingham, or Myles Birket Foster, and you will discover the reality.

The Burlingham timbers were of course for the most part decorative facings, with the one-inch boards nailed to the brick. If there is an overhanging wall, the boards are nailed onto the timber frame. When decorating, if the timber needs preserving, an absorbent mid-brown colour should be used, which will take away the harshness of the black, and prevent the flaking seen on the painted wood of some houses. The dowels at the timber joints are purely decorative. Quite properly, the top side of the timber is protected by a lead flashing.

As a sign of the trouble that the architect took to make the outside timber appear solid, perhaps as a consequence of the advice from Baillie Scott, the surface was formed with marks made with an adze, as if recently hewn from woodland. This finish can also be seen on internal timbers in the inglenook fireplaces.

The painting of the oak and the plaster on Burlingham's houses was not commonplace until the 1960s, or even later. Some, such as 32, Ganghill remain unblemished. Burlingham moved away from the half-timbered concept after 1929, and some of the houses in Ganghill have timber spanning the whole front elevation.

Tile Hanging

Tile hanging on walls is very much a feature of older cottages in Kent, Sussex and Surrey. This is often seen on the first storey wall, and on gables and dormer windows. In timber-framed houses tiles were there to protect the oak timbers from the weather; it was more expensive than covering them with plaster but became common in Sussex and Surrey. In 1910 Lawrence Weaver recorded that the use of tiles in this manner was rarely present before 1700, yet other authorities such as Adrian Tinniswood in his book *Life in the English Country Cottage* claimed that tiles were present in the south-east in the 16th century.

Tiles are used as an alternative to half-timbering, or roughcast on gables and upper storey walls. Burlingham has ensured that the tile hanging seen at Stoke Park Farm is replicated in an attractive manner. The bottom tiles were proud of the walls beneath; thus the rainwater mostly fell away from the walls.

As one looks at cottages in Surrey villages that carry these weather tiles, it becomes apparent that there are many differently shaped tiles in use. It is known that each area tended to manufacture its own form of tile. Even

151 *Various styles of tile are used on this Surrey cottage.*

in Abbotswood, different shapes, rather than the simple rectangle can be seen. That on Stoke Park Farm has to the front a covering of pointed tiles not common in Surrey. Perhaps they were made in the local clay works at Burpham. To the rear of the farmhouse these are continued, but on the gable they are rounded, similar to ones from Ewhurst. On the front of South Stoke there are three bands of Ewhurst tiles, which may be a deliberate copy of the farmhouse, and on Waysend, the sister house, the tiles are quite plain. Tiles were also hung on chimneys of the early houses. Burlingham's Queen Anne style houses have fine examples.

Wood Facings

A popular feature of the Surrey style is the use of stained wood facing on the walls – this is called weatherboarding or clapboarding. This provided a covering for the wooden frame in order to prevent rotting by rain. The wood did not last as long as tiles or plaster, but at least the boards were cheaper to replace when necessary. This covering is evident in old buildings as you pass through many Surrey villages; it is not a common feature in Abbotswood, but can be seen on Littlefield and The Orchard. The largest expanse of wood could, until a short while ago, also be seen at The Corner House, when it covered the whole of the front of the property, at the first floor. In 2000 this was replaced by tiles. It is not surprising that a barn covered in wood planking can be found at Stoke Park Farm.

152 *These Burlingham buildings reflect the weatherboarding at Stoke Park Farm.*

Cement Render

Baillie Scott:

> On the exterior of the house a cemented stone wall is dull.

In order to enliven plain walls, Baillie Scott advocated the use of a trowel and wooden float to create a rippled effect that would attract light. This can be seen on his design at Church Rate Corner, Cambridge, and is replicated in Abbotswood at West Hill House, The Corner House and at Archways in Fairway.

Rough Cast Render, or Pebbledash

Roughcast was a simple finish, and a rather inexpensive one, which provided a contrast against brick and the half-timbering. It formed an important aspect to the Arts and Crafts designs of Voysey who used it in many of his buildings. At various times it was popular with many of the other Arts and Crafts masters. This is a mixture of cement with crushed stones or shingle, and gives a less than uniform surface. Burlingham used the roughcast method, but with a mixture of mixed stones and a light mortar, which has not always stood the test of time. Most of this finish has been painted white and can be seen in Fig. 164.

Pebbledash forms a major part of the finish on suburban 1930s houses, and comprises small stones sprayed by hand on to a wet plaster surface. It is less attractive, due in part to its commonality. The rear of The Hazard has recently been treated with pebbledash, but retains the natural light brown colour.

Other Types of Decoration

Some of the early houses have plaster decorations on the exterior known as pargeting, showing garland motifs.

153 *Church Rate Corner and West Hill House.*

Occasionally large walls are broken up using vertical vents such as seen at Wey-ne-Shing and Sunnymead.

WINDOW SHUTTERS

Window shutters were exceptionally used on Hestercombe, but were used as a formal part of the design on the bungalows. These can be seen in Fig. 114.

BARGEBOARDS

On a number of gables there are bargeboards helping to keep the rain off the walls. In the later houses in Abbotswood, Burlingham went to the trouble of attaching ones with intricate carvings. Examples can be seen on Wykeham Lodge, Westcott and others.

ROOFS

The designers of Arts and Crafts houses paid much attention to the size and style of the roof. One may think that they believed in the 'bigger the better' concept. Burlingham did not let them down. The pitch of the roofs are around fifty degrees, far greater than a modern house, and in several cases the roof stretches from the apex down to the eaves at ground-floor level. Examples include The Cottage, Wey-ne-Shing, Wykeham Lodge, Westcott, and The Hazard. This type of roof was much favoured by Lutyens.

Inside the roof space of The Hurst can be seen a timber lining. More usually, whilst there appears to be a lining, there were simply planks of triangular sectioned wood used as battens, on which the tiles were hung. This gives some protection to the roof space, but not much. Before the First World War, this was lined with a hessian material, and after this period the planks were bare. Under the apex of the gables, a covering of planks can be seen.

154   *Pargeting.*

155   *Decorative bargeboards.*

156   *The long roof is not uncommon in Abbotswood.*

157 *Attic lining and planks for tile hanging look similar.*

Mini-Roofs

On a number of occasions Burlingham designed walls with a small tiled roof to join the main house to a yard or a garage. At Friars Oak, the courtyard entrance has such a wall, similar to those attaching the garage at Littlefield.

Drainpipes

The external guttering and drainpipes were made of cast-iron. Some of the drainpipe hoppers were splendid, and embellished with patterns but the norm was a simple cast-iron type. Today, when replacements are required, all too often plastic piping or guttering is used which weather from black to a grey/black colour after a few years.

158 *A mini-roof.*

Chimneys

One would expect houses of this Arts and Crafts type to have overpowering chimneys where the greater size of the roof is offset by the size of the chimney. This was not the case for Burlingham. Where the roof is large, such as at Wey-ne-Shing, the size has been offset by other means; in that case by a dormer window.

Exceptionally, The Hurst has tall diagonally set chimneystacks, very much in the Arts and Crafts style. Others in Abbotswood are more conventional, but still maintain interest. Even Stoke Park Farm

has a central chimneystack of a moderate size. Perhaps Burlingham took his style from there, using relatively simple designs, which were mostly neither plain nor spectacular. Those at The Cottage are the more interesting in their size and proportion to the house. Some early designs feature windows in the chimneystack at ground-floor level.

The removal of chimneys invariably spoils the design.

GABLES

Gables are a common feature on the Abbotswood houses. They add to the complexity of the design, and enhance the appearance. These features are both at the end of roofs, and at right angles, proving additional rooms. The decoration is of varying types including half timbers, roughcast, tile hanging and, exceptionally, brick. The most spectacular gables are at Albury, which has six in all.

The gablet, a small gable, is seen on early Surrey buildings. Except for that at The Hurst, it was not used by Burlingham until after the

159 Drainpipes and hoppers come in all sizes.

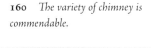

160 The variety of chimney is commendable.

161 *The perfect, well balanced gable, with planking under the eaves.*

First World War. These are a method of altering the size of a house plan, whilst keeping the correct roof angles. In medieval houses they were open, providing an exit for smoke before the use of brick chimneys. This is evident at Stoke Park Farm. Sometimes gablets were used by Burlingham to differentiate house designs such as that between Littledene and White Gates.

Splash-Backs

Most gable ends reveal a pronounced rise at the end of the roof line. This is known as a splash-back. It helps to divert the rainwater from the gable end, particularly where there is virtually no overhang. This is a feature of the older houses in the south of England, where the rainfall is less than in the north, and the overhang at the gable edge is only a few inches. In the north of England, the overhang was a lot greater and the splash backs were not required. The gable at Hillcrest is a prime example with an edge of no more than two inches. Also to be noted is the lip above the window to help take the rainfall away, and at the bottom of the overhang, too. The windows are almost flush with the wall (*see* Fig. 163). The splash-back was also present on some bay windows including those at Oakdene and Red Cottage.

162 *A gablet.*

In recent restorations builders have perhaps not appreciated the significance of this feature, and on restoring or changing roof structures have removed it!

Sprockets

The roofs and gables invariably have sprockets. These are rectangular pieces of wood placed on the end of the rafter to angle and lift the last few tiles at the bottom of the roof; this can clearly be seen on the white gable end in Fig.164. The idea was that this would slow down the water as it came off the roof, and into the gutter – a feature no longer seen on modern roofs.

First-Floor Overhangs and Jettied Gables

In line with the Tudor image, a large proportion of the houses have upper storey floors overhanging the lower ones by two feet or so. These extensions are held up by extended beams, and sometimes have the additional support of small brick buttresses, or stone or wooden frames at the ends. Invariably the outer wall is a wooden timber frame, with either tile hanging, roughcast rendering or half-timbering.

Dormer Windows

Small dormer windows are an attractive feature on many of Burlingham's designs. Sometimes they are gabled, and sometimes hipped. The sides, or cheeks, may be tiled or roughcast. Often they stand alone, but sometimes they are incorporated into the roof at a junction. Occasionally they are formal, and symmetrical, at other times they are purposefully asymmetrical. All are small, and have a cill to keep the water away from the joinery; these are so much more attractive than the modern roof lights.

163 *A splash-back.*

164 *A sprocket can be seen on this unsupported overhang. Examples of different buttresses are shown.*

Porches

Baillie Scott:

> Circulation was removed from the hall to avoid draughts and maintain privacy. A broad and welcoming front door generally opened onto a hallway which contained a separate access for servants and a direct route to the staircase.

165 *There are many types of dormer windows to be seen.*

Churston and Aoetearoa were the first houses to be built. Burlingham designed the houses with the porch to the right of the front. Lutyens, Baillie

Scott, and C.R. Mackintosh all used this feature, giving the emphasis on the size of the house, rather than the grandeur of the entrance. As if to de-emphasise the entrance even further, not only did these porches contain a plain door and a small porch roof supported by two wooden brackets, but the boundary to the plot was just six feet from the door. With a canopy measuring seven feet wide, and five feet to the front, this left just one foot before the hedge. The entrance was intentionally far from impressive.

With few exceptions Burlingham preferred an integral, but open, entrance porch, more in line with the statement above. Visitors would enter the walls of the house while they waited for the bell to be answered. Most of the porches were enhanced by an open wood structure and let into the house through brick faced walls whilst others were more elaborate with York stone surrounds such as at The Lair and Albury. Hestercombe and Upmeads were the exception, having an enclosed porch, with fine stone around the entrance door.

166   *The entrance porch at Aoetearoa is unassuming.*

VERANDAHS AND LOGGIAS

Baillie Scott:

> In the quest for healthy living, the beneficial effects of sunshine were much appreciated. He tucked a sheltered, sunny verandah under the roof of even the smallest houses.

167   *Porches were a significant feature for Burlingham's houses.*

168 *Several verandahs remain.*

Long before the plethora of plastic or wooden conservatories, Burlingham incorporated verandahs and loggias into his designs. This gave the owner the opportunity to enjoy the pleasures of the garden within the confines of the home. The difference between the two is that the loggia was generally enclosed and the verandah had at least one open aspect. The best examples of a loggia are to be seen at Lorraine and Friars Oak, which are enclosed, having large windows and a door onto the patio. The verandahs at Albury, Waysend and Red Cottage are in their original form, whilst those at The Odd House, Brookdale and Oakdene have been absorbed into the drawing rooms.

Windows and their Different Forms

Baillie Scott:

> He believed that bay windows generated and addressed an important point in the garden. Usually south facing they provided an alcove for sun and light. In early houses they tended to include a window seat.

Houses, designed prior to 1918, had high quality lead casement windows in mostly pine frames. Sometimes the inner and outer cills were made of oak along with the bottom of the frame, while the top of the frame and the mullions were of pine. At this time pine was sometimes referred to as deal, which was a generalised name for fir or pine timber, especially in cut form.

Until building stopped in 1916, the opening windows had a metal frame rebated into the wooden surround. The hinged and glazed metal frame was let into this frame. When the window was fixed, the leaded lights were fitted directly into the wood frame. After the First World War the more expensive external metal frame was done away with, and the opening windows, still in a metal frame, fitted straight into the pine frame.

Sometimes the shape of the glass was mixed. As an example, The Cottage has diamond shapes at the front and square at the back, which is exactly as shown on the original plan. In the 19th century, the first Arts and Crafts houses had mostly square panes although vernacular houses tended towards the diamond shape.

The wooden frames, made of 4in x 3in timbers, were pegged together using single dowels. The number and size of frames differed depending on use. In some houses Burlingham gave the impression of grandness by creating a window with six lights, still seen at Hillcrest, having two six-inch mullions. Whilst not visible from the outside, this served for two rooms, but gave the impression that it was a very large window in just one room. On a smaller scale The Gate House had a four-light window for two bedrooms, again split at a large mullion, as did the designs for Red Cottage and South Stoke. Voysey was renowned for long multi-mullioned windows.

Some of the earlier Abbotswood houses have larger horizontal window openings measuring 25in x 20in, rather than the later ones in slightly narrower windows at 19in x 16in. The former are half the length of the window, while the post-war ones measure one third of the overall length.

The window furniture was to style. Some elements were cast, and others wrought. There is little doubt that these were purchased to order from Guildford Glass and Metal, rather than using the local blacksmith as did the early Arts and Crafts architects. A threaded hole for a grub screw to lock the windows can still be seen.

Whilst no longer permissible today, these houses have windows that feature the glass very close to the outside. The gable at Hillcrest clearly shows how the window forms part of the wall. It is a comment often quoted by the Arts and Crafts enthusiast from Guy Dawber that windows 'should be treated as organic parts of the wall and not mere openings surrounded by stonework. Windows should always give a sense of enclosing, or of separation from the outside'. Perhaps,

170   *Window sizes changed.*

as a continuation of the wall, Burlingham achieved this in Abbotswood. Roderick Gradidge comments that a modern house cannot comply with this ideal because bye-laws now require that the window glass has to be recessed by at least four inches, thus providing a drip head to direct the falling rain away from the window glass, and also require a sill to take the rain away from the wall beneath. This can be seen in Fig. 164 above.

Baillie Scott:

> Wherever possible the living spaces were lined up along the south front of the house. If the plot orientation allowed, they opened up to the garden through bays, garden rooms, and verandahs.

Again with an Arts and Crafts influence, some double windows open from the sides and permit a double opening from the ground or first floors onto the garden, making the house and the garden as one. Bay windows are a common feature.

Sadly, the time has come when owners believe that the old windows are no longer worth preserving. Sometimes it is easier for the builder to go to a convenient salesroom that caters for the 'ordinary', or there may be a belief that plastic windows are better for the environment, which is doubtful if the build

171 *The more usual window fittings.*

172 *Bay windows gave a closeness to the garden.*

173 *The most popular front doors were solid planks.*

costs are taken into account, together with the relatively short lifespan. Many of the original windows have lasted over 90 years, and are still giving good service. Already at Aoetearoa plastic windows put in a few years ago have been replaced.

Windows that give the same appearance as the originals are available, and existing windows can be double glazed. Those at Westward Ho are a case in point where the restorers went to the trouble of using the original windows and bringing them up to modern standards using plain glass, double glazed, with adhesive metal strips to give a similar appearance to the originals. A purist might baulk at this, for the originals presented the Arts and Crafts ideal of varying reflections for the myriad of panes.

Baillie Scott:

> Small panes would create a varied quality of light, whereas the large sheet of glass had only a 'blank and vacant stare'. Generally the mullioned windows were in timber with metal opening casements, and they were positioned flush with no protruding cill, allowing for the surface of the wall to remain undisturbed.

174 *Some doors were special to the design.*

The good thing about replacement plastic windows is that they can be replaced in wood and metal by the next discerning owner.

EXTERNAL DOORS

The majority of front doors are of a ledged and braced design, made of seven or eight solid planks, about 4½in wide, with a moulding at each edge. The planks are

175   Scullery doors.

grooved at each internal side and a strip of wood joins the planks together. These are then attached to the cross members using dowels. Each door measures 6ft 6in x 3ft 6in. Other types of front door are also to be found.

Doors to the scullery and outhouses were solid, too, but of a lesser quality.

Door Furniture

Moving with the times, and to help the postman, many front doors now have enlarged letter boxes. The original letter boxes had a much smaller aperture, measuring 5in x 1³/₈ in, and quite sufficient for the size of letter used in the 1920s. These still exist at The Odd House and The Lair. Some letter boxes have solid handles which enable the door to be closed when there is no opening handle or latch.

The external door handles and latches were invariably of wrought iron, with a cottage-type latch, so common in the Lutyens-designed houses. some have a crafted Arts and Crafts style heart-shaped motif. After nearly 90 years of use the hinge pins are often worn thin, and need careful replacement.

On front doors, strength mostly took precedence over style, and hidden hinges were the norm, sometimes using decorative plates for effect. Ornate hinges were sometimes used.

Locks would have been present on all external doors. A simple attached lock was found on the minor doors, but the front door would have had a cylinder Yale-type lock, first introduced in Victorian times. Banham was

176   Letter boxes were small and varied.

another make frequently used. A careful examination of the older doors will sometimes reveal the filling of an old hole when the lock has been repositioned or replaced by a more sturdy Chubb lock.

Motor Houses

When Abbotswood was conceived in the mind of the developer, the car was in its infancy and extremely expensive to buy and to run. The horse-drawn carriage was still a popular form of wheeled transport, and most people walked to and from work. Thus the garage, more correctly called the motor house, was seldom a feature on the earliest houses.

Nevertheless, Abbotswood must have been one of the first areas in Guildford that catered for the motor car. In the 1920s, when a semi-detached house cost about £300, and cars of quality including the Alvis, Lagonda and Sunbeam cost up to £1,000, only the wealthy could afford them. Even the more down-to-earth cars in the 1920s, such as the mass produced cars from Austin, Ford and Morris, were in the region of £200. Thus 'motor houses' were not common, except in Abbotswood!

The first garage to appear on an original house plan occurred in 1914 for The Cottage. Many owners had garages built soon after they moved in. The detached motor house at Albury, built in 1927, with a room over the car is a fine example. So, too, is that at The Lair, which still has the original sliding doors so often seen on coach houses. Westward Ho and Brookdale each had a garage built with accommodation over it, but both have been demolished.

In 1923 the first truly integral garage in Abbotswood was built at South Stoke. When Wykeham Lodge and The Hazard were built in 1924 they had garages built into a lower ground floor, let into the hill, and entered from the rear of the property. The latter still has the garage in place today.

177   *Cottage-type latches.*

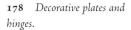

178   *Decorative plates and hinges.*

179 *A selection of garages.*

The later integral garages at West Hill House and The Corner House brought criticism from the planners, who insisted that the garage ceilings should be of concrete in order that, should there be a fire, the maid in her bedroom above should be protected. This was a far cry from the early garage at Littlefield, built in 1915, with a wooden floor stipulated on the plans.

The more usual garage built for the smaller cars of the day, such as the Austin Seven, would have been similar to that still seen at Sunnymead.

GARDEN DESIGN AND TENNIS COURTS

Burlingham did little about garden design. The three plans that contained sketches for gardens were for The Croft, Littlefield, and Abbots Trace. It is not known if the designs were adopted. Most owners created gardens using an abundance of York stone for patios and walls. Invariably the deeds contained a covenant to the effect that the owner had to maintain a hedge to the border fronting the road which determined that the gardens would be enclosed rather than open plan as seen in Ganghill.

Local firms such as Astolat of Godalming designed some of the gardens, particularly in Trodds Lane and Merrow Downs Estate, from 1927 onwards.

Many gardens contained a tennis lawn, one of which was at Hillcrest, which is still in use today. The ground was prepared with proper drainage and had a nearby tap for the water supply. The same flat areas used for courts can still be identified in the gardens of The Gate House, Littlefield, Wey-ne-Shing, Westcott, The Lair, Lorraine, Waysend and Upmeads. A court once existed at Eaglehurst, as the photograph below shows. Tennis parties were clearly a feature of the period and nearly a third of the Abbotswood houses had a court in the garden.

TRADESMEN AND THE GARDEN ENTRANCE

Today we can still see evidence that a tradesman would not be expected to use the main entrance to make deliveries.

At Albury, there are to be seen in the hedge metal posts for the main gates and, a few feet away, another set of posts for a smaller gate for the tradesmen. The current driveway entrance was established later in 1929. A little further along at The Lair there is again evidence of the posts for the small tradesman's entrance. Where there are still the original hedges, similar evidence may be found elsewhere on the estate. The tradesman's entrances at Wey-ne-Shing and South Stoke are still in use today.

EXTENSIONS

One of the endearing features about a true Arts and Crafts house is the fact that it is asymmetrical, and the architect invariably designed it not to look new. This

180 *Eaglehurst in the 1920s, and Hillcrest today.*

was often achieved by making portions of the house appear to have been added at different dates. Using this analogy, it is hard to object to later additions, so long as they are in keeping with the area and the general style.

The current trend of replacing windows has already been mentioned, and in the same light a conservatory that suits the current occupant can always be removed if originality is something a future occupant is seeking. The large-scale additions seen at Littlefield, Westward Ho, and Brookdale are interesting. Those that have retained the Arts and Crafts style are to be congratulated.

It should expected that houses will be altered and improved. Indeed, a house that is 400 years old and has not been changed is likely to have been condemned long ago. As long as the original Abbotswood houses maintain their unique character, change should be welcomed. To do as the recent owners of The Gate House, Upmeads and The Hurst have done, and go the extra mile to restore and preserve original Arts and Crafts features should be considered the epitome of good taste.

Internal Features

It is often the interiors that suffer most at the hands of the new owner or developer. The lives of a modern-day family have changed out of all recognition from those of the Edwardian period. Double glazing and central heating; modern kitchens with utility areas for tumble dryers, washing machines, dishwashers and water softeners; top of the range bathrooms; en-suite rooms with power showers; eating in kitchen areas rather than dining rooms; television rooms; computer rooms – such a list reveals how our lives have changed. Long gone is the need for a scullery, a coal store, and the maid's bedroom. In acknowledgement of these new needs, the pressure for a complete re-fit more often than not wins the day.

Fortunately there are sufficient features that remain in some of the houses to enable recognition of the original design, if an owner wishes to retain some originality, or restore what has already been lost.

Entrance Vestibules

Very much as seen at the Stoke Park Farm, the entrance is often just a small vestibule. Burlingham used this in a number of houses including The Gate House, The Hurst, and Wey-ne-Shing, with a then dramatic entrance to an open hall, with doors leading to the main rooms.

Staircases

The balusters are broadly of two types. The Hurst has the most expensive and extensive with the stairs leading to a gallery above the hall-cum-billiard room. These were made of oak, with barley twists in the centre, and square into the stair rails. The rails and the plain newel posts were the same as those used in all the other houses. The balusters in the other houses were made of plain deal and painted.

The early top rails were below the newel post top, whilst the later ones were flush, which makes them much more tactile. The top rail and the newel post were made of oak, or another hardwood. All newel posts had dowels to attach these to the lower side string, which in turn, more often than not, was attached to panels being the sides of a cupboard below the stairs.

WINDOW SEATS

Enhancing the view of the garden from the interior, there is sometimes a window seat. More often than not these were panelled, with a wooden ledge for a long cushion and storage space beneath.

CEILING DECORATION

In the larger houses plaster sculptures provide decoration showing fruits and flowers. A smaller version is to be found at Wykeham Lodge. The panels were purchased in strips and let into the ceiling.

The Hurst has decorative exposed beams in the billiard hall. Several 1920s houses have various beams in the entrance hall, drawing room and dining room. Most of these are structural, and some even pegged.

181 *Balustrades before (top) and after the First World War.*

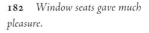

182 *Window seats gave much pleasure.*

183 *Acorns, fruits and grapes.*

Art Deco

The later houses designed by Burlingham in Abbotswood were of the Art Deco period. Although there are almost no related items to be seen, ceiling lights from Wey-ne-Shing prove the exception.

Internal Tiles

Baillie Scott:

> It is difficult for the building artist to find a modern glazed tile which he can use. The manufacturers have all aimed at a mechanical regularity of shape, uniformity of pattern, and staring glassiness of glaze which make practically all modern tiles impossible. Only in the old Dutch tile does the glaze have a thick and creamy quality of subtly varied tones; and in form, texture, and patterning, they are full of individual character.

In the kitchens and larders the white tile was prevalent. In bathrooms there might have been a little colour, yet around the fireplaces they were heavily coloured in greens, blues, and sometimes a floral decoration. Where there is an impressive fireplace, Burlingham turned to the Dutch tile. The tiles prior to the First World War are of a lighter blue, and those after the war were generally darker and have a blue circle around the subject.

Parquet Flooring

184 *Beams became popular in later designs, and were sometimes held by pegs.*

Most flooring is tongue-and-grooved deal wood planking, measuring 4in wide, and ¾in thick – a difficult size to replace in the age of the metric measurement. Carpets were invariably not wall to wall, and the planks would have been stained or painted by the skirting. Some of the larger houses have parquet flooring on the ground floor, such as Wey-ne-Shing and Albury. In Upmeads, there is a sunken central area for a carpet in both the drawing and billiard rooms; this must have been a special order, for it does not appear in the twin house, Hestercombe. Some medium-sized houses such as Sunnymead and The Lair also have parquet flooring. Invariably the parquet flooring had a double band at the outside which would have been cork filled to allow for the expansion of the wood and prevent lifting should the floor become wet through cleaning or spillage.

185 *A rare Art Deco feature light.*

As an alternative to parquet flooring, and where there was a requirement for a polished wood floor, smaller planks made of elm or oak were laid down measuring seven feet in length, and just 3½ inches in width. This can be seen at The Gate House in the large entrance hall.

SKIRTING BOARDS

Generally these were 4½in deep with a plain chamfer, made of deal and painted. In keeping with the Queen Anne style, at Hestercombe and Upmeads, these were considerably deeper at 12 inches and had a moulded chamfer for decoration.

DELFT RACKS

The early houses, Churston and Aoetearoa, have a delft rack on the walls on the first floor, which takes ornaments and plates. This is very much a leftover from Edwardian times.

PICTURESQUE LEADED LIGHTS

A favourite Arts and Crafts feature was the use of coloured glass. This was used in jewel-like abstract patterns and figurative designs. More often than not they presented idealised country views. This is not common in Abbotswood but can still be seen at four houses The Gate House has a floral ceiling decoration. Sunnymead and The Lair each have a landing window showing a lake, trees and a sailing boat which are similar, but not the same, in each house. To have been identical could have resulted in an accusation of its being machine-made, and that would not have done for an Arts and Crafts house. Smaller round examples exist at Churston.

PANELLING

Panelling in the form of doors and cupboards is to be seen in most of the houses. However, it is a special feature of polished and stained wood in the entrance hall at The Hurst, The Gate House and Albury. It is also present in the drawing rooms in the larger houses, Hazlewood, Lorraine, and Friars Oak. Exceptionally, the smaller house, Red Cottage, has a panelled drawing room. This is of oak except

186 *Two sizes of skirting board with parquet flooring.*

187 *A delft rack.*

188 *Before the First World War coloured glass was popular, a river with trees and a lake.*

189 *Panelling: oak, maple and pine. Even the painted panelling looks attractive.*

190 *The indicators found in most kitchens.*

at Albury, where the panelling is extra special, being made of the most attractive maple and walnut.

The construction of the panelling and the size of the panels was very similar to that by Baillie Scott at Storey's Way, Cambridge, except that for Abbotswood the dowelling is not present. Invisible joints are used instead. This is shown in Fig. 146.

The dining room at Friars Oak is different, having large painted panels similar to those found in the hallways at Upmeads and Hestercombe. These panels are of very thin deal, although it is thought that some of this type at Upmeads were oak. The Hurst also has half panelling in the dining room. In lesser houses panelling took the form of cupboard surrounds and under stairs-areas. This was invariably pine and consequently painted.

Servants

It would be expected that the majority of houses had living-in staff to do the cleaning and the cooking. The original plans show that most two-storey houses had four or five bedrooms. The smallest bedroom was invariably intended for the maid, and often marked as such on the plans. The kitchen and scullery were small, and quite out of keeping with today's standards when so often the lives of the family are centred around an extravagant kitchen.

There would have been a series of bell pushes in the rooms and a central box to indicate where the call was from, along with a bell. Each box would be marked to meet the needs of the house. Some of these are still found and even work! Where they have been removed, evidence of their previous existence can usually be found in the loft where there is a plethora of bell wire attached to the timbers.

The bell pushes would have been made of brass or the then modern material, bakelite.

Fireplaces

Baillie Scott:

> He saw the fireplace as 'practically a substitute for the sun', drawing the family to its warmth. Its treatment reflected above all a 'breadth and simplicity' which gave it something of the scale of the open hearth of old houses. The fireplace was generally recessed in its own inglenook, carefully positioned to avoid drawing draughts across the room. The inglenook contained a simple settle and wherever possible a small window for light.

On the ground floors, a fireplace existed in the main rooms and sometimes in the hallway, too. The latter was an attempt by Burlingham to reinforce the Arts and Crafts concept, when the hearth was very much to the fore. The Lair, South Stoke and The Croft are examples of where a corner fireplace was to be found in the bedrooms, dining room and hall respectively.

191   *Ground-floor fireplaces.*

Tiles were a usual feature in the main reception-room fireplaces of the early houses; as already described they were patterned blue delft tiles. This was a common Arts and Crafts feature and almost the same designs are to be found in the grander houses of the time such as Blackwell, designed by Baillie Scott in 1898.

Before the First World War the main fireplaces had a stone surround incorporating a floral motif. Others had a tall painted wood surround of distinctive design. After 1920 the reception-room fireplaces were generally made of different forms in brick, giving a country-cottage air.

On the upper floors, in all but the smallest bedrooms would have been small cast iron fireplaces, varying in design, sometimes with decorative tiles. These would only have been lit in exceptional circumstances such as very cold weather or the illness of an occupant when additional heat was a necessity.

HEATING CHAMBERS AND RADIATORS

Prior to the First World War, houses generally relied on fireplaces for warmth. Only the larger of Burlingham's houses had radiator heating

powered by coal-fired boilers located in a 'heating chamber'. Warming the cast-iron radiators and the hot water system, these were unlikely to have been very efficient.

At other times the kitchen stove would have provided hot water for the house.

Ventilators

Ventilators measuring 12in square were made of perforated metal and evidence of these is to be found in the ceilings of upper-storey rooms. Today they are considered a waste of valuable warm air and have either been blocked up or removed entirely. When the houses were built a draught of air was considered a requirement for the escape of fumes from gas appliances.

There is a cryptic comment in Burlingham's own hand on the plans for The Hurst. It reads 'NB. If insisted upon, rooms where tops of windows are less than 7ft 6in above floor level will be provided with ventilators in ceiling – but very unnecessary in a house of this class and when fireplaces are provided.' The same type of construction was used for wall ventilators in larders and toilets.

192 *Upper-floor fireplaces.*

Bathrooms

Baillie Scott:

> The bathroom was usually placed directly above the kitchen, to simplify plumbing.

At the turn of the 20th century, for some middle-class homes bathrooms were considered vulgar. It was a sign that you could not afford to have servants to bring jugs of hot water up to the bedroom for a hip bath.

Even when there was a bathroom, it was for everyone to share. At Standen, near East Grinstead, a house designed by Phillip Webb in 1891, there were 12 first-floor bedrooms for the Beale family and their guests, with just one bathroom. The habit of washing with a jug and a bowel in the bedroom was still the norm. Cottages built in Guildford Garden Estate in the early part of the 20th century had three bedrooms, a living room and a parlour with a W.C. reached through an external yard, and no bathroom.

Areas such as Abbotswood led the change towards more regular bathing. The only early bathroom remaining is at The Hurst and evidences a propensity for white tiles, which enabled owners to see a relatively clean wall surface.

Water Closets

The building of Abbotswood was a time when the government of the day was trying to improve sanitary conditions for the population. The planning applications evidence these concerns and full details of water closets and utilities had to be given. Not unexpectedly the W.C.s of 1912-25 have nearly all been replaced by modern appliances. The comforts of an internal toilet are seldom fully appreciated by the young of today. The thought of having to go outside on a winter's night, even when the toilet is within the walls of the building, is indeed a chilling one.

193   *An early bath.*

194 *Internal doors.*

Today, people take for granted the use of multiple bathrooms and toilets, particularly in larger houses. When occupants had to share a toilet, the use of a chamber pot was common; thus relief could be obtained during the night without disturbing others. The ceremony of emptying the pot each morning will be fresh in the memory of some readers.

Internal Doors

The quality of the internal doors varied from a simple plank door at The Red Cottage to an elaborate panelled sliding door at Upmeads. In between there was a more common approach with painted pine doors having mostly symmetrical panels. The measurements were 2ft 6in x 6ft 5in. Only in the last house to be built, The Odd House, did the asymmetrical style of the 1930s appear with two long lower panels, and a squat upper panel. Doors to the kitchens and the scullery were planked with external latches, thus giving a country furniture effect.

The Arts and Crafts house had doors carefully positioned to protect the comfort and privacy of the occupants. They usually opened inward towards the far corner of the room, so that the complete interior was not revealed at

195 *Door furniture.*

once. On hearing the door handle turn the occupants would have a moment to ready themselves for the visitor.

This era witnessed the introduction of the fitted cupboard in which the clothes were usually laid flat on shelves. Only a third of the space was devoted to hanging dresses and skirts. Before that, in Victorian times, heavy free-standing wardrobes and chests of drawers were the order of the day.

Door Furniture

Most internal doors have copper or brass handles, a hard task to polish, and others wrought iron, wooden or bakelite. In several of the larger houses the very high-class handles match those of the windows; in others, they were plainer with round or oval handles. In The Red Cottage they were befitting the plain country-style doors and made of wrought iron. Each door would have been lockable, and a keyhole cover was the norm. There are a number of houses with finger plates.

Some houses, such as Wey-ne-Shing, had on the lower floors a more expensive metal set of door furniture including finger plates, while those upstairs had a dark wood finish.

196 *Small cupboards have separate locks.*

197 *The cookers had mostly white tile surrounds.*

Small cupboard doors, such as those under the stairway, have smaller round knobs of metal or wood, and again have locks, presumably to protect the supply of fine wines.

Kitchens

Baillie Scott:

> The north side of the house was typically lined with the service spaces – staircase, porch, scullery, and kitchen entrance …
>
> The kitchen was always envisaged as a formal space … even modest middle-class households expected to employ domestic help, at the very least a live-in maid. The family domain was kept separate from the kitchen and from the servant's circulation routes. Judicious planning and high window sills prevented too much of an invasion of privacy. Typically the kitchens contained both a cooking area and a separate scullery with sink, as well as a pantry, larder, Coal store and servants' W.C. The early kitchens were always on the north side of the house, with separate access by a back door. Only later, when the lady of the house did the cooking, would kitchens be moved to the south side of the house, overlooking the garden.

The current trend is to change our kitchens every few years, or at the very least when one moves into a house. Therefore the likelihood of having an original kitchen in a house that is 90 years old is remote. Some will have retained the old kitchen area, but more usually this will have been joined with the scullery. Sometimes the floor will be a mixture of solid floor and floorboards indicating this.

When The Hurst was considered for a listing by English Heritage, thankfully both the scullery and the kitchen were very much as they were when the house was built. The cooking was done on a cast-iron range, heated

198 *The dresser at The Hurst.*

by coke or coal, with double doors and hotplates. The fuel also heated a water boiler; there would have been smaller versions for the lesser houses. Some had gas cookers, as quoted on the plans for Hillcrest, which were becoming more reliable. The cooker area frequently had a tiled surround.

The original double cooker remains at The Hurst, and the tiled cooker surround at The Cottage now houses the heating boiler.

The kitchens invariably had a built-in dresser, but most have long since gone. A wall cupboard at Sunnymead still exists, and a dresser at The Hurst.

THE SCULLERY

Kitchens were used for cooking and storage. The washing and ironing of clothes and cooking utensils was done in the scullery, and the house plans usually show a sink with a wooden draining board where the maid would have carried out the hand washing. Invariably there would have been a solid red-tiled floor, and possibly a drain to the outside to take away spilt water. The equipment would have included a mangle for wringing the clothes, and a drying horse raised by a pulley fixed to the ceiling. Off the scullery was often the coal store, and a larder. To the outside would have been a lobby, or in the bigger houses a yard, and from these there would be a toilet for the use of the maid and the gardener.

In the scullery at The Hurst there was a Belfast-type ceramic sink with wooden drainers each side, along with original cupboards, pantry and coalhole, as shown in Fig. 88. A similar but smaller sink was found in the maid's bedroom.

LARDERS AND PANTRIES

Some houses had butler's pantries, but all had larders of one sort or another. Generally a larder was for meat, fish, vegetables and general food stuff and normally had a slate shelf. This is still to be seen at Wykeham Lodge and The Cottage. Conversely, a pantry was used for the storage of bread, cakes and dairy produce.

In the days before freezers and refrigerators, keeping food fresh was a challenge. These rooms were usually built against a north- or east-facing wall where it was coolest. The windows were small and protected against flies with a mesh cover when opened.

LOFT LADDERS

All houses had a loft, often used for storage. The developers sometimes assisted with the installation of a quite complicated ladder which was counter-balanced and would be brought down safely. A few still exist today.

199   *A small sink.*

200   *Loft ladders.*

Cellars

Only The Hurst was designed with a cellar. On the plans this was marked as 'Wine or Game Larder.'

Utilities

The developers of Abbotswood proudly exclaimed in their advertisements that these were 'New houses with every modern convenience, and enjoying all the amenities of the town in the way of electric light, gas, water supply, telephone, etc.'

At the turn of the 20th century, some new houses were being built without electricity, gas or mains drainage. In 1910 only five per cent of houses had electricity. Guildford town relied mostly on gas for street lighting for the whole time that Abbotswood was being built.

The records of the Lighting Committee of the Guildford Borough Council give evidence that in 1921 Burlingham requested electricity to four new houses. The cost was to be an estimated £325, and he offered a payment of £75 from the owners of the estate, and guaranteed a minimum payment of £50 per annum for the supply of electricity for each of the first three years.

Woodland Setting

A woodland appearance for the estate was encouraged by the planting of large trees in the gardens and roadsides. These were particularly Horse Chestnut, Scots Pine, Beech, Oak, Lime, Poplar, Willow and Yew.

House Prices

The cost of the houses was very much a moving target. In order that the standards of the estate should reflect the quality of house expected, the deeds invariably contained a minimum cost of building. In the early days this ranged from £500 to £1,000. In 1925 Eaglehurst sold for a massive £3,825, when General Longbourne of Loseley was developing Guildown Estate, selling houses at a minimum of £2,000.

Contemporary advertisements put the price of the more expensive houses into perspective. In 1934 new semi-detached houses were for sale at £675 in Ash Grove on the Woodbridge Estate. At the Winterhill Estate, 200 yards past the *Green Man* inn at Burpham, new luxury detached houses were for sale at between £700 and £950. Around the same time The Gate House sold for £4,200.

In 2006 a house in Abbotswood sold for almost £2,000,000.

Eleven

The Histories of the Burlingham Houses

An examination of each house follows, starting with information about the name. Next to each name is the date that each name was first recorded, which might have been on the deeds or in the *Street Directories*. In Abbotswood, house numbering did not come into effect until about 1942.

The owners of each house are listed from the time they were built. The primary source of this information is the deeds and, where they are not available, reference has been made to the *Land Registry* and *Guildford Street Directories* by either Kelly's or Lasham's (both hereafter referred to as the *Directories*) for the period to 1969. Thereafter the electoral register has been used.

> *Author's Observation*: I am grateful to the many owners who have assisted by providing copies of the deeds to their house. It is a bonus when the original deeds have been retained. More often than not, they have been split from the other documents once the land became registered. It is a reflection of the paperless society we have today that once a good title is proven, the use for these old documents diminishes significantly. After that point these fascinating papers, often written in beautiful copper plate script on vellum, have little intrinsic value and are of interest only to historians or discerning owners. All too often they are retained by previous owners, or simply thrown away. People moving houses should be encouraged to pass these documents to the next owners.

Where deeds are not available an on-line search at the Land Registry, for just £3, will reveal details of the sale by Alfred Taylor of the property to the first owner, as well as the covenants, the names of the current owners, any charges against the property, and for recent sales the amount they paid. For a similar sum a site map is available, too. Today, little is secret.

The *Directories* help to indicate when a house was first occupied, and when it was left vacant. They also help to confirm ownership, or lettings. They even show when the army officers received promotion, about which they were no doubt pleased to tell the enquirer at his annual return.

However, use of the *Directories* does create an element of doubt. They were created by the representative from say Kelly's *Directory* walking around the estate, knocking on doors, or enquiring of neighbours, in order to obtain the details of the occupant. Because he was enquiring about the occupant, rather than the owner, problems occur. The owner might have been the lady of the house, whereas the man is invariably named, owner or not. The fact that a house may have been jointly owned mattered not, and there were no joint names in the *Directories*. The responder may be a tenant. When nobody was present, guesswork came in, or there is a blank.

The change of house names and the fact that houses were split over two parishes added to the confusion. Until 1933, the *Directories* indicated that the reader should refer to the Worplesdon section for the northern area of Abbotswood. In the 1935 edition this no longer applied, reflecting the 1933 parish boundary changes. Fresh enquiries started after the previous edition was printed. Therefore the information was likely to be at least 12 months out of date, a fact confirmed when the *Directories* are compared with the more accurate deeds.

Just to make matters more problematic, the houses referred to as Hestercombe and Upmeads had drives that joined the London Road, rather than Abbotswood. This must have confused the producers of the *Directories*, because sometimes they were listed as parts of Abbotswood, sometimes part of the London Road schedule of properties, and at other times left out of the *Directory* completely. Land Registry records show that the numbering only referred to London Road. It is just a coincidence that The Hurst is the 46th house in Abbotswood, and the next-door neighbour is 47, London Road. In practice the house numbered 45, and 'next door', is over half a mile away at the other end of Stoke Park!

In order to establish ownership over the last 38 years, reference has been made to the electoral register. This records anyone who is living at the house and in their 18th year. Therefore it is with great difficulty that the owners, or indeed the parents, in the house can be identified. Thankfully most long-standing neighbours have long memories.

With these caveats, this book provides as accurate a list of owners as possible, with those recognised as tenants marked accordingly. Apologies are given for any omissions and inaccuracies.

As an aside, it is rather sad to note that the stress of moving must have been as great in the 1920s as it is today. On several occasions the deeds indicate that the husband died within a year or so of moving in, leaving his wife to sell and move on, or alternatively to stay in the house as the new owner.

1, The Gate House

Name: 1914, The Gate House

The house name is synonymous with that of the Gates family, of Cow & Gate. Bramwell Gates lived here and Ernest Gates lived at The Croft.

DESIGN 3 – This imposing house was built in 1914. The exterior is almost as it was when it was built, save that additional rooms for the surgery were built on to the right side. These have recently been replaced by a garage. Internally, restoration work has reinstated many of the Arts and Crafts features. As with the majority of the Abbotswood houses, the kitchen and scullery have been combined and altered to form a modern kitchen, but the main ground-floor rooms are used as they were intended by Burlingham.

Entry is through an exterior porch, a small vestibule, and then into a large inner hall, with an exquisite fireplace, oak panelled walls, and a multi-light window. These attractive features still exist, save that the partitioning wall has been removed, leading the visitor from the entrance porch straight into the grand hall.

OWNERSHIP

1915	W.R.B. St J. Gates	1949	R.O. Dowdeswell
1919	F.H. Franks	1954	D.H. Bennett
1930	W. B. Thorpe	1987	R.J. Bennett
1935	N. Drake	2006	Myles Gilbert

DEEDS

A search of the Land Registry revealed that Alfred George Taylor sold the property to Walter Rougier Bramwell St John Gates on 14 March 1919. However, this was not the whole story. Because this house was referred to as The Gate House in the *Directories* from 1915, it was likely to have been built in 1914; it follows that Bramwell Gates was probably in occupancy shortly after that time as the *de facto* owner.

The conveyance dated 1919 was in fact the initial sale of the property to Frank Harold Franks, a successful and well known local coal merchant. The deed reveals that Bramwell Gates, then of The Paddock, London Road, Burpham, had agreed to purchase The Gate House from Taylor for £2,800, but had not conveyed the money. The sale to Mr Franks was for £3,500 thus Franks paid Taylor the £2,800 he was owed, and £700 to Gates.

We cannot tell if Taylor encouraged Bramwell Gates to buy the house on a delayed payment system in order to be able to show that the important people of Guildford, such as Gates, wanted to live there, or if it was just that Gates did not have the funds available.

On 24 March 1930, Franks sold the house to Wilfred Bertram Thorpe, from Wandsworth Common, for £4,750. In turn, Thorpe sold the house to Norman Drake on 12 August 1935 for £4,200. Mr Drake came from Honley near Huddersfield.

Reginald Owen Dowdeswell, a stationer, of Byeways, Farley Green, Albury purchased the house from Drake for £7,750 on 19 August 1949. Searches dated 1949 reveal that the boundary-to-boundary width of the Abbotswood road was 47 feet, and that of the A3 trunk road just 50 feet.

On 31 May 1954 Dowdeswell sold The Gate House to Donald Harry Bennett, a 'Doctor of Chiropractic' for £6,750. Because of the restrictive covenants, Mr Bennett provided an indemnity to Alfred Taylor against 'all claims actions and costs' that might arise out of a change of use of the premises, and in return Taylor agreed to its use as a surgery on 6 April 1954. Clearly, a chiropractor was considered to be neither a surgeon nor a physician.

Despite the change of use, the structure was initially left unaltered. The kitchen was used for the x-ray equipment, and the dining room and the drawing room were each used as a surgery. The grand hall was a waiting room, and the study a changing room.

In 1956 Bennett submitted plans for an extension which would release all but the study and the dining room for domestic accommodation. The plans were refused and on appeal to the Minister of Housing and Local Government the rejection was upheld. In December 1956 revised plans were submitted with a letter implying that the applicant appreciated there was a problem for the neighbours and further extensions would be curtailed. This was sanctioned in January 1957. Tony Vokes, of The Lair, recalls his father trying to assist the first Mr Bennett with his battle with the local authority planners who had been encouraged by local residents to reject plans for treatment rooms as part of an extension to the house. A plan for a further extension, taking the building to within five feet of the boundary, was submitted and sanctioned in January 1964, despite previous assurances.

After the turn of this century, attempts to sell the land for flats was declined by the local council, and a further plan involving turning the house into a nursery school attracted considerable local opposition mainly due to the probable danger to children caused by the nearby main road. At the end of 2006 Russell Bennett, who had followed his father as a chiropractor, moved the practice away from Abbotswood.

The house was purchased in 2006 by the current owner, Myles H.M. Gilbert, and with Karen Smith he decided to turn it back into a private house and, as appropriate, reinstate the Arts and Crafts style features.

2, Hazlewood

Name: 1914, Hazlewood

Design 2 – Building started for this house in 1913; it was one of the very first houses to be constructed.

From the outside, the front this house looks very original. In the early 1980s the then owners erected an addition to the rear of the house to create a substantial kitchen. Subsequently it was decided that for the long term good it was appropriate to replace the external windows and door woodwork.

Ownership

1914	G. J. Jacobs	1959	Raymond B. Ham
1922	Mrs G. J. Jacobs	1969	Ronald E. Frost
1933	W. A. Gammon	1981	Peter and Mary Roberts
1948	Mrs W. A. Gammon	1998	Neil Afram
1953	Thomas Walter Saint		

Deeds

A search at the Land Registry revealed that on 20 April 1914 the property was sold by A.G. Taylor to George James Jacobs.

In 1913, a Mr G.H. Jacobs purchased the plot on which Aoetearoa was built, and then a further plot next door in 1916, on which Homewell was built in which C.J. Jacobs lived from 1921. There was most likely a family connection.

On 9 February 1998 Mr (Neil) Nabil Hanna Afram purchased the property.

201 *Hazlewood, as it was in the 1920s.*

4, The Croft

Name: 1915, The Croft

DESIGN 7 – Externally this house has changed little, save for the conservatory at the rear. The long open entrance porch and the jettied gable at the side are distinctive features. Internally, the drawing room has been enlarged, but the fireplace, with the carved stone surround and coloured tiles, remains an important element of the whole.

OWNERSHIP

1915	E.R. Gates	1962	Mr and Mrs A. Solomons
1920	T. Coulthard	1963	Mrs B.P.M. Palmer
1922	R.E. Way	1984	Dr and Mrs A.S. Atkinson
1933	Mrs R. Way	2001	Alan and Fridrun Williams
1935	Maj. A.D. Sloane		

DEEDS

On 26 February 1915, A.G. Taylor sold Ernest Rayer Gates, of 'Pedwell', Guildford, a plot of land for £225. At the rear it bordered the farm buildings of Stoke Park Farm, then occupied by Richard Blake, and to the front, the New Road in Abbotswood. This was the first deed showing the wall for the archways at the entrance to Abbotswood to be in situ on the block plan. Hazlewood had already been built. Any house built was to cost not less than £700. Gates' signature was witnessed by A.C. Burlingham.

On 12 July 1915, a mortgage for £650 was taken out by Gates with London and Manchester, concurrently a second mortgage in the sum of £250 was obtained from A.G. Taylor. It notes that '… the dwelling house now erected thereon or some part thereof and know as The Croft …'

On 25 December 1915 A.G. Taylor sold a strip of land to the side of The Croft, where the modern Elmhurst now stands, for the sum of £196 10s. On the same day, Gates took out a mortgage with A.G. Taylor, in the sum of £196 10s., at a rate of five per cent from 5 December 1915. Both Taylor mortgages were re-conveyed on 17 December 1917.

The later mortgage stipulated that the mortgagor will keep the property in good repair and '… also insured against loss or damage by fire and (during the present or any future war) against aircraft or bombardment to the full value thereof …' This was included long before aircraft were the weapon they became, and the bombardment would have been mostly land artillery, perhaps anticipating an invasion. The earlier mortgage of 12 July contained no reference to war protection.

The mortgage contained reference not only to 'the power of leasing given to a mortgagor in possession by virtue of the 18th section of The Conveyance Act 1881 shall not be exercised … the mortgagee shall not be answerable for any involuntary losses which may happen in or about the exercise or execution of the power of sale …' but also that the '… mortgagor hereby attorns tenant to the mortgagee of the heriditaments hereby mortgaged at the yearly rent of £9 16s. 6d. … but so that such rent shall be applied in or towards satisfaction of such interest …' In a later mortgage dated 21 April 1920 this rental has become a peppercorn.

Christmas Day 1915 was clearly very busy, for Taylor also gave Gates access to the farm road at the rear of the property, with Gates acknowledging that there was no right of way. For access he paid, if demanded, 1/- per annum.

On 28 January 1918, a further strip of land, just 20ft wide, bordering The Croft on the north side, was sold by Taylor to Gates for £52 10s. – this land was abutting farm buildings then occupied by Allen Ansell. There is a note that the construction of a Motor House would be allowed on the purchased land subject to the consent of Taylor, but no further house would be allowed.

Gates sold to Thomas Coulthard, an engineer from Lancaster, all the land comprising The Croft for £2,300 on 20 April 1920. This had, we assume, cost Gates just £1,324, plus interest on his various mortgages, and thus gave him quite a profit. Coulthard took out a mortgage on 21 April 1920 with William Farwell Ashcroft, a solicitor, in the sum of £2,200 at six per cent. On 15 March 1922 the Croft was sold for £2,400 to Rupert Edward Way.

An abstract of title dated 1922 has a map of part of the estate attached, which shows a right of way through the five-acre paddock between Thorneycrofts and Abbotswood and indicates a footpath to Stoke Church.

On 7 July 1922, a further strip of land, now making up the plot for the bungalow, was sold by Symes of Stoke Park Farm for £150 to Rupert E. Way. However, it prohibited the use of the New Road for certain farm vehicles.

R.E. Way died on 23 April 1933, and in 1934, the property was let out under a tenancy agreement to Alfred Bates from 31 December 1933 to 11 March 1934 for the princely sum of £45, fully furnished. On 16 April 1935, Rosalia Way, the widow of R.E. Way, sold the entire plot to Major Arthur Douglas Sloane for £2,200 – the reduction on the total purchase price was perhaps a sign of the bad economic climate at the time.

In August 1962 Sloane sold the property, for £10,700, to Alexander and Zena Jean Solomons. Alexander was a jeweller. They continued to live there until they sold The Croft, and built Elmhurst in their 'widows plot'. In the meantime they sold the two pieces of land to the north of 'The Croft' on 29 April 1963 to Cecil Thomas Corps and Edith Alice Corps to enable them to build the current bungalow next door. This was subject to a planning application dated November 1962, revised in January 1963, with plans produced by Douglas Steer of Woking.

By a conveyance dated 11 December 1963, the Solomons' sold The Croft, for £8,300, to Beatrice Mary Pauline Palmer, wife of Eric H. Palmer.

The bungalow called Hurdestoke, at the back of Elmcroft and The Croft, with an entrance on to the farm lane was built in the late '60s. Hitherto the land would have partly belonged to the owners of Stoke Park Farm and partly Elmcroft.

Alan Stanley Atkinson and Pamela Mirian Atkinson bought The Croft on 31 August 1984 and sold it on 4 October 2001 to Alan Keith Williams and Dr Fridrun Felicitas Williams.

5, Churston

Name: 1915, Churston; 1917, Westwood Cottage; post-1942, Smallacre

DESIGN 1 – This property was one of the two of the earliest houses in Abbotswood, with the plans approved in December 1912. The outside structure at the front and the sides is mostly original, with roughcast walls, relieved by brick patterns at each corner. The main entrance was once at the side, but has recently been replaced by a large covered porch at the front. This has brought a symmetry to the house, inside as well as outside.

The side entrance, a delft rack, some internal fireplaces, along with coloured window lights with a floral pattern, are all evidence of the Arts and Crafts style.

OWNERSHIP

1913	Mrs E.D. Falkus with A.C. Burlingham-residing	1950	O.H. Hopgood
1917	E.W. Hopewell	1955	Peter D. Davey
1919	Rt. Hon. Mrs E.W. Hopewell	1991	Michael and Susan Davey
		1993	John and Sissel Jewhurst
1928	Miss Constance (tenant)	2003	Paul and Natasha Halliwell
1932	Hon. Mrs Hopewell		

DEEDS

A search at the Land Registry reveals that on 25 January 1913 A.G. Taylor sold the property to Eva Dorothy Falkus, wife of H. Falkus.

On 23 October 2003, Dr Paul John Halliwell and (Natasha) Inderjit Kaur Halliwell, purchased Churston.

6, The Cottage

Name: 1915, The Cottage; 1917, Florence Lodge; 1919 Abbots Lodge

DESIGN 6 – This is one of the most attractive houses in Abbotswood. It is not large and imposing, but small and crammed full with Arts and Crafts features. The plot was purchased by R.U. Falkus on the same day that a Mrs E.D. Falkus purchased the plot next door, which became Churston.

Importantly, the house has not been changed by way of disproportionate additions. It is a compact and very original house, well placed in a large garden and just as Burlingham intended. The brick buttress at the front door is a later addition.

A most charming dwelling, one of which Burlingham would be very proud.

OWNERSHIP

1913	R.U. Falkus	1937	F. C. Weller
1915	H. Morse	1939	Lady Biscoe
1919	O.J.A. Harrison	1942	Sir Roydon Dash D.F.C.
	(P.J.A. Harrison – 1924)	1962	Lady Dash
1924	Mrs M. Langtree	1966	Mr and Mrs W.J. Luxton
	(Mrs O. Langtree – 1927)	1983	Niels and Elizabeth Laub

DEEDS

The deeds reveal that this house was built on a plot purchased for £100. The initial conveyance is dated 25 January 1913 and was from A.G. Taylor, of 16, Southwark Street, in the County of London, Surveyor, to Mr Richard Uriah Falkus, of South Hill, Guildford. The agreement stipulated that the cost of the house should not be less than £500, and a planning application was submitted in November 1914.

On 18 May 1915, Mr Falkus, 'of Churston', obtained a mortgage of £450 at a rate of £4 10s. p.a., from London and Manchester Industrial Assurance Company Limited. The deed was witnessed by A.G. Taylor, hardly a disinterested party.

The house was sold by Falkus to Herbert Morse, from Shanklin, Isle of Wight, on 13 October 1915 for the sum of £600, with the existing mortgage still intact. The new owner became the mortgagor, and the mortgagee remained London and Manchester. Thus the total purchase price was £1,050. The signature of Mr Morse was witnessed by Amelia Jeffery of 10, Dapdune Crescent, Guildford who after her signature added, 'Wife of T.W. Jeffery' as a description of her status.

On 9 September 1915 Taylor gave the right to use the lane at the back of the property for the sum of one shilling each year, if so demanded. This lasted until 1966.

Herbert Morse died on 28 June 1918 and on 31 January 1919 his executors, Amyas Morse and Margaret Hannah Fell, had the property re-conveyed to them. The deed was signed on behalf of the mortgagee by a J.A. Woodward and W.H. Brown, directors. By that time the name of the house had been changed to Florence Lodge and was sold on 7 January 1919 for £1,200 to Edith Mary Harrison. In May 1923 she redeemed her tithe responsibilities for £4 6s. 9d.

On 29 September 1924, Mrs Harrison sold the property, now called Abbots Cottage, to Mrs Mabel Langtree of 31, Stanhope Gardens, South Kensington, for £2,200. The signature of Mrs Harrison was witnessed by Miss E.B.F. Chalk, described as 'domestic servant', also of Abbots Lodge.

Mrs Langtree, a widow, entered into a mortgage agreement on 30 September 1924 with Charles Style Humphreys of Kinturk Castle Pollard in the Irish Free State, Herbert Ogilvie and William Brodie in the sum of £1,350, with interest at 5 per cent p.a. This was re-conveyed on 16 July 1937 when Mrs Langtree sold the property to Frederick Charles Weller for £1,700. The conveyance was witnessed by Capt. Touzel of Craig Cottage.

The property was sold to Dame Dorothy Eva Biscoe, of 100, Oakley Street, Chelsea, on 15 December 1939 for £1,825. On 14 September 1942 it became the property of Mr R.E.A. Dash, later to be Sir Roydon Engerfield Ashford Dash, for £2,250. On 10 February 1962 it was conveyed by him to Lady Joan Pritchett Dash. Further comment about Sir Roydon is made in Chapter 13.

On 28 June 1966, for £9,800 Lady Dash sold the property to William John Luxton C.B.E. and Megan Luxton. In turn they sold it, on 21 October 1983, to the present owners Niels Hieronymus Laub and Elizabeth Anne Laub.

Mr Luxton understands that The Cottage was the subject of a prize for Burlingham.

7, Aoetearoa

Name: 1916, Aoetearoa; 1917, End House; 1919, Milestones

In the *Directories* of 1916 the name Aeotea Roa was used. Enquiries reveal that the visitor to the house was quite often inaccurate with the scribing of names. Therefore the name is most likely to have been Aoetearoa, the name of a Pacific Island off New Zealand. There may have been a connection with the 4th Earl of Onslow, at one time Governor of New Zealand. Whatever the true reason, by the time the 1917 edition was published, it had become known as End House, and then Milestones. This caused confusion with the property called Lorraine which, from 1917 to 1921, was also called Milestones.

DESIGN 1 – This house has retained the side door with the small roof, so indicative of the Arts and Craft designers.

The early black and white photographs reveal that the front elevation is unchanged, save for the removal of the chimneys. At the rear there was once a first-floor balcony, overlooking the large and long garden. As with all the roughcast rendered houses the original plaster colour was retained well into the 1960s.

Inside there remains some of the Edwardian delft racking, evidence of a corner fireplace in the hall, and original drawing-room fireplace.

It is understood that the house was badly damaged by a fire in the 1930s, caused by a maid drying clothes too close to an open fire.

OWNERSHIP

1913	G. H. Jacobs	1952	Harold Joseph Davis
1916	C.L. Jacobs, residing	1970	Florence Mary Davis; d.1977
1919	W. Mitchell Gauld	1975	Vivian and Iris Read
1926	Herbert Thompson J.P.	1995	Peter and Lynn Ferguson

In November 1914 Mr A.V. Falkus was living at the sister house, Churston. It is a reasonable assumption that this house was also built by then, and that the building work had commenced in 1913. Because it did not appear in the *Directories* until 1916, it was probably not occupied until late 1914, or even 1915.

DEEDS

A search at the Land Registry revealed that the property was sold on 29 July 1913 by A.G. Taylor to George Hilder Jacobs. In 1916 he purchased the plot for Homewell.

From 1952 the owner was H.J. Davis of J.T. Davis Ropes, of Bow, London, later part of British Ropes. He was also a Director of Hall's Barton Ropery Co. Ltd, 96/98 Leadenhall Street, EC3, which had a head office in Hull.

On 15 February 1995 the property was purchased by Peter John Ferguson and Eluned Mary Ferguson.

8, Homewell

Name: 1921, Homewell; 1944, Homeland; 1988, Old George

Design 11 – Built in 1920, Homewell is one of five properties of the same design which were the first houses to be built in Abbotswood after the First World War.

The rear elevation has a splendid half-timbered jettied gable. The verandah construction can still be determined, although this has long since been converted to an internal eating area. The internal configuration has changed with the dining room and the kitchen/scullery areas having been reversed. The hallway has been absorbed into the drawing room to make it bigger, and an attached garage was added to the front of the house in the 1980s, but has now been demolished. The upstairs rooms are almost unchanged save for one small bedroom becoming an open landing.

The most endearing feature is the drawing room. Mr Jacobs had this built when he also owned the early house next door. He must have known about the superior fireplaces in the other early houses, so he had built a very grand fireplace. It has a carved wood surround, some of which is probably from a Tudor or Jacobean house, and a stone and brick fireplace, to which is attached white and blue delft tiles, found in only two other post-war houses in Abbotswood. See Fig. 120.

This property is currently being extended.

Ownership

1916	G.H. Jacobs	1984	Mr and Mrs R.A. Henderson
1921	C.L. Jacobs – resident		
1924	R.H.B. Bryant	1988	Mr and Mrs C. Baker
1934	E.R. Manley M.A.	2007	Fareydood and Nahid Farkhondeh
1950	Mrs E.D. Manley		

Deeds

The deeds evidence that the indenture for the sale is dated 31 December 1916, and that land was sold for the sum of £125 by A.G. Taylor to George Hilder Jacobs. Taylor had previously sold the next door property to G.H. Jacobs in 1913. On both occasions the address given for Mr Jacobs was Pendinas, Austen Road, Guildford. This supports the assumption that a relative of Mr Jacobs, a C.L. Jacobs, first lived in Aoetearoa, and then at Homewell, effectively as a tenant.

On 24 June 1924 G.H. Jacobs, still of 'Pendinas', sold the property to Robert Henry Baker Bryant, from Birkdale, for the sum of £1,850. The house was referred to as Homewell, and the signature was witnessed by Cecil Hart, solicitor.

The property was sold by R.H.B. Bryant to Eric Rundell Manley, a schoolmaster, on 22 March 1934. The price paid was £1,650, some £200 lower than 10 years previously. This loss was perhaps reflective of the difficult economic climate of the day.

On 21 October 1944, E.R. Manley borrowed £1,000 from his wife, Edith Dorothy Manley, and in so doing took out a mortgage in her favour over the house, for repayment on 25 December 1944, and with interest at four per cent p.a. His signature was witnessed by M. Glover of Sunnymead. The mortgage was re-conveyed on 18 October 1950, and added to the type is the comment that Mrs Manley repaid the mortgage herself, with interest and costs, following the death of Mr Manley on 3 September 1949. By an assent also dated 18 October 1950, the house passed from the personal representative of E.R. Manley to Mrs E.D. Manley. She died on 3 June 1982.

On 17 October 1984, Mr Syson, on behalf of the estate of the late Mrs Manley, sold the property to Robert Anthony Henderson and Lauren Adele Henderson for £102,000. On 15 May 1988 the Hendersons sold the property to Christopher Robert Baker and Belinda Jane Baker.

Early in 2007 Mr Fereydood Farkhondeh and Mrs Nahid Akhnan Tabinzi Farkondeh purchased Homewell, now known as Old George.

9, Littlefield

Name: 1917, Littlefield; 1931, Abbots Cottage

DESIGN 7 – This house is twinned with The Croft. There are subtle differences and importantly the front elevation has bay windows on both floors instead of just the ground floor. Furthermore, for external decoration, Burlingham used wood facings on the first floor, which was carried forward to the external garage, built at the same time as the house. This was attached to the house by a small wall with a short tiled roof.

In 2006 the original garage which was built with a wooden floor was demolished. The floor had been replaced many years before, but when demolition took place the walls that held the joists were revealed. The house has been significantly enlarged with a two-storey extension. The brickwork and lintels have been accurately copied, and the oak and pine window frames have been replaced by modern plastic.

Ownership

1915	A. Burningham	1953	L.R.G. Errington
1923	A. Burningham and H. I. Harvey F.R.C.S.	1957	Wing Commander James Morgan D.S.O.
1926	Mrs Burningham and H.I. (J.) Harvey	1965	Robert and Rosemary Munro
1927	Mrs Burningham	1990	Stephen Thomas Murphy and Pamela Mary Murphy
1928	Maj. H. Hughes (to move to Hillcrest in 1931)		
1931	Charles Lewis Saunders	1992	Arthur James Turner and Darrell Jane Turner
1940	F.J. Hubble		
1943	A.C.D. de Helme	2001	David and Alison Stubley
1950	Charles Yates		

Deeds

A search at the Land Registry reveals that A.G. Taylor sold the property on 31 June 1915 to Alfred Burningham. This must have caused great confusion at the time bearing in mind the significant presence of Alfred Claude Burlingham.

On 17 January 2001 the property was purchased by David Peter Stubley and Alison Julie Stubley.

13, Wey-ne-Shing

Name: 1924, Wey-ne-Shing, Wayneshing and Weynishing; 1926, Bradfield; 1932, Hawkshield; 1937 Grasmere

Design 16 – This house was built to order, and the new owner was able to personalise it and create a unique property.

The house is now central on the plot. At one time it had a large garden stretching down to the meadows on the hillside. The view across the river valley to Stoughton would have been uninterrupted. To make the best of this Burlingham designed a verandah leading from the sunken hall, in the corner of which stands a large red-brick fireplace.

All this, with the original doors and windows, makes it a very attractive house.

Ownership

1921	W.W.E. Smith (land only)	1963	Bill and Lorna Dunne
1924	Col. N. Smith	1986	John Frederick and Alison Margaret Clements
1926	Henry Eade Churchman	1989	Dr and Mrs S. Davies
1932	George Fullerton Ross	2008	Andy Corner and Sian Powell
1937	Norman Clifford Turner		
1938	David W. Turner		

Deeds

A search at the Land Registry revealed that A.G. Taylor sold the property to Wilfred Wool Edmund Smith on 3 October 1921. This was most likely a relative of Col. N. Smith, the first resident. He gave his address as, Noesleigh, York Road, Guildford.

A subsequent owner, H.E. Churchman, was responsible for the building of Orchard Neville in 1931, and in 1933 Ederline. Agreements exist between Mr and Mrs Dunne and the owners of the spur road in 1984, and again in 1985 regarding the construction of a dwelling in the garden, which had entry on to the spur road. In 1984 they also sold off land that they owned towards the river, to enable Bovis Homes to build nine houses in Westward Ho.

Mr and Mrs Clements purchased the property from the Dunnes and sold it on 28 September 1989 to Stuart James Mansell Davies and Margaret Maureen Davies.

On 22 May 2008 Andrew Martin Corner and Dr Sian Margaret Powell became the new owners.

14, Westward Ho

Name: 1923, Westward Ho; 2001, Bell House

Design 17 – Westward Ho is of a design that mirrors that at Hillcrest. The house was considerably extended by the first owner, and these extensions were mainly removed and replaced with larger additions in 2001, including a third floor in the roof space. The remaining original features include the inglenook fireplace, the panelled doors, window fittings, and the jettied roughcast gable to the rear.

Ownership

1923	Mrs H.H. Evill	1965	G.J. Van Der Wurf
1927	Maj. Arthur Frederick R. Hunt D.S.O.	1968	M.G.R.Unwin
1941	Capt. R. Edwardes	1970	Colin and Diana Haley
1945	R.L. Tillett	1999	Garth Nicholls and Fanny Bridges
1960	Exors. R.L. Tillett	2001	Michael and Chris Kirby
1963	Elwell Investments Limited		

Deeds

The indenture dated 22 October 1923 between A.G. Taylor, still of 'Stowford', and Henrietta Hortense Evill, wife of Douglas Claude Strathern Evill, of 33, Tavistock Place, Russell Square, London WC2, conveys the land, " … together with the dwellinghouse erected thereon or some part thereof and known as 'Westward Ho' Abbotswood Guildford', in the sum of £2,775. Chapter 13 features information about Douglas Evill.

Ada Mary Edwardes, wife of Richard Edwardes, a retired Captain in His Majesty's army, sold Westward Ho for £4,750 in 1945 to Russell Leslie Tillett of 18, St Swithin's Lane in the City of London, Chartered Accountant. On 29 April 1960 Russell Tillett died. On 12 February 1963 the executors, being his son, David Rupert Tillett and Wilfred Edward Howard, sold the property, for £10,950, to Elwell Investments Limited.

On 26 February 1968 Gerardus Johannes Van Der Wurf sold to Michael George Redpath Unwin the house and a much reduced garden for £13,325. This left Van Der Wurf with the roadway for Westward Ho, and the land on which Nos. 1, 2 and 3 Westward Ho now stand. On 31 July 1969, Rutherford Developments Ltd, of Hillingdon House, Harrow, sold 2, Westward Ho, for £14,500, to P.A. & C.Y. Toovey.

In April 1970 Westward Ho was sold by Mr Unwin to Dr Colin Andrew Charles Haley and Mrs Diana Pearl Haley. On 22 October 1999 the house was sold by Diana Haley to Judy Susan Tania Bridges (otherwise known as Fanny Bridges). Fanny Bridges and Garth Nichols, or Mr and Mrs Nichols, as they now are, set about an enlargement of the property, replacing some of the earlier 1924 additions to the house built by Evill. On 12 November 2001 it was bought by Michael Francis and Christine Anne Kirby.

15, Wykeham Lodge

Name: 1926, Wykeham Lodge; and sometime after 1957, Coppice Mead

DESIGN 19 – This is one of three houses built to approximately the same design. Wykeham Lodge had a garage on the lower ground floor, which has been converted into living accommodation. Otherwise the house is externally as it was built, along with a later wood-clad garage.

The many original internal features include the ceiling beams in the hall, the fireplaces, and the beams in both the drawing room and the dining room.

OWNERSHIP

1925	Mrs V.M.B. Robinson	1963	Reginald E.P. Rickinson and Molly Rickinson
1927	Andrew Percival Crosby		
1957	Mrs D. M. Crosby	1973	Michael and Brenda McCarthy
1961	Group Captain B. Sampson O.B.E.	1975	Peter and Olivia Harwood

DEEDS

An examination of the deeds revealed that on 12 January 1925 A.G. Taylor sold the property, for the sum of £2,775, to Violet Mary Boileau Robinson, the wife of Frederick Percy Robinson of Church Croft, Effingham. It was recognised as being part of the arable field enclosure No. 44, as shown on the original farm deeds. The size of the plot remains today as it was at the time of the sale. The house deeds allowed for a further garage to be built on the land in addition to that on the lower ground floor.

On 31 January 1973 an outline planning application was submitted for the existing garage to be re-sited and the erection of a two-storey detached dwelling. This was declined because of the lack of sufficient width. In 1974 a further application was made for the erection of a replacement garage with a flat over it for an elderly relative – this was again declined.

On 5 September 1975 the current owners, Peter Herbert Harwood and Olivia Harwood, purchased the property.

16, *The Odd House*

Name: *1926, The Odd House;*
1953, Hatchgate

DESIGN 21 – This is the last house designed by Burlingham on the estate. The 1930s type panelled doors show that styles were changing. The elevation above the river valley led to the inclusion of a verandah which has now been absorbed into the drawing room.

Externally, the house has retained its character with its brick facings and original windows. The external roofed porch is an addition, although it simply extends the original porch for which the original beam remains.

OWNERSHIP

1926	R.E. Bryan and R.A. Seargantson	1953	Mrs Phyllis M. Fawell
1933	Algernon E. Webb	1969	Derek Moncur Hatton
1937	John Wheeler	1976	Mr and Mrs G. Whitby
1939	Herbert Malpas	1997	Mr and Mrs M. Drinkwater
1948	Frederick James Hull	1999	Dylan and Nicky White

DEEDS

On 10 September 1926 the property was sold by A.G. Taylor and Onyx Property Investments to Ralph Edward Bryan and Rowena Alice Seargantson.

On 3 December 1976 Derek Moncur Hatton sold the property to Gerald and Patricia Alice Whitby.

On 2 November 1979 the Whitbys sold a plot of land in the garden for a new house, together with a further portion of the garden to make the road into Westward Ho. They sold the house to Martin and Misa Drinkwater, who, in turn, sold it on 10 May 1999 to Dylan Glyn and Nicola Susan White.

17, *West Hill House*

Name: *1926, West Hill House; 1953, Westhill*

DESIGN 20 – This house is unique in Abbotswood, being the only one to have the external walls plastered in a cement render, creating a pattern by sweeps with a wooden float. This was a popular finish with the likes of Baillie Scott as shown in Fig. 153 and is also seen on the ground floor at The Corner House.

Ownership

1926	Mrs E. Chambers	1979	John Roger Churchouse and Rosamund Esther Churchouse
1934	Richard G. Ward		
1953	Alex C. Durie	1996	John Charles Holden and Linda Holden
1955	Mrs Durie		
1957	Col. Ernest S. Brockman	1998	Vorley Investments
1975	Frank and Patricia Dewhurst	1999	Wilrich and Susan Schroeder (tenants)
1977	Dr David Moule	2003	Sam and Kate Samaratunga

Deeds

A search at the Land Registry revealed that the property was sold on 31 December 1926 by The Onyx Property Investments to Elizabeth Chambers, wife of A. Chambers.

On 11 July 2003 Dr Varuna Sanjaya and Kathryn Fiona Samaratunga purchased the property.

18, Westcott

Name: 1925, Westcott; 1983, Mead House

DESIGN 19 – The entrance hall has the same beam feature seen in the other two houses of similar design. Because this house is not built on a slope, there is no lower floor garage. It has the same attractive half-timber features as Wykeham Lodge, including the decorative bargeboards. A large conservatory has been added to the rear.

Ownership

1924	Mrs V.M. Burke	1984	Mrs Patricia Smith
1945	G.E. Pearson	1986	Christopher Jordan and Pauline Kay Sneddon
1953	A. Rendall		
1965	Lionel E. Wood	1993	Philip Charles Molyneaux Beardwood and Mrs Susan Jane Beardwood
1967	George Beedell		
1980	Michael and Jean Newman		
1981	Alan and Katherine Elizabeth Gavaghan	2005	Peter and Amanda Regan

Deeds

A search of the Land Registry revealed that by a conveyance dated 31 July 1924, A.G. Taylor sold the property to Mrs Violet Maude Burke, wife of John William Burke. She sold the property to Gerald Ernest Pearson on 26 November 1945, who in turn sold it to Antony Rendall on 26 May 1953.

Peter William Regan and Amanda Maxine Regan purchased Westcott on 24 May 2005.

19, The Corner House

Name: 1926, The Corner House,
1928, Penkenna

Design 20 – Burlingham chose to clad the first floor with timber, a feature not seen elsewhere in Abbotswood. This has recently been replaced by tiles.

The entrance porch has a particularly attractive cement redered brick pillar. Most of the windows have original brick mullions and, unlike at the twin house, they remain unpainted.

Ownership

1926	Mrs E.S. Ellis	1972	R. and Mrs M.J. Thomas
1929	C.E. de Maligny	1975	Mr and Mrs H. Simpson
1960	Mrs A.G. Johnson	2000	David and Veronica
1967	A.R. and Mrs J. Yates		Campbell

Deeds

Inspection of the deeds reveals a conveyance for the sum of £2,900, dated 26 February 1926, from A.G. Taylor and Onyx Property Investments, to Ellen Sophia Ellis.

On 25 July 1928 a mortgage was taken out with London and Manchester, for £2,000 at 5½ per cent, by Ellen Sophia Ellis, the wife of Reginald Ernest Ellis. Reginald Ernest Ellis stood as surety. The name had changed to Penkenna.

On 7 June 1929 the property was sold to Charles Eugene de Maligny, an insurance manager, for £3,350. De Maligny died on 10 May 1960, 31 years after buying the house, and on 9 August 1960 a grant of probate was issued. The Executors received a permit to built a house or bungalow on the adjoining land on 29 June 1960. In August 1961 detailed plans were approved and this became 19a, Abbotswood.

The property was sold by the Joint Executors, Midland Bank Executor and Trustee Co. Ltd, and Jane Elise Van Dyck de Maligny on 22 September 1960 for £7,350, to Amy Gollan Johnson.

Amy Johnson sold it to Alexander Royden Yates, a dental surgeon, and Jean Yates and moved to Hillcrest. In May 1972 the Yates' sold Penkenna to Roy Thomas and Margaret Joan Thomas. On or around 17 March 1975 Harry and Gladys Simpson bought the property.

Harry Simpson died on 18 September 1988, and Gladys died in 1999. Her family made an unsuccessful attempt to obtain planning permission in the garden between this house and 20a, Abbotswood. The Simpsons were great friends of the former Prime Minister and his wife, Sir John and Lady Major. Chapter 13 provides details of the relationship.

On 31 March 2000 the current owners, David Sterling Reddick Campbell and Veronica Janet Mary Campbell purchased The Corner House.

20, South Stoke

Name: 1925, South Stoke

DESIGN 18 – South Stoke is twinned with Waysend, and differs in that it has an internal garage. The early addition of a shed, integrated into the garage, with an extension of the long sloping roof, adds to the charm.

Internally the interesting features include original fireplaces, some of which are placed in the room corners, and original fittings and joinery. The fitted cupboards in the kitchen have been retained during recent improvements.

OWNERSHIP

1924	W.E. Murphy	1967	W.R. Hancock
1948	Mrs E.D.F. Murphy	2002	Paul and Pamela Gillingham
1954	D.M. Mills		

DEEDS

By a conveyance dated 7 February 1924 A.G. Taylor sold this property to William Edward Murphy for £2,190. Murphy's address is given as 39, Lombard Street, London EC3. On the plan, attached to the conveyance, Hillcrest and Westward Ho are shown as complete.

By an indenture dated 10 June 1925, a further plot of land with an 80ft frontage and adjoining South Stoke was sold by Taylor to Murphy for the grand sum of £270.

With the deeds is an Agreement dated 20 March 1933, whereby William Murphy stood as a guarantor. The Guildford Light and Coke Company undertook to lay a gas main in a new road off Epsom Road, Guildford. At the expiry of each 12 months commencing 31 July 1933, the company would produce figures giving gas usage. If in any of the five subsequent years the company received less than £16 for the gas supplied through the main, Murphy undertook to make up the difference. Burlingham entered into a similar agreement for houses in Abbotswood. This document had nothing to do with South Stoke, but shows how Murphy had other interests in Guildford.

A further document of interest included a letter dated 22 December 1931, which was addressed to William Murphy, at Messrs J.A. Wattie & Co. Ltd, 39, Lombard Street, London EC3. Presumably this was his place of work. The letter was from Chas Osenton & Co., Chartered Surveyors of Old Jewry, also in the city of London, who had an office in Guildford. It referred to a second letter, which was addressed to a J.S. Latham, against whom the cost of dilapidations was claimed following a rental of the property referred to as Pareora, Epsom Road, Guildford.

Latham had entered into an agreement in 1928 with James A. Wattie Esq., presumably the owner, and during the rental period caused considerable mess and damage. The list runs for 11 typed pages, and refers to 10 bedrooms, three bathrooms, a morning room, billiard room, drawing room, dining room, all the servants' work areas, a stable-block with a living room, two bedrooms, a coach house and a lodge. Outside were two orchards, a tennis court, kitchen garden, rose garden, herbaceous borders, and even pigsties. Wherever this was on the Epsom Road, it must have been an extensive property, and Murphy was charged with sorting out the problems after the rental.

William Murphy died on 18 February 1947. On 30 April 1954, William Murphy's widow, Mrs Emily Dorothy Forbes Murphy, and Albert Henry Throssell, both acting as executors, sold the property for £5,050 to David Murray Mills. The conveyance did not include the plot purchased in June 1925, on which was constructed Lydford Cottage in 1958. The house is well built in the Burlingham style.

Subsequently William Russell Hancock and Margaret Broleen Hancock bought South Stoke and on 31 March 1967 sold the piece of garden with a frontage of 60 feet, which is now Moonfleet. This was developed by Bardolin Securities Limited.

On 31 July 2002 Bill and Margaret Hancock sold South Stoke to Paul Martin Theodore Gillingham and Pamela Christine Gillingham.

21, Hillcrest

Name: 1923, Hillcrest

DESIGN 17 – The house was originally an 'L' shape, and was extended in 1987 to provide an en-suite bathroom to the main bedroom, a further bedroom and a third reception room.

When built in 1922-3 Hillcrest mirrored Westward Ho where many of the same features were recognisable until the latter was extended in 2001.

In Hillcrest, the narrow entrance hall leads to a drawing room which features an oak beam in the fireplace alcove. The larder, coal store, W.C. and scullery have been absorbed into a modern kitchen with breakfast room. On the first floor original fireplaces remain in two of the bedrooms along with all the original panelled doors. The leaded lights are rectangular at Westward Ho and diamond shaped in Hillcrest.

Externally, there are overhangs in half timber, with oak and plaster rendering on one, and roughcast on the other. In order to retain the style, the 1987 extension, which provided a further bedroom, a bathroom and a third reception room, has a similar overhang. At the front entrance, the original curved doorframe and curved window remain but the latter is to the front instead at the side. In 1986 the external roofed porch was constructed.

When Mr and Mrs McCandlish Wilson purchased Hillcrest in 1970 they did so without the garden plot on which Bornholme was constructed in a 'modern' style in 1972. Planning for Bornholme was initially refused. The plot was restricted in size so that the original grass tennis court at Hillcrest could be retained. It is still used today for play, including the annual ladies day for Abbotswood Women In Touch.

202 *Hillcrest, prior to an extension.*

Ownership

1923	Doresa Family Trust Residents: Mrs and Mrs Basil Doresa	1939	Frank Roffey BSc. PhD. (tenant)
1930	Capt. P.C.W. Tatton-Tatton (tenant)	1953	Leslie George Newland (tenant)
1931	Maj. Hy. Hughes (tenant) [previously at Littlefield in 1928-31]	1959	Douglas M. Cobban (tenant)
		1963	Capt. Peter Constantine Doresa M.C.
1935	Col. Hy. Hughes (tenant)	1967	Mrs A.G. Johnson
1937	Major Charles Theodore Foster M.C. (tenant)	1970	Mrs and Mrs R. McCandlish Wilson
		1982	Michael and Georgina Drakeford

Deeds

On 11 June 1923 A.G. Taylor sold the land with the house already constructed to a consortium of individuals being: Constantine Doresa, Basil Spiro Doresa, Irene Laing Murly Gotto and William Leach Lewis, comprising the Doresa Family Trust.

The *Directories* evidence the residents, of which there were many from 1930. In fact the house was held in trust by the Doresa family during this time and given as a wedding present to Peter Doresa, who took up residence in 1963. He sold the orchard plot before leaving. Chapter 13 contains references to Peter.

On 20 March 1967, Amy Gollan Johnston, having sold The Corner House, paid £9,500 for the property. In turn she sold it for £15,000 on 30 June 1970 to Mr and Mrs R. McCandlish Wilson who had moved from The Hazard. This is Abbotswood's equivalent of musical chairs.

On 11 October 1982 Michael William Drakeford and Georgina Ann Drakeford purchased Hillcrest.

22, Sunnymead

Name: 1917, Sunnymead and Sunnymede; 1932 Long Hayes and before 1962 Leaf House, thereafter Langton House

DESIGN 8 – This house has remained unchanged externally since it was built before the First World War. The stone surround to the entrance porch, with the stone balls on the small walls, are just as they were designed.

Inside the alterations are few, and the house retains the original internal panelled doors, the fireplaces in the sitting room and dining room, as well as most of the window fitments. Even the scullery area has the original doors to the various sheds, stores and W.C. for the staff.

Such an original example of Burlingham's works is hard to better.

Ownership

1916	Dr R.H. Lucy
1932	George Ernest Woodward C.B.E.
1940	Mrs M. Glover
1957	Mrs G.M. McNabb
1962	Vernon and Vera Goodeve

Deeds

A search at the Land Registry revealed that A.G. Taylor sold the property on 10 November 1916 to Reginald Horace Lucy.

It appears that on 12 October 1961 Gladys Mary McNabb transferred land to Peter Noel Scarfe which facilitated the building of a bungalow in the grounds, now known as 22a, Abbotswood.

Sunnymead was bought for £7,000 by Vernon Clifford Goodeve and Vera May Goodeve on July 1962. And at that time, the general and water rates amounted to £107 10s. 6d. per annum.

23, Postland

Name: 1922, Postland

DESIGN 9 – The modernisation to the windows and the interior has not detracted from the early post-war design for this one of five similar bungalows. Importantly the wood pillars in the porch remain. The owner, buying the plot before the house was built, was able to alter the living room to reflect an Arts and Craft style by the inclusion of an inglenook fireplace.

Ownership

1920	T. Ashby	1957	Mrs G. Hooper
1925	John Edwin Furnass	1961	Mr and Mrs Ronald S. Fairall
1939	Edgar Stark	1992	Basim and Margaret Rashid

Deeds

A search at the Land Registry reveals that on 25 February 1920 A.G. Taylor sold the property to Thomas Ashby. The normal covenants applied, with the proviso that any house built on the land shall have a cost of not less than £800. On 20 April 1920 a further piece of land adjoining the original plot was sold between the same parties.

From the date of the land purchase, being 25 February and that of the planning consent being 25 April, it appears that Taylor sold just the land and afterwards built the property to order.

On 17 July 1992 Basim Rashid and Margaret Rashid purchased the house from Mrs Doris Fairall.

24, Albury
Name: 1922, Albury

DESIGN 12 – This house was built for William Leighton after he had purchased the plot. Thus, he was able to influence the design.

From an architectural perspective this is a most interesting house with six gables. The walls are a mixture of half-timbering, roughcast and brick. The original verandah remains. Inside, the wall panels are unlike the oak type seen elsewhere on the estate. Here they are a lavish maple, which shines a different hue as the angles of view change. The ground-floor fireplaces are splendid and quite original.

Even the detached garage, erected in 1929, which has a chauffeur's accommodation above, is of interest architecturally.

Ownership

1920	W.T. Leighton	1977	James and Jennifer Dixon
1944	E.S. Phillips	1986	John and Janet Smith
1953	James Smith	1995	Robin and Angie
1957	Mrs R.C. Smith		Cregeen

Deeds

A search at the Land Registry reveals that on 10 August 1920 the land was sold by A.G. Taylor to William Todd Leighton. On 18 September 1920 a further plot of land was conveyed between the same parties.

William Leighton is believed to have been a director of John Moon and Son Limited, the timber merchants situated where the Debenhams building now stands. It was wood from this yard that was washed downriver in the floods of 1900 and demolished the Town Bridge.

With the earlier conveyance were covenants that unusually allowed for the building of two houses, at a net cost of not less than £1,250 each.

On 27 September 1995 the current owners, Robin James Cregeen and Angela Dawn Wyatt Cregeen, purchased the property.

25, *Aysgarth*
Name: 1922, Aysgarth

DESIGN 9 – There have been a number of additions over the years including extending the living space into the roof. The timber posts in the porch have been retained.

OWNERSHIP

1920	P.B. Addington	1940	William Smith
1926	Mrs L.M. Hewetson	1953	Philip Thompson
1933	Capt. John Samuel Pike Touzel (tenant)	1957	William and Nancy Pringle
		1978	Trevor and Ellen Bolton
1937	T.J. Tarry		

DEEDS

A search at the Land Registry reveals that by a conveyance dated 14 June 1920 A.G. Taylor sold the plot to Paul Bernard Addington. Because the planning approval was not forthcoming until 27 April 1920, Mr Addington made the purchase against plans, perhaps at a discount. This would help the cash flow for the developer who was committed to build at least four other bungalows at this time.

Henry Thomas McAuliffe and Paul Bernard Addington sold Aysgarth to Mrs L.M. Hewetson on 10 December 1926. The introduction of McAuliffe as a vendor is not clear; it is possible he had lent money and taken a charge over the property. On 15 March 1937 Mrs Hewetson, then of Red Tile Cottage, Drayton St Leonard, Oxfordshire, sold the property for £1,330 to Thomas Joseph Tarry. The fact that Mrs Hewetson, a widow, had been living away from Abbotswood for a while would lead to the assumption that Capt. Touzel, a resident in 1933, was renting the property. In 1937 he went on to buy Craig Cottage.

On 25 July 1978 Trevor Eric Bolton and Ellen Caldwell Bolton purchased Aysgarth.

26, The Lair

Name: 1918, The Lair; 1924, St Valery

DESIGN 8 – The central front elevation of this house looks much as it did when built. To the right-hand side there is an extension to the dining room, and to the left, a south-facing glass conservatory. At the rear are extensions next to the drawing room and the scullery. The large drawing room remains a significant feature. The bedrooms are virtually unchanged from their original design and contain original metal fireplaces.

The garage was built around 1928 with a square pitched roof, crowned with a weather vane, and remains quite original to this day.

OWNERSHIP

1917	H. Greenfield (tenant)	1927	Edward H. Curtis
1918	Mrs M. Lang	1939	Mrs C.I. Curtis
1923	Mrs E.B. Lawley	1944	Frederick J. Hubble
1924	Mrs F.M. Cherry	1952	Tony Vokes

DEEDS

The property was constructed in 1916; the first resident, probably in 1917, was an H. Greenfield. It is likely that this person rented the property from Mr Taylor until a buyer could be found.

On 7 May 1918 A.G. Taylor sold the property for £1,470 to Mrs Muriel Lang. The house was referred to as 'The Lair' in the indenture, and the plot measured 60ft wide by 190ft long. Her husband was Mr T. Lang. On 7 April 1920 Taylor sold the adjoining plot to Mrs Lang for £275. It measured 100ft x 190ft, and more than doubled the size of the first purchase. This allowed room for a tennis court and a double garage.

Mrs Lang sold 'The Lair' to Mrs Emily Blanche Lawley, a widow, on 17 April 1923, for £2,362. It is worthy of note that the signature of Mrs Lawley was witnessed by a Captain W.J.W. Cherry, described as a master mariner at 122, Leadenhall Street, London EC. The title of Captain is obtained from the *Directories* rather than the deeds. Mrs Lawley paid £5 17s. 4d. to the Ministry of Agriculture and Fisheries on 24 May 1923 in respect of a Tithe Redemption No. 34729 at 'The Lair'. The words 'The Lair' were crossed out and 'St Valery' inserted. Perhaps the new owner did not like to be referred to as the lioness. This respite did not last for long, as a year later, on 29 May 1924, Mrs Lawley died.

An indenture dated 29 July 1924 details the sale of the property by the executors of Mrs Lawley, being Henry Vassar Lawley and Ernest Norman

Lawley, to Florence Margaret Cherry, described as the wife of William George Wray Cherry, of St Valery, Abbotswood. It was he who had witnessed the purchase of the property by Mrs Lawley in 1923, just 15 months before, where the sale price was £2,362 again. A co-executor, Frederick Theodore Lawley, an engineer, had previously renounced probate.

By a conveyance dated 21 October 1927, Mrs Cherry, now described as a widow, sold St Valery for £2,947 to Edward Herbert Curtis, an 'editor'. By an assent of the late Mr Curtis date 31 January 1939, Clara Ida Curtis, now a widow, and as personal representative, vested in herself the property. Mrs Curtis died on 17 December 1943. Lloyds Bank, as executor and trustee, sold the property on 15 March 1944, for £3,600, to Frederick Joseph Hubble.

Gordon Heatherton Vokes (Tony) purchased the property on 12 August 1952 and lived there with his mother, Mrs E. Vokes.

27, Hutton Ambo

Name: 1922, Hutton Ambo; 1941, Neilston; 1954, Piel Wyke; 1967, Greenmantle

DESIGN 9 – This is probably the most original of the five bungalows of this design. The Crittal windows remain, together with the timber supports for the porch. Inside a feature archway separates the two reception rooms from the bedrooms and the kitchen area.

OWNERSHIP

1921	Maj. W.R. Stainforth	1954	Reginald B. Mills
1941	Capt. J.S.P. Touzel	1967	E. A. Burton and
1950	Mrs A. Touzel		Mrs A. S. Burton
1954	C.W. Renard	1970	Bob and Joan Thomas

DEEDS

On 29 July 1921, A.G. Taylor sold Hutton Ambo to Major William Rede Stainforth of Cambridge Lodge, Stanhope Lines, Aldershot, Hampshire for £1,650. He concurrently took out a mortgage with London and Manchester.

An extract in the deeds shows that the property was sold to Capt. John Samuel Pike Touzel on 29 September 1941, who had been responsible for building Craig Cottage. On 6 November 1950 it passed to his widow, Mrs A. Touzel. On 13 April 1954 the personal representatives of the late Mrs

Touzel sold the property to Constant William Renard. Shortly afterwards on 12 October 1954 it was sold to Reginald Bertram Mills.

Mr Mills sold Hutton Ambo on the 21 September 1967 to Edward Arthur Burton and Amelia Selina Burton, when the name was changed yet again, this time to Greenmantle. In December 1970 the current owners, Dr Robert and Joan Patricia Thomas, purchased the property.

28, Greta

Name: 1922, Greta; 1930, Tyrol Lodge

DESIGN 9 – This bungalow has been changed significantly over the years by previous owners and now provides considerably enhanced accommodation.

OWNERSHIP

1921	B.J.H. Billing	1948	Hugh F. Lindo
1930	F. Horstmann	1961	Leslie and Norah Reed
1932	Mrs F. Horstmann	1993	Stephen and
1935	Mervyn Clarence Johnson		Gillian Arien Birch
1936	Ernest George Manning	1996	Simon and Jane Exton
1944	Mrs K. Durrant	2003	Reeve and Bridget Martin

DEEDS

A search at the Land Registry reveals that the property was sold on 31 March 1921 by A.G. Taylor to Bertram Joseph Harrild Billing. On 8 November 1922 a further plot of land was sold between the same parties.

In January 1928 Mr Billing purchased 2, Fairway from Mr Burlingham and Ernest Taylor. It was also designed by Burlingham. The Wall Street crash took place in 1929; selling Greta might well have been a problem.

On 18 February 2003 the current owners, Reeve Daniel Martin and Bridget Martin, purchased the property.

29, Brookdale

Name: 1922, Brookdale; 1973, Damansara

The reason for the name change is that a one-time owner used the 'widow's plot' to build a new bungalow for her own use, and in order to retain the name and number of her home simply kept that of Brookdale, 29,

Abbotswood, and renamed and re-numbered her old house Damansara, 29a, Abbotswood.

DESIGN 11 – This house was one of five of the same design. Not long after it was built in 1921 additions were constructed including a garage with living accommodation for staff; perhaps the chauffeur. This has recently been replaced. The drawing room was enlarged by the absorption of the verandah some while ago.

Using the builders Deeks and Steere plc, extensive alterations have recently been carried out and the owners have successfully managed to retain the Arts and Crafts style.

OWNERSHIP

1921	G.F. Middleton	1971	Mrs A. Hunt
1923	Col. Alfred Bryan Bethell	1973	Mr and Mrs T.P. Furlonge
1950	Edward Arthur and Peggy Smith	1977	Kevin and Gillian Dennis
		1996	Robert and Jill Symonds
1957	Mr and Mrs B.F. Hunt	2001	Peter and Samantha Gissel

DEEDS

On 15 September 1921 the property was sold by A.G. Taylor to George Francis Middleton. In 1923 it was purchased by Colonel Bethell, C.M.G., D.S.O., D.L., who lived there until 1950. He is referred to in Chapter 13.

Mr and Mrs Smith lived there until 1957 when the house was bought by Bernard Francis 'Mike' Hunt and Audrey Mary Hunt. When Mike died in 1971, Audrey had the bungalow next door built, into which she moved, selling the original house to Timothy Patrick Furlonge and Peggy Ernestine Furlonge on 21 May 1973. In order that the new bungalow should not become a house one day, Mrs Hunt insisted that there should be a restrictive covenant allowing the property to have only one storey. Mike Hunt is also referred to in Chapter 13.

On 26 July 2001 Peter Gissel and Samantha Jane Gissel bought the house.

30, Erlesdene

Name: 1924, Erlesdene and Erles Dene; 1950, Friesdene; 1963, Tankards; 1968, Arrochar

DESIGN 14 – This house is twinned with Iomhar. It has a roughcast front and an original attached porch, rather than the enclosed type hitherto favoured by Burlingham. The exterior is generally original. Alterations have been carried out to the interior and, where possible, the deal doors have been retained.

Ownership

1922	Mrs M.A. Alder	1968	Prof. Malcolm B. Waldron and Josephine Waldron
1936	J.W. Wilton	1975	Brian and Susan Macfarlane
1937	William Curwen Barrett	1993	Graham and Elizabeth Rowlands-Rees
1938	Mrs Barrett		
1950	Arthur Edward Hare	1998	Anthony and Ruth Ashton
1953	Roger Frederick Lawrence		
1963	L.E. Davies		

Deeds

A search at the Land Registry reveals that the land was originally conveyed on 17 October 1922 by A.G. Taylor to Mary Ann Alder, the wife of Ralph L. Alder.

In January 1936 a further piece of land was conveyed by Taylor to John William Wilton.

On 8 September 1998 the current owners, Anthony Edward Ashton and Ruth Irene Ashton, purchased the property.

31, Eaglehurst

Name: 1924, Eaglehurst

This house is clearly of different style from the rest of the estate, being of Edwardian design. The plot was purchased by a builder for his own occupation, using a design of his own architect, rather than that of Burlingham. This house boasts many impressive features already fully described.

Ownership

1922	Mrs A. Wheeler	1969	Harri P. Mostyn and Eluned E. Mostyn
1925	Mrs A.M. Hobbs		
1948	Hilary D. Brown	1976	Mr and Mrs F. Dorman
1955	Thomas C. Thorp	1996	Terry and Sue Newman
1969	M.P.H. Williams/ A. & J. Simmons Ltd		

DEEDS

On 8 October 1922, for £490 A.G. Taylor sold the land to Alice Wheeler, wife of William John Wheeler. A further deed dated 25 May 1923 resulted in the purchase of a rectangular strip of land running the length of the rear garden of Iomhar. The garden of Eaglehurst included part of the copse identified in early maps, and the new piece of land extended the area of woodland.

Whilst the absence of both a planning application at the Surrey History Centre and a record in the Planning Committee's minutes mean a lack of evidence, it is quite likely that Mr Wheeler was the developer of the site and the house was built between 1922 and 1923. On 7 May 1925 Alice Wheeler sold Eaglehurst to Alice Maud Hobbs, the wife of Bedo Hobbs, for £3,825. The large plot measured 258ft x 205ft wide and extended as far as Iomhar.

Guildford's antiquarian bookseller, Thomas Colebrook Thorp, purchased Eaglehurst around 1955, and came to live with his wife Helena. On 12 February 1969 there was a transfer of land from A. & J. Simmons Ltd, and Michael Pollock Howell Williams for £10,950. The amount indicates that the house in the garden of Eaglehurst had been built on a plot measuring 70ft x 257ft.

Hal and Lyn Mostyn purchased Eaglehurst in 1969, and they sold the house to Frederick William Dormon and Norma McArthur Dormon on 1 November 1976.

Terry and Sue Newman purchased Eaglehurst on 15 April 1996.

32, Iomhar

Name: 1922, Iomhar; 1941, Lea Cottage

DESIGN 14 – Iomhar is twinned with Erlesdene. Apart from the back, where there is a large extension, externally it remains very much as it was designed. The walls are clad on all elevations with tiles at the first floor, matching into the side of the small roof at the bays. There is an external porch, and above this is a square window with a dormer roof and timber and plaster facing.

The lead casement windows and the correct fittings have been retained. So, too, has a four-plank front door with the decorative hinge plates. Internally, there are correct panelled pine doors, and in particular a long half-width cupboard door of the type also seen at Sunnymead.

Ownership

1922	Elliott Kitchener	1954	E. Lund-Yates
1929	Mrs M.E. Kitchener	1961	Hugh H. Thomas
1941	John A. Loudon	1965	F.G. De Saulles
1948	John B. Fletcher M.B.E.	1992	David and Irene Pardo

Deeds

On 1 September 1922 A.G. Taylor sold the property to Mr Elliott Kitchener who was related to the Earls Kitchener. He died in 1929 leaving the property to his wife, Mrs Maude Elizabeth Kitchener. Chapter 13 gives details of this illustrious connection.

In order to facilitate the building of new houses in Abbotswood Close, part of the land belonging to Iomhar was sold by Hugh Howell Thomas to Business Property Finance Co. Ltd in August 1963. Thereafter Iomhar was known as 1, Abbotswood Close.

Conditional outline planning consent for the formation of an access road to the land at the rear of Iomhar and The Hazard was given in September 1963. In 1964 an application for a bungalow in the garden of Iomhar was refused, but the erection of a garage and a two-storey extension for Iomhar was approved.

On 7 April 1965 Hugh Howell Thomas, on the direction of Small Traders Finance Company Ltd, sold the property to Frederick George De Saulles. He paid £6,500 to Mr Thomas, and £1,500 to the finance company. From the plan attached to the sale document it is clear that the garden of Iomhar had by then been further reduced in size, and that the initial planning refusal had been rescinded. The bungalow, known as 2, Abbotswood Close, was subsequently constructed. Four houses were eventually built in the garden of Iomhar.

Fred and Gloria De Saulles lived there until the current owners, David Colin Pardo and Irene Anne Pardo, purchased Iomhar on 2 September 1992.

33, The Hazard

Name: 1925, The Hazard

DESIGN 19 – This house has tile hanging rather than the half-timbering seen at the other two house of similar design. To the rear there is unpainted rendering, which is gratifying to see. Amazingly the lower ground floor garage is still intact.

Inside the beams in the hall, drawing room, and dining room remain.

Ownership

1923	A.C. Burlingham	1981	Roger and Maria Vellacott
1924	B.K. Finnimore	1984	Nagila Selmi
1950	Thomas Foster	2002	Dudley Penrose for the
1953	R.M. Wilson		Dudley Penrose Trust/
1970	Mr and Mrs A. Staits		Four Seasons Trust

Deeds

A search at the Land Registry revealed that on 3 September 1923 A.G. Taylor sold the property, likely to be just the land, to A.C. Burlingham. Together with the normal covenants was a stipulation that no more than two houses should be built on the land, at a value of not less than £1,000. On 24 September 1924 Burlingham sold the property to Benjamin Kington Finnimore.

Mr and Mrs Roger McCandlish-Wilson lived at The Hazard from 1953 to 1970. Having sold the garden for the building of four houses, they sold the property to Alan and Sonia Staits, and moved to Hillcrest.

The Hazard was purchased on 20 May 2002 by Dudley Charles William Penrose, and it is now used by the Penrose Trust.

The property is currently owned and utilised by the Dudley Penrose Trust, also known as the Four Seasons Trust.

34, Waysend

Name: 1925, Waysend; 1935 Ways End

As the name implies, this house is at the end of the original Burlingham houses, at the most northerly point of the estate. Alternatively this could have been created as a joke by Dr Billingshurst, for a Rupert Way was living at The Croft at this time!

Design 18 – This house is of the same design as South Stoke but instead of an internal garage there is in its place a large verandah with the north side enclosed.

The house was little changed by 1970, reflecting middle-class life of the early part of the 20th century, with a tradesman's entrance to the back door, the kitchen windows shielded by a heavy yew hedge from vistas of the garden, and bells in the main rooms and an indicator in the kitchen for the staff.

The currents owners make the interesting comment that the house has evidence of inter-war origins indicated by the style of the internal doors which had wide panels. These, they believe, were apparently not found before the First World War when panels were limited to the width of a single plank before the construction of plywood, and rarely seen after the Second World War when flush panels became the norm.

Ownership

1923	A.C. Burlingham	1970	Business Property Finance Company Limited
1925	Dr W.B. Billingshurst		
1953	T. Cohen	1972	Sir Anthony and Lady Vineall
1963	Mrs C. Cohen		

Deeds

Deeds of 3 September 1923 provide evidence that A.G. Taylor sold the land to A.C. Burlingham. As with The Hazard, it was stipulated that up to two houses might be built. This presumably gave Burlingham authority for these two adjoining plots to be built more densely than elsewhere in Abbotswood – this he declined to do. Having been constructed in 1924, it was firstly owned by Dr Walter B. Billingshurst who extended the property to allow for a surgery for his patients.

It has only had three 'families' owning the house in its 83 years. After Dr Billingshurst, the next owners were Mr Theodore Cohen and Mrs Carol Cohen from 1953. Mrs Cohen died in 1970. Her executors made a number of unsuccessful attempts to pull down the house and build six dwellings. Permission was eventually given for part of the garden to be sold and the last three and the most northerly houses at Abbotswood Close to be built. Hence they appear to be of a quite different design when compared with the first houses.

Among the reasons given for the rejection was that the additional traffic on to the London Road was unacceptable. The new A3 by-pass had not then been built, and it was considered that the carriageway to the main road was too narrow.

The portion of the land sold in 1972 contained a tennis court and a small pavilion; the foundations of the latter still remain in the garden.

On 11 April 1972 the current owners, Anthony John Patrick Vineall and Dorothy Vineall, purchased the property from Business Property Finance Company Ltd. Around that time they bought back some of the land sold for Abbotswood Close from the developer who had no use for it. Chapter 13 provides the details of Tony's 2002 knighthood.

35, Littledene

Name: 1923, Littledene; 1953 Dene House; 1963 Quinton Lea

DESIGN 15 – This house is twinned with White Gates, except that Littledene has no gablets on the roof. The external facing of roughcast matches that of

Erlesdene. Save for the updating of the windows, Littledene has not been changed significantly at the front.

Ownership

1922	Mrs J. Smith	1965	Peter George and Judy Skinner
1927	Major F.R. Savage	1975	John and Lorna Clayton
1940	A. N. Duder	1983	John and Janet McLean
1950	L.H.V. Longmore M.D.	1989	Mr and Mrs Price
1953	Edward St John Harden	1993	Kirritkumar and Hasmita Shah
1955	Edward S. Holcroft and Mrs R.M. Holcroft		
1963	Derrick Roy and Joan Bettison		

Deeds

A search at the Land Registry revealed that the property was sold on 2 August 1922 by A.G. Taylor to Jane Smith, the wife of Henry E. Smith.

On 16 August 1963, the land was transferred from Katherine Mary Ruth Holcroft, Ronald Godfrey Potts and Cyril John Milford Abbott to Derrick Roy Bettison. He built the new house, 35a, and on 16 February 1965 Littledene was sold to Peter George Skinner while he and Joan moved into the new house.

On 28 April 1993 the current owners, Kiritkumar Jayantilal Shah and Hasmita Kiritkumar Shah, purchased the property.

36, White Gates

Name: 1924, White Gates; 1925, Birch Tree Cottage; 1953, Birchwood Cottage

DESIGN 15 – Until very recently White Gates had been little changed since it was built and was in the same family from 1927 to 2006. It is twinned with Littledene.

A recent restoration has seen the interior completely updated. The roughcast on the exterior has been replaced with smooth plaster and the front door and porch have received a plastic make-over. The additional accommodation in the roof is lit by two dormer windows at the front; this and the large extension to the rear, coupled with the removal of the chimneys, has disproportionately altered the overall dimensions. Two similarly sized properties are being constructed in the garden.

203 *White Gates before restoration.*

Ownership

1923   H. R. Hannard
1926   S.T. Gotelee
1962   Mrs J. Gotelee and later the Gotelee Trust
2005   James Kingerlee

Deeds

A search at the Land Registry revealed that on 25 April 1923 A.G. Taylor sold the property to Harry Russell Hannard.

Mr and Mrs Gotelee lived at White Gates from 1926. After Sydney Gotelee died in 1962, Jessie Gotelee continued to live in the house with her adopted daughter Mary. After Mrs Gotelee passed away, the Gotelee Trust became the owners of the house, and Mary had the right to live there for her natural life. Chapter 13 features more information about Mary.

On 31 August 2005 the house was purchased by James Edward Kingerlee and he and Glenda commenced development.

37, Red Cottage

Name: 1922, Red Cottage

Design 11 – Burlingham lived here for two years. He changed the design by doing away with the verandah outside the drawing room, and extending that room to the length of the house. Perhaps to encourage a later sale, he then panelled it in oak, and installed a fireplace with a stone surround and delft tiles on the inside. He later added a garage with roughcast rendering and pargeting in the form of a flower garland alongside a detached verandah, which is visible in an early advertisement. The internal doors had simple wrought iron handles, with catches rather than locks.

The house has recently been refurbished and, save for the modern windows and the French windows by the verandah, initially looked original from the exterior. In 2008 a planning application was submitted for the removal of the verandah, to facilitate the construction of a large house in the modestly sized garden. The verandah and garage have now been demolished.

204 *Red Cottage shortly after construction.*

205 *Red Cottage – Rita Burlingham on the steps of the patio.*

Ownership

1920   A.C. Burlingham

1923   Mrs A.S. Butler

1936   George Leslie Pearse

1965   Hilary Chaird

1967   Alex and Louise Hannah

1973   Anthony and
Dorothy Hopper

1993   Keiko and Yasunao Yokota

1997   Albert Robert Gasser and
Pamela Carole Gasser

2006   Zarah Smith

Deeds

Burlingham lived at Red Cottage from mid-1921 to 1923, prior to moving to his new house, Newlands Cottage, in Trodds Lane, Merrow. A search at the Land Registry revealed that on 10 May 1923 A.C. Burlingham sold the property to Annie Sarah Butler.

On 14 March 2006 Zarah Clare Smith purchased the property.

38, *The Orchard*

Name: *1923, The Orchard*

DESIGN 13 – It had been intended in the original plans that this property should have a thatched roof, but this did not come about. The two interesting features are the inglenook fireplace and the external wood facing on the gable end.

The builder was Mr W. Bullen.

OWNERSHIP

1921	H. Falkus	1948	Arthur William England
1928	William Bernard Manley, Barrister-at-Law	1950	Leonard Gumby M.C.
		1955	Mrs Gumby
1937	Edward Owen Fox M.R.C.S. L.R.C.P.,	1963	Cedric Needham
		1969	Colin and Anne Knight
1938	William Knox	1973	Stanley and Margaret Holland
1939-43	no entries		
1944	Arthur Evans	1995	Sian Gregory-Smith

DEEDS

A search at the Land Registry reveals that on 30 July 1921 A.G. Taylor sold the property to Hubert Falkus, an accountant. In 1914 Mr H. Falkus was listed in the *Directories* as living at Churston.

On 18 January 1995 the current owner, Delyth Sian Gregory-Smith, purchased the property.

39, *Lorraine*

Name: *1915, Lorraine; 1917, Milestones; 1921, Greystones; 1931, Holybourne, and later changed back to Greystones*

There was some confusion with the name 'Milestones' because it was concurrently used for two Abbotswood properties.

DESIGN 2 – The occupants over the years have cherished the original features and most have been retained. Of particular note is the exterior, which has an outstanding timber and plaster three-stage gable, with a useful splash-back at the apex.

The details have been fully described and do not need repeating. This is just a fine example of this architect's work.

Ownership

1915	Mrs A.C. Dufort	1948	Mrs N.H. Scott
1915	Burningham (a tenant, pending moving to Littlefield)	1957	Mrs P.J. Henderson
		1962	O.P. Edwards
1916	Mrs Colthurst (a tenant)	1963	G.A. Mills
1921	Miss H.C.S. Gordon (Hon. Mrs A. Gordon, in residence)	1966	J.D. Davis
		1971	Christopher and Wendy Fuller
1931	Mrs M.H. Complin		
1938	The Misses Complin	1983	Ian and Eileen Chapman

Deeds

By the deed of sale dated 30 April 1915, Alfred Taylor sold the property to Mrs Anna Caroline Dufort for £1,900. The vellum deeds, written in copperplate longhand, with the original signatures and seals, include an attached plan of this house.

A further deed, also dated 30 April 1915, is an indenture for a mortgage with London and Manchester Industrial Assurance Company Limited in the sum of £1,250 at 4½ per cent with Mrs Dufort as mortgagor. It seems likely that Mrs Dufort used this as an investment property for most of the period. The addresses on the deeds were firstly Cadogan Place and latterly Thurloe Place, Kensington.

When Mrs Dufort sold the house to Miss Gordon on 18 October 1921 for £2,900, the deed referred to Milestones. However, Mrs Nesbitt-Dufort's signature was witnessed by Margaret Frances Risbridger, of Greystones, Abbotswood. Perhaps that was the day the name was changed again. It is assumed that she was either staying with Mrs Gordon at the time or was a servant. The *Directories* of 1922 listed The Hon. Mrs A. Gordon as living at Greystones. Mrs Dufort had changed her name to Mrs Nesbitt-Dufort on 2 January 1917, and on 3 June 1915 London and Manchester changed its to London and Manchester Assurance Company Limited. Confusion all round.

The searches at the Land Registry reveal the following information about subsequent purchases:

16 February 1962:	Ozanne Peter Edwards: Price paid £7,750
22 November 1963:	Geoffrey Anthony Mills: £11,500
23 June 1966:	John Derek Davis, and Peggy Jean Davis: £12,750
4 August 1971:	Christopher Alan Fuller: £18,500

When carrying out building work at Lorraine a postcard dated 28 August 1918, stamped with two half-penny stamps, was found, addressed in pencil to 'Master Alastair Gareth, Orchard Cottage, Burpham, Guildford, Surrey.' The card has printed on it a cat and the pencil script appears to read: 'Dear Alastair, Fancy a pussy cat having a cup of tea. I am glad to hear that you are getting such a big boy. Aren't you glad you are always having to live in the lovely country. Baby is so like you and has made friends with all the boys and girls in the house. Hug and kiss …'

We can but wonder if this was a homesick little boy with a card of encouragement from an aunt perhaps. The First World War was just a few weeks from its end. The franking stamp starkly stated 'Buy National War Bonds NOW'.

It would have been pleasing to tie this up with the Orchard Cottage in Abbotswood, but it was not built until 1921 at the earliest. It is likely that the card was sent to Orchard Cottage, 15, New Inn Lane, Burpham.

In 1972 a planning application was made for a bungalow and garage in the garden of Lorraine. This was rejected because of the additional traffic across the opposing traffic stream on to what was then a busy trunk road, which would interfere with the free flow and safety of the traffic. A planning application for a detached five-bedroom house with a garage was rejected in 1979 for basically the same reason.

On 26 August 1983 Ian Frank Chapman and Eileen Mary Chapman purchased Greystones.

40, Friars Oak

Name: 1917, Friars Oak

DESIGN 2 – This well kept house is twinned with Lorraine. The rear gable is tiled rather than half-timbered, and the dining room has exquisite panelling, not seen elsewhere in Abbotswood. The plot was extended to include the land on which Craig Cottage was later constructed. This is another prime example of Burlingham's work.

OWNERSHIP

1917	Mr and Mrs C.M. Holloway	1955	Leonard A. Morgan
1922	John Harold Archer	1965	Mrs L. Morgan
1948	Trevor L. S. Baynes	1967	David Lloyd
	M.D., F.R.C.S. Eng	1968	Ernest R. Nuttall
	Obstetrician and	1968	Mr and Mrs
	Gynaecologist		A.W. Barnard

1973	Colin and Anne Knight	1988	Michael and Stephanie Ferdenzi
1973	Helen Alexander	1994	Graham and Sue Hibbert
1984	Patrick and Barbara Nash		

Deeds

By a conveyance dated 19 December 1918 A.G. Taylor sold the plot and other land to Clarence Morgan Holloway and Annie Holloway. 'A sub-purchaser', John Harold Archer, appeared to be the person to whom the covenants applied. This does not equate with the first resident shown in the *Directories* as C. Morgan in 1917, and C. Morgan Holloway in 1918. In 1922 the 'sub-purchaser', J.H. Archer, was the only resident.

On 2 December 1968 a mortgage was taken out by Alan Walter Barnard and Pearl Anna Barnard with the London and Manchester.

The current owners, Dr Graham Hibbert and Susan Mary Hibbert, purchased the property on 19 September 1994.

42, Abbots Trace
Name: 1922, Abbots Trace

DESIGN 10 – Abbots Trace was not designed with the timber posts at the front seen on the other bungalows. An extension has been built on the right, extending the roofline.

The original windows remain.

Ownership

1920	P.A. Belton	1957	George K. Le Grys
1922	C.G. Howard	1976	Patrick and Louise Pollard
1924	Geoffrey Milner	1982	Claude and Peggy Langley
1926	J.C. Taylor	1988	Peggy Langley
1930	Miss M. Wright	1991	James and Ragna Eynon
1953	Roy N. Price		

Deeds

On 21 October 1920 the Land Registry shows that the property was sold by A.G. Taylor to Percy Alfred Belton.

On 13 December 1991 James and Ragna Eynon purchased the property.

43, Rosedene

Name: 1921, Rosedene; 1948,
Bay Tree Cottage

DESIGN 9 – This was the last of the five early bungalows to be built. Extensive alterations have been carried out, including additional living space in the roof, making for improved accommodation.

OWNERSHIP

1921	S.W.H.R.D. Perrett	1953	William Hilary Rickinson
1922	W.L. Pinniger	1975	Ellen Bray
1930	Mrs Florence Medwin	1976	John and Phyllis O'Neill
1943	James Kemble F.R.C.S., Ch. M.	1977	Roger and Joan Spong
1948	Harry Finch, Solicitor and	1980	Joan Spong
	Commissioner for Oaths	1981	James and Patricia Youngs
1950	H. Gifford	1985	Alex and Jacqueline Johnson

DEEDS

The Land Registry records show that the property was sold on 30 June 1921 by A.G. Taylor to Samuel Wilfred Henry Reynolds Dickeson Perrett. On the same day Mr Perrett also purchased Oakdene, next door. He soon sold Rosedene, and until 1929 continued to live at Oakdene.

On 11 June 1985 the current owners, Alexander Yiannikos Johnson and Jacqueline Ann Johnson, purchased the property.

44, Oakdene

Name: 1922, Oakdene

DESIGN 11 – One of five similar houses, this was built facing north, at right angles to the road. At one time the driveway came onto the plot from the direction of Rosedene, where a newer house now stands.

A flat-roofed addition was added in 1930, providing an extension to the scullery area and a repositioned bathroom on the first floor. The drawing room was extended by enclosing the verandah. The windows have been replaced with metal Crittal types.

The open side lobby, leading to the scullery, remains, when all others of this design have been enclosed. The half-timbered jettied gable is particularly attractive.

Ownership

1921	S.W.H.R.D. Perrett	1943	Maj. Ronald Curtis, and from 1944, Lt. Col. Ronald Curtis
1929	H. Thorpe		
1931	William C. H. Tyler	1950	Hilary Walton
1938	Comdr. Vaughan Alex Edward Hanning-Lee, DSO, OBE, RN (Rtd.)	1953	Mrs M. Walton
		1953	N.A. Ovington
		1967	Mr and Mrs J.I. Robertson.
1940	Mrs M.E. Pinker	1979	Ian and Rosemary Spence

Deeds

The property was sold on 30 June 1921 by A.G. Taylor to Samuel Wilfred Henry Reynolds Dickeson Perrett.

There was a transfer of the property on 2 May 1967 between Norman Allan Ovington and the purchasers, John Ireland Robertson and Olive Kathleen Robertson, which contained an additional covenant relating to fencing on the property. The Robertsons paid £8,400 for the house. In 1969 the erection of a garage was approved by the authorities.

On 19 November 1979 the present owners, Ian Gerald Spence and Rosemary Elizabeth Adalaide Spence, purchased the property.

45, Crossways

Name: 1922, Crossways

Design 11 – This is much on a par with the others in this group of five houses. Improvement work has been carried out over the years from as early as 1926. Nevertheless, the side and rear view offers a glance at the original Burlingham design, as seen on this early photograph.

Ownership

1920	Mrs E.M Wyllie	1978	Derek and Hilda Hill
1927	Philip Peebles J.P.	1985	Anthony W. and Jane E. Derbyshire
1963	Mrs A. Peebles		
1972	Michael John Christopher Wetz	2001	Andrew and Vivien Cornish
1976	Alexander and Isobel Parker		

Deeds

A search at the Land Registry reveals that on 30 August 1920 A.G. Taylor sold the property to Elsie Maude Wyllie, wife of D.S. Wyllie.

The present owners, Andrew Dennis Cornish and Vivien Cornish, purchased the property on 2 August 2001 from Tony and Jane Derbyshire.

46, *The Hurst*

Name: 1916, The Hurst; 1924, Woodways

Design 4 – This is the premier house in Abbotswood and richly deserves the listing afforded by English Heritage.

The Hurst is still on a plot of the original size. Some who saw the recent building of a new house in its grounds in 2002 might have thought that the original plot was being encroached upon. This was not the case. In 1925 the owners acquired this adjacent plot when purchasing the main house.

The excellent restoration has ensured that this house remains a prime example of the Arts and Crafts style. Externally, it has changed little except that the ground-floor verandah has been enclosed. It has a complexity that could be questioned, yet it knits together to form an impressive whole. Local residents are delighted that The Hurst was saved from demolition.

Owners

1916	Commander C.T. Oldham R.N. (tenant)	1996	Church of Jesus Christ of Latter-Day Saints
1925	H. Somerset Bullock M.A.	2000	Borme Homes Limited
1963	Mrs H.S. Bullock	2001	Mr and Mrs D.R. O'Flaherty
1972	Colonel John Coupland and Mrs D. Joy Coupland	2006	Paul and Wendy Kenyon

Deeds

A search of the Land Registry reveals that the property was first subject to a sale when, on 14 July 1925, A.G. Taylor sold it to Herbert Somerset Bullock, a book editor. It was to remain in the family until 1996. Before that it was rented.

The Bullock family included three daughters, Joy, Nancy and Hester. The voters' register shows that in 1963 Dorothy J. Bullock, Mary M. Bullock and Nancy E. Bullock were all residents. Nancy and Hester still live in Guildford. In 1995 Joy, then a widow, sadly died at the house.

From 5 March 1996 the property was owned by The Church of Jesus Christ of Latter-Day Saints. Details of the efforts by residents to retain this house are given in Chapter 14.

Borme Homes Limited purchased The Hurst on 27 April 2000 and on 27 April 2001 sold it to Susan Margaret O'Flaherty and David Richard O'Flaherty. On 11 August 2006 Paul Mark Kenyon and Wendy Joanna Kenyon purchased it.

47, Hestercombe

Name: 1917, Hestercombe; 1919, Ardenholme

DESIGN 5 – This house is one of a pair designed by Burlingham with the same floor plan, yet differing sufficiently to make each house unique and special. Hestercombe has two matching herringbone brick-faced gables on the south wall.

Inside, the wall panels, the large sliding doors into the billiard room from the hall, and the symmetrical drawing-room and dining-room doors leading to the verandah and the garden all go to provide a quality not often seen. The removal of the glazing bars on the ground-floor windows overlooking the garden has improved the garden view from the inside.

It remains a truly magnificent property.

OWNERS

1917	Struan (tenant)
1918	Mrs B. Mitchell (tenant)
1924	Miss A.M.V. Clavering
1937-9	missing from directories
1943	Maurice H. Cawson (M.H. Cawson & Co.)
1953	Mary Louise Adgey-Edgar
1970	Elizabeth Mary Robertson, wife of Charles Graham Robertson
1976	Peter James Hillard Ferris and Mrs Valerie Joan Ferris, together with Frank and Kathleen Shuttleworth.
1982	Alexander and Jill Erskine, together with Sidney and Nora Palmer
1986	Bernard and Carol Stevens

DEEDS

The Land Registry documents show that A.G. Taylor sold the property to Augusta Maria Valentine Clavering on 15 July 1924, 10 years after it had been built.

For £8,500 in July 1953 the property was purchased by Mrs Adgey-Edgar, wife of Captain Walter H. Adgey-Edgar.. Mrs Robertson bought it for £18,950 in July 1970, and Mr and Mrs Ferris, together with Mr and Mrs Shuttleworth, were recorded as the proprietors in 1976, when £38,500 was paid.

In April 1986 Bernard John Oswin Stevens and Carol Anne Stevens became the owners.

49, Upmeads

Name: 1917, Upmeads; 1928, Abbotsmead

When the entrance to Upmeads was moved from the London Road to one in Abbotswod, the number 49 was no longer appropriate. The nearest true number was 38 for Orchard Cottage. The thinking was that the next property, on the old tennis court called Lawnlands, should be 38a, and Upmeads, because at that time it had dual occupancy, should be 38b and 38c, and thus the posts at the two entrances for Farthings now proclaim the house to be 38d. The post office has a lot to answer for. How much more attractive it would be to use names.

DESIGN 5 – Early maps show that there was a private lane along the northern boundary, towards the river. This was lost when the Weylea Farm development took place.

This house, twinned with Hestercombe, was built on one of the largest plots in Abbotswood comprising 1½ acres, and second only to The Hurst. The extensive front garden was bordered by the London Road, which the house faced, and the rear garden had a tennis court and a kitchen garden.

At the rear of the house the original sash windows with the correct glazing bars have been retained. On the rear elevation, rather than being gabled, the roof is continued with a splendid plaster cornice.

There is little to add to the comments made about Hestercombe. Both have been well cared for and Upmeads has recently undergone a sympathetic upgrade using Deeks and Steere plc.

Upmeads is yet another excellent example of Burlingham's work.

OWNERSHIP

1917	Miss Johnson (tenant)	1949	J.W. Bland
1919	Miss Johnson and Miss Wright (tenants)	1959	Miss M. Perman
1923	G.D. Russell	1968	Mr and Mrs A.R. Worthington
1927	Mrs E.F. Gross	1981	Mr and Mrs H. Roberts and Mr and Mrs D. Loble
1937	W. Gross		
1938	B.C. Lucas	1991	Mr and Mrs F. Barber
1945	Mrs M. Lucas	2006	Peter Tolhurst

DEEDS

The deeds reveal that Upmeads was first sold on 10 September 1923 by Alfred G. Taylor to George Dearie Russell. He sold it to Edith Florence Gross on 17 March 1927 and her relatives, being Muriel Edith Sutcliffe and Kembo Abbot Cronin Gross, on 28 April 1938 sold it to Bernard Chaytor Lucas. It passed to Margaret Lucas on 18 June 1945 and on 3 August 1949 she sold it to John William Bland.

The property was sold on 30 September 1959 by Mr Bland to Miss Molly Claudia Perman for £8,500. Mr Bland went to live at Lawnlands from this time, which is a property built in the portion of the garden away from the London Road, once encompassing the tennis lawn – hence the name. Upmeads was later owned by Andrew Ralph Worthington and Tessa Helen Worthington. The property and the adjoining land, was sold on 1 September 1981 by Mr and Mrs Worthington to Herbert Charles Percy Roberts, Doris Daisy Roberts, David Peter Loble, and Jacqueline Marion Loble.

On 17 January 1991 Frank Antony and Carole Jean Barber became the owners of Upmeads. The name was changed from Upmeads to Abbotsmead around that time. In turn they sold it on 30 June 2006 and, Peter Tolhurst and Yuko Nozawa arrived.

Author's Recollection: I can recall looking at this building on my way to work in Guildford in the 1960s. It was slightly elevated and the long drive meandered to the front door. From this angle, the house gave a sense of grandeur. The garden was later taken for a new and attractive house called Farthings.

Twelve

Housing Developments, 1926-39

H ouse building continued apace to try to satisfy the insatiable demand for affordable middle-class homes. Generally the styles were becoming more predictable, but there were still pockets of development that catered for the more discerning buyer.

During this period of intensive building of suburban houses the names of builders we still see today were much in evidence, such as Costain, Wates, Wimpey and Laing. In 1919 there were eight million houses fit for occupation in Britain. By 1939 this had grown to 12 million. Many of the new houses would be semi-detached, built in fields surrounding towns, and along roads in ribbon developments. Whilst the houses were of varying designs, something akin to the Arts and Crafts style was very popular for the private house. There is reason to believe that this was so because a lot of the council-built properties were quasi-Georgian, and the new mock-Tudor style was an easy way of differentiating the two types.

Jacobethan houses, influenced by the styles of Elizabeth I and James I, were easily identified by the half-timbering, sometimes 'jettied', herringbone brickwork, leaded windows, and red-brick or pebbledash walls, sometimes with an integral garage as car ownership became more common. The houses in Abbotswood could fall into this category save for the fact that they were designed too early for this mass market period, were individually designed, and far more reflective of the Arts and Crafts Movement.

The next stage was the Modern Movement, the designs of which gave more light into the dwellings. This is often recognised by the horizontal Crittal metal windows and white exterior walls, with the occasional flat roof. Some would claim that even the basic tenets of the Modern Movement were influenced by the Arts and Crafts style, but the new designs were applied with the inevitable use of modern production methods.

Hollywood Moderne was seen in the 1930s, which was the Modern Movement incorporating Mexican or Mediterranean influence, originating in California, or more precisely Hollywood. White rendering of the walls combined with a green or blue pantiled roof were giveaway features. Burlingham occasionally used this design in Fairway and Ganghill.

During this period between 1926 and 1939 there were three houses built in Abbotswood, but not designed by Burlingham. Nevertheless, they are of a similar style and standard to the post-First World War properties on the estate.

These are as follows:

3, Abbotswood, Orchard Neville

Name: 1932, Orchard Neville;
1952, Brooklands

Originally called Orchard Neville, a reference to the first residents, the Neville family, it was later changed to Brooklands. This no doubt reflected an admiration by the owners for the motor racing circuit of that name in Weybridge.

PLANNING

- Pn 6986 dated 12 November 1931, approved 24 November 1931
- Proposer: Mr H.E.Churchman; Architect and builder:
  R. Holford & Co., Walnut Tree Close, Guildford

207   *Orchard Neville.*

COMMENTS

This well proportioned property has retained much of its originality. The construction is of brick with roughcast, and a tiled roof with gablet ends.

An open roofed porch leads through a solid oak door to a central hall, with an oak panelled staircase and single square balustrades faced alternately. The doors, also of oak, are stained, along with the door surrounds. On the first floor the doors are made of pine and the door furniture made of bakelite. In the sitting room there is an original brick fireplace. Stained wood picture rails are found throughout the house.

Externally, most of the windows are original, made of cedar, with metal wood frames. The wood frames are squared off, and smaller than those seen in the Burlingham houses. The windows are by Crittal, with external hinges. Those on the upper floor have protruding hinges to allow for window cleaning from the inside of the house.

208   *The rear of Orchard Neville.*

209 *The entrance and stairs and exterior bay window.*

Ownership

1931	H.E. Churchman (land only)
1932	Rev. William Neville M.A.
1940	Mrs M. Neville
1952	Mrs H.M. Walton
1981	Ken and Pat Fisher

Deeds

The plot was initially part of the garden of Hazlewood, purchased by G.J. Jacobs in 1914.

There was a supplementary agreement dated 3 October 1916 between A.G. Taylor and Mr Jacobs. The details are not fully known, but it is understood to have modified restrictions and conditions such as reducing the minimum value of any new house from £900 to £800. This could indicate that Mr Jacobs was already intending to sell some of the land for development, which of course he did some time later when the plot was purchased by Henry Eade Churchman who lived at Wey-ne-Shing. He was clearly a property man, for not only was he involved with this house but also Ederline. When he applied for planning permission for Orchard Neville, Churchman was living at 1, Clarendon Terrace, Kemp Town, Brighton.

Mr Churchman sold the house on 20 July 1932 to William Neville, Muriel Neville, Wilfred John Brymer and The Rev. Canon Charles Bower, Clerk in Holy Orders. The Nevilles held title at the Land Registry through a Good Leasehold title. The Rev. Neville lived in the house until 1940, and Mrs Neville until 1952. The agreement to sell and then lease probably had something to do with his occupation as padre.

On 14 March 1952 Brymer and Bower sold the property to Hilda Mary Walton for £7,550. The deeds referred to 'All which said piece of land is delineated and shown on the plan drawn on a conveyance dated 30 April 1914 between A.G. Taylor and G.J. Jacobs and is coloured pink together with the messuage or dwellinghouse erected thereon and formerly known as 'Abbotswood' but now known as 'Orchard Neville …'. Between 1952 and 1981, Sidney Edgar Mann and Anthony Geoffrey Stoughton-Harris became Trustees, and Mrs Walton and her husband Leonard Walton took out a lease.

A draft conveyance dated 1981 shows the intention for (1) Sidney Edgar Mann and Anthony Geoffrey Stoughton-Harris (both selling the fee simple in possession as trustees) and (2) Leonard Walton and Hilda May Walton, of 'Brooklands', 3, Abbotswood (selling as leaseholders and beneficial owners) to sell to Kenneth Brian Fisher and Ann Patricia Fisher.

10, Abbotswood, Ederline

Name: 1935, Ederline; 1948, Kingfishers

PLANNING

- ✎ Pn 7384 dated 15 August 1933, approved 18 August 1933
- ✎ Proposer: H.E. Churchman; Architect and builder:
    R. Holford & Co.

210 *Ederline.*

Comments

Ederline is situated at the end of the 'spur' road, which first appeared on the plans submitted for Wey-ne-Shing in 1921, when it was described as 'farm track'. It still forms part of the property of Ederline, and leads to other properties. Annesley, Brownrigg and Hiscock, architects in Guildford, submitted a planning application on 7 February 1933 to concrete the lane between Wey-ne-Shing and Littlefield.

The planning application was submitted by Mr Churchman who had previously purchased both the plot and the track from Samuel Symes at Stoke Park Farm. The block plan shows that the rear garden of Ederline backs on to Farm Lane, which led at that time to the fields at the west of Abbotswood.

The house comprised of three reception rooms and four bedrooms. In recent years much internal renovation and improvements have been undertaken.

Ownership

1922	Land only to Samuel Symes	1964	Mr and Mrs M.H. Lowson
1933	H.E. Churchman		
1935	William Sibbald Campbell M.D. and Helen Marshall Campbell	1966	Mr and Mrs J.A.B. Stewart
1950	Ernest Harold Edwin	1993	Mr and Mrs P. Bazin
1955	Robert Officer and Elsie Margaret Officer	2007	Andrew and Cynthia Crossley

Deeds

A Land Registry search revealed that A.G. Taylor sold the land to Samuel Symes on 27 December 1922. Mr Symes had purchased the farmhouse in 1919 and this was a quite separate transaction.

At some point in time Mr Churchman purchased the land from Mr Symes. Because there was an agreement (to enable the laying of a water drain) between Mr Churchman and the Mayor, Alderman and Burgess of the Borough of Guildford dated September 1933, it is likely to have been shortly before then. On 2 May 1935 Mr Churchman sold the property to Dr and Mrs Campbell.

The covenant differed from those on other properties in that it stipulated that 'the Purchaser shall not at any time hereafter use the property or any part thereof for the erection of rows or groups of cottages or for allotments or small holdings or for the erection of any factory or for any offensive noisy or obnoxious or dangerous trade business pursuit ….'. This appears to reflect the fact that the property was being sold by a farmer who did not wish to have his livelihood encroached upon.

On 10 June 1964 Elsie Margaret Officer sold the property to Murray Hough Lowson and Ella Fenton Lowson. They sold the house to John Anthony Benedict Stewart and Geraldine Margaret Stewart in 1968, who in turn sold to Philip Mark Bazin and Georgia Bazin on 10 August 1993. Chapter 13 includes references to John and Geraldine.

Andrew and Cynthia Crossley purchased the property on 11 July 2007

41, Abbotswood, Craig Cottage

Name: Craig Cottage

PLANNING

- Pn 8500 dated 12 October 1936, approved 18 October 1936
- Proposer: Captain J.F.P. Touzel; Architect: R.H. Matthews, Weller's Gate, Burpham; Builder: R. Holford & Co.

COMMENTS

This is a tile-hung building comprising four bedrooms and a box-room, with an integral garage. The interesting front porch is not original.

OWNERSHIP

1936	Capt. J.S.P. Touzel	1963	Leo and Audrey Cornish
1941	Maurice W. Bray	1981	John and Elizabeth Homer
1953	Mrs G. Bray	2000	David and Elizabeth Young
1953	Michael W. Spratt	2003	Robert and Phillipa Cane

211　*Craig Cottage.*

Deeds

John Harold Archer, of Lorraine, purchased this plot from A.G. Taylor on 19 June 1919 to enlarge his garden. He in turn sold it on 10 November 1936 to Capt. John Samuel Pike Touzel, who had received planning approval a month before.

Capt. Touzel was no stranger to Abbotswood having previously rented Aysgarth from 1933 to 1938. He later lived at Hutton Ambo from 1941 until his death in 1950. In March 1971, Leo Trevor Cornish sold part of his garden to Staryn Limited for the building of 41a, Abbotswood.

Lizzie Young, when living at Craig Cottage from 2000, wrote *The Reading Group* under her pen name of Elizabeth Noble, and is referred to in Chapter 13.

Phillipa Jane Cane and Robert Arthur Cane, purchased the property on 10 October 2003.

Fairway and Downsway,
the Trodds Lane area and Ganghill

From the deeds available, and the evidence from the planning applications, it is clear that about half of the plots in these areas were sold individually and were subsequently built by developers other than Onyx Country Estates. Houses understood to have been built later than 1939 have mostly been omitted from the following lists.

Fairway

There are a number of houses in Fairway and Trodds Lane for which the original plans are not available for inspection at the Surrey History Centre and thus the names of the architect and builder cannot be verified. Importantly, plans are missing for 14 houses built from 1929 to mid-1930, submitted by Claude Burlingham on behalf of Onyx Country Estates Limited. By a process of elimination, it can be ascertained whether Burlingham was indeed the architect for these otherwise non-attributed houses. No other architect applied for planning permission in these roads at the time that the houses were built. Subsequent searches at the Land Registry confirm the date of the initial sales on behalf of Onyx Country Estates. If another developer is included in the purchase, such as at number 36, Fairway, it can be assumed that Burlingham was not the architect and the plot alone was being sold.

Furthermore, where it has been decided that Burlingham could be the architect, the design has to contain features seen in his other houses. Houses thus identified as being by Burlingham have the date of the sale stipulated. In all, an estimated 25 houses in Fairway were designed by A. Claude Burlingham.

No. 1
For: Onyx Country Estates
Architect: A.C. Burlingham
Builder: A.E. Stanley
Plans approved: 6 January 1931

This is the only flint clad house. It was built in the style of the flint cottage in the grounds of Downside, the demolished house nearby.

No. 2
For: Onyx Country Estates – Type C
Architect: A.C. Burlingham
Builder: A.E. Stanley
Plans approved: 4 January 1927

No. 3
For: Onyx Country Estates – Type A
Architect: A.C. Burlingham
Builder: A.E. Stanley
Plans approved: 4 January 1927

No. 4
For: Mrs N.G. Marson
Architect: Not given
Builder: J.M. Rutter & Co.
Plans approved: 26 October 1927

No. 5
For: Onyx Country Estates – Type B
Architect: A.C. Burlingham
Builder: A.E. Stanley
Plans approved: 4 January 1927

No. 6
For: Onyx Country Estates – Type C
Architect A.C. Burlingham
Builder: A.E. Stanley
Plans approved: 4 January 1927

No. 8
For: G.C. Rattey, of Downside, Merrow
Architect: J.W. Shaft
Plans approved: 13 July 1937

No. 10
For: Onyx Country Estates – Type A, handed
Architect: A.C. Burlingham
Builder: A.E. Stanley
Plans approved: 4 January 1927

No. 11
For: Onyx Country Estates
Architect A.C. Burlingham
Builder: A.E. Stanley
Plans approved: 25 September 1928

No. 12
For: Onyx Country Estates
Architect: A.C. Burlingham
Sold by Onyx on 1 March 1930
    to Harriet Lizzie Herbert

No. 13
For: Onyx Country Estates
Only possibly designed by A.C. Burlingham.
Sold to Basil Peacock on 1 July 1931 by Onyx

The symmetry to this house, and the method of supporting the gable ends, call into question the possibility that this house was designed by Burlingham.

No. 14
For: Onyx Country Estates
Architect: A.C. Burlingham
Builder: A.E. Stanley
Sold by Onyx to Geoffrey Gibbs on
    6 May 1932

No. 15
For: F.K. Lamb
Architect: L. Hiscock & C.J. Moureau
Builder: R. Holford & Co.
Plans approved: 13 July 1937

No. 16
For: Onyx Country Estates
Architect: A.C. Burlingham
Plans approved: 15 November 1938

No. 17
For: Onyx Country Estates
Architect: A.C. Burlingham
Sold to Hilda and Winifred Hole
    on 31 December 1941

This house is included because it was built for Burlingham's sister.

No. 18
For: Miss Hilda Hack
Architect: James Ransome & Coote
Plans approved: 17 January 1939

No. 19
For: Mr J.G. Hampton
Architect: N.L. Smith
Builder: Hampton & Son, Pall Mall SW1
Plans approved: 30 April 1935

No. 22
For: Onyx Country Estates – Type C, handed
Architect: A.C. Burlingham
Plans approved: 20 August 1938

No. 23
For: C.J. Kent
Architect: E.C. Kent of Searle & Searle,
	Paternoster Row, EC4
Plans approved: 15 March 1938

No. 24
For: Onyx Country Estates
Architect: A.C. Burlingham
Plans approved: 24 August 1934

No. 25
For: L.R. Hiscock
Architect: L.R. Hiscock, of Annesley
Brownrigg and Hiscock
Builder: Mr Ashenden
Plans approved: 27 February 1934

No. 26
For: Onyx Country Estates
Architect: A.C. Burlingham
Builder: A.E. Stanley
Plans approved: 31 July 1928

No. 27
For: Onyx Country Estates
Architect: A.C. Burlingham
Plans approved: 16 May 1939

No. 28
For: Onyx Country Estates – Type P
Architect: A.C. Burlingham
Sold by Onyx to Dorothy Andrews
	on 12 January 1931

No. 29
For: Onyx Country Estates
Architect: A.C. Burlingham
Sold by Onyx on 17 March 1930 to Anne Coles

No. 31
For: Onyx Country Estates
Architect: A.C. Burlingham
Plans approved: 20 August 1938

No. 32
For: Onyx Country Estates
Architect: A.C. Burlingham
Builder: W.J. Wilkinson of Farnham
Plans approved: 25 August 1939

No. 33
For: Major Helps
Architect: Charles Whitby, Epsom
Builder: H. Ashenden
Plans approved: 28 November 1933

No. 34
For: Dr W. Thornly
Architect: Charles Whitby
Builder: H. Ashenden
Plans approved: 28 November 1933

No. 35
For: Mr W.H. Schilch
Architect: J.R. Moore
Planning application: 5 April 1937

No. 36
For: Clarke, Gammon & Emerys
Architect: R.G. Bowers, Cheselden Road,
	Guildford
Builder: R.G. Bowers
Plans approved: 15 March 1938

No. 37
For: Mr A.W. Lightbody
Architect: Messrs Annesley Brownrigg
	and Hiscock
Builder: Holfords
Plans approved: 18 August 1933

No. 38
For: Onyx Country Estates – Type P
Architect: A.C. Burlingham
Sold by Onyx to Lady Eleanor Leticia Paddison
	on 25 June 1929

No. 39
For: Onyx Country Estates – Type B
Architect: A.C. Burlingham
Builder: A.E. Stanley
Plans approved: 27 September 1927

No. 40
For: Onyx Country Estates – Type Q
Architect: A.C. Burlingham
Builder: A.E. Stanley
Plan approved: 27 April 1928

The design of this house was particularly impressive. To the front were two large gables, with a central door. Hidden from the front was a side double garage. The fascia comprised oak half-timbering, partly rendered panels and partly filled with herringbone bricks. Internally there were seven bedrooms. Subsequent owners have changed the original front.

No. 42
For: Mr A.E. Baynes – Type K
Architect: A.C. Burlingham
Builder: A.E. Stanley
Plans approved: 27 September 1927

No. 43
For: Onyx Country Estates – Type L
Architect: A.C. Burlingham
Plan as for No. 1, Downsway
Dated 7 June 1929

No. 44
For: Onyx Country Estates
Architect: A.C. Burlingham
Plans Approved: 31 March 1931

No. 214
For: Onyx Country Estates
Epsom Architect: A.C. Burlingham
Rd.Plans Approved: 31 March 1931

A planning application dated 12 March 1931 for these last two houses was placed before the committee with the comment that 'it would be suicidal' not to allow two houses on the plot nearest the road. These are relatively small houses and, whilst not shown on the plans, the entrance to 'Archway' was to be through an archway in the high flint wall. Number 44, Fairway has been much altered. Archway was of the same design, but with a cement rendered facing rather than plain brick. The tell-tale wooden beam at the porch to the front door is a typical Burlingham feature.

212   1, Fairway.

213   *2, Fairway.*

214   *3, Fairway.*

215   *5, 6, 10, Fairway.*

216   *11,12, 13. Fairway.*

217   14, 16, 17, Fairway (clockwise from top left).

218   22, 24, 26, Fairway (clockwise from top left).

219 27, 28, 29, Fairway (clockwise
from top left).

220 31, 32, 38, Fairway (clockwise from above).

221 39, 40, 42, Fairway (clockwise from top left).

222 43, 44, Fairway and 214, Epsom Road, through the archway (clockwise from top left).

Downsway

Most of the houses in Downsway are of a high quality, built in the 1930s. Five are known to be by Claude Burlingham.

No. 1
For: Onyx Country Estates – Type L
Architect: A.C. Burlingham
Builder: A.E. Stanley
Plans approved: 25 June 1929

No. 2
For: Mrs E.B. David
Architect: G.E. Clare, Harrow
Plans approved: 22 July 1930

No. 3
For: Mr G.R. Strong
Architect: A.L. Abbott FRIBA
Builder: Y.J. Lovell, Gerrards Cross.
Plans approved: 26 November 1935

No. 4
For: Mr A. Gostelow
Architect: Alfred Gostelow & Sons Ltd
167, High Street, Guildford
Builder: Walter Davis, Gomshall
Plans approved 10 November 1936

No. 5
For: Mr H.E. Roscoe
Architect: A. Westbrook
Builder: R. Holford & Co.
Plans approved: 27 March 1935

No. 6
For Mr J.A. Hughes
Architect: H. Osborn FFAS, Chichester
Builder: Chapman, Lowry and Puttick,
    Haslemere
Plans approved: 12 May 1936

No. 7
For: Mr C.F.S. Hole
Architect: A.C. Burlingham
Plans approved: 2 April 1936

No. 8
For: Miss Savage
Architect: L.R. Hiscock, Guildford
Builder: R. Holford & Co.
Plans approved: 2 April 1936

No. 9
For: Onyx Country Estates
Architect: A.C. Burlingham
Plans approved: 15 November 1938

No. 10
For: Walter Davis
Architect: Alfred Gostello & Sons Ltd
Builder: Walter Davis
Plans approved: 2 April 1936

No. 11
For: Onyx Country Estates
Architect: A.C. Burlingham
Plans approved: 24 August 1934

No. 12
For: Onyx Country Estates
Architect: A.C. Burlingham
Builder: A.E. Stanley
Plans approved: 28 January 1930

223   *1, 7, 9, Downsway.*

224   *11, 12, Downsway.*

Trodds Lane

Eight houses in Trodds Lane are recognised as having been designed by Claude Burlingham.

No. 2 – June Croft
For: Onyx Country Estates – Type D
Architect: A.C. Burlingham
Builder: A.E. Stanley
Plans approved: 27 September 1927

No. 3
For: Onyx Country Estates
Architect: A.C. Burlingham
Sold to Stanley Charles Godfrey
on 13 July 1928

Greys
Architect: A.C. Burlingham
Built in 1923 for Hilda Hole, the sister of the architect

Newlands Cottage
Architect: A.C. Burlingham
Built in 1923 for Burlingham and his family.

No. 32 – Little Court
For: Onyx Estates
Architect: A.C. Burlingham
Builder: A.E. Stanley
Plans approved: 30 January 1928
and revised 27 March 1928

Beech Chase
For: Onyx Country Estates
Architect: A.C. Burlingham
Builder: W.G. Sheppard
Plans approved: 4 January 1927

Greatford Cottage
For: Rev. B.W. Peacock
Architect: A.C. Burlingham
Plans approved: 15 February 1927

Greatford House
For: Rev. B.W. Peacock
Architect: A.C. Burlingham
Plans approved: 15 February 1927

225 *2, 3, Trodds Lane.*

226   *Trodds Lane (left),*
32, Beech Chase (right).

227   *Greatford House (left top and bottom),*
Greatford Cottage (right), Trodds Lane.

Abbotsway

All but one of the pre-1939 houses were designed by Claude Burlingham.

No. 1
For: Onyx Country Estates – Type E
Architect: A.C. Burlingham
Builder: A.E. Stanley
Plans approved: 31 January 1928

No. 2
For: Onyx Country Estates – Type E
Architect: A.C. Burlingham
Identical plans approved for No. 1, Abbotsway,
    31 January 1928

No. 3
For: Onyx Country Estates – Type P
Architect: A.C. Burlingham
Sold to Cecelia Bertha McIver on
    20 December 1933

No. 4
For: Onyx Country Estates – Type P
Architect: A.C. Burlingham
Sold to Sidney Charles Godfrey on
    13 January 1930, having previously bought
    3, Trodds Lane in 1928.

No. 5
For: Miss M.R. Martindale
Architect: Allen Chandler
Plan approved: 30 December 1929

No. 6
For: Onyx Country Estates – Type P
Architect: A.C. Burlingham
Sold to Archibald Davie on
    18 September 1933

228   *1, 2, Abbotsway showing an unusual front porch.*

229 *3, 4, 6. Abbotsway.*

Three Pears Road

The name Three Pears comes from the three pears in the heraldic shields found on the doors at the Abbot's Hospital in Guildford, more correctly known as 'The Blessed Trinity Hospital', the Governors of which sold Hall Place Farm.

Initially plans were approved in September 1927 for the Type-C houses in Fairway and Three Pears Road. Abbots Ann was subject to a planning change with a large gable to the left, and an extended roof line for a further gable at the end. This allowed a further bedroom, making five in all. A feature chimney, with Bargate stone and three steps, quite like that at Newlands Cottage, together with an extended porch, made this house most attractive.

230 *Door at Abbot's Hospital.*

No. 2 – Abbots Ann
For: Onyx Country Estates – Type C
Architect: A.C. Burlingham
Builder: A.E. Stanley
Planning approved: 31 January 1928

No. 4
For: Onyx Country Estates – Type B
Architect: A.C. Burlingham
Builder: A.E. Stanley
Planning approved: 4 January 1927

No. 6
For Onyx Country Estates – Type D
Architect: A.C. Burlingham
Builder: A.E. Stanley
Planning approved: September 1927
    for June Croft

231 1, 3, 5, Three Pears Road.

1, Three Pears Road (and above).

3, Three Pears Road.

5, Three Pears Road.

Epsom Road

When Hall Place Farm was purchased in 1927, the farmhouse and farmyard buildings were either side of the Epsom Road. The farmyard buildings were next to the church and, save for a small shed, they were replaced by the three houses listed below.

The 17th-century farmhouse, shown in Fig. 43, was restored in 1928 by Claude Burlingham. Some of the large beams predate the house. He had started work without applying for planning permission and, whilst it was granted in January 1928, he was ticked off for the misdemeanour. The position of the front door was changed and the original door was re-used internally. The work included the installation of new W.C.s, a revised kitchen, a porch and a lobby area. The ground-floor fireplaces were 'modernised' and reduced in size, but these have now been opened out again. The windows were replaced where required. However, Burlingham managed to keep to the shape of the Victorian frames, and use the Abbotswood style metal frame for the glass.

No. 226
For: Onyx Country Estates – Type L
Architect: A.C. Burlingham
Sold to William Fish on 1 June 1929

No. 228 – Tithe House
For: Onyx Country Estates – Type Q
Architect: A.C. Burlingham.
Sold to Cecelia Theodora Barton
    on 1 August 1934
The name is a clue to its origins.

No. 230
For: Onyx Country Estates
Architect: A.C. Burlingham
Builder: A.E. Stanley
Plans approved: 31 July 1928 as for 26, Fairway

Strangely both 226 and 230 look symmetrical which is unlike Burlingham's designs. Close examination reveals that the right-hand-sides are later additions.

232 *226, 228, 230, Epsom Road.*

Ganghill

On 9 July 1929 the land was purchased from 5th Earl of Onslow by Claude Burlingham and Ernest Taylor. Various planning applications for the road, the entrances, and even a bridge at Ganghill ensued.

The first application was submitted in June 1929 when Burlingham sought approval for the layout of a new road on the south side of the London Road in Ganghill Copse, and later the gate piers and end wing walls at the entrance.

In September 1929 Burlingham submitted a further application for a road extension, this time incorporating a design for a bridge. This took the road over the railway line at the end of the present Ganghill to extend the estate further into the Ganghill Copse. Whilst approved by the Council, these plans were not put into effect. Shortly afterwards, a further application sought to extend the road to the left at the T junction, rather than over the railway. It identified 11 plots, with names of nine prospective purchasers given as Walton, Peddie, Hutt, Thomson, Woods, Colley, Smart, Jeffries, and Ticehurst.

In the period up to 1939, Claude Burlingham designed 12 houses in Ganghill.

No. 2
For Onyx Country Estates
Architect: A.C. Burlingham
Builder: A.E. Stanley
Plans approved: 28 April 1931

No. 3
Architect: Margary & Scott
Builder: Armstrong Estates
Plans approved: 29 October 1935

No. 4
Architect: Margary & Scott
Builder: Armstrong Estates
Plans approved: 29 October 1935

No. 5
Architect: Margary & Scott
Builder: Armstrong Estates
Plans: Not available
First sold: 1 May 1937

No. 6
Architect: H.Y. Margary
Builder: Armstrong Estates
Plans approved: 28 August 1936

No. 7
Architect: H.Y. Margary
Builder: Armstrong Estates
Plans approved: 17 December 1935

No. 8
Architect: Margary & Scott
Builder: Armstrong Estates
Plans approved: 29 October 1935

No. 9
For: Onyx Country Estates
Architect: A.C. Burlingham
Builder: A.E. Stanley
Plans approved: 1 April 1930

No. 10
Architect: H.Y. Margary
Builder: Armstrong Estates
Plans approved: 12 October 1937

No. 11
For: Onyx Country Estates
Architect: A.C. Burlingham
Builder: A.E. Stanley
Plans approved: 30 September 1930

No. 12
For: Onyx Country Estates
Architect: A.C. Burlingham
Builder: A.E. Stanley
Plans approved: 17 April 1931

No. 13
For: Mr P.D.D. Innes
Architect: not known
Builder: Eden & Brown
Plans approved: 28 July 1931

No. 14
For: Onyx Country Estates
Architect: A.C. Burlingham
Builder: A.E. Stanley
Plans approved: 28 April 1931

No. 26
For: Mrs Ramsden
Architect: R.H. Matthews
Plans approved: 11 May 1937

No. 27
For: Onyx Country Estates
Architect: A.C. Burlingham
Builder: A.E. Stanley
Plans approved: 14 October 1929

The final designs of 27 and 29 differed somewhat
from the initial sanction.

No. 28
For: Mrs J.H. Jones of Hastings
Architect: A.B. Westbrook
Builder: R. Holford & Co.
Plans submitted: 6 March 1935

No. 29
For: Onyx Country Estates
Architect: A.C. Burlingham
Builder: A.E. Stanley
Plans approved: 14 October 1929
As for No. 27

No. 32
For: Mr Goode-Parker
Architect: A.C. Burlingham
Builder: not known
Plans approved: 14 October 1938

No. 34
For: R.O. Gerard
Architect: A.R. Drowley, Byfleet
Builder: R.O. Gerard
Plans approved: 26 April 1932

No. 35
For: Mr S.S. Mitchell
Architect: D.J. Barry
Builder: R. Holford & Co.
Plans approved: 31 March 1931

No. 36
For: Onyx Country Estates
Architect: A.C. Burlingham
Builder: A.E. Stanley
Plan approved: 28 April 1931

No. 37
Architect: A.C. Burlingham
Builder: A.E. Stanley
Plans approved: 29 October 1929

No. 38
For: Capt F.B. Baker
Architect: J. Barrington Baker
Builder: H.C. Beagley, Shalford
Plans submit: 11 September 1929

No. 40
Architect: A.C. Burlingham
Builder: A.E. Stanley
Plan approved: 1 April 1930

No. 41
Architect: H.Y. Margary
Builder: Armstrong Estates
Plans submitted: 7 January 1935

No. 42
Architect: A.C. Burlingham
Builder: A.E. Stanley
Approved: 29 October 1929

No. 43
For: Mr W.G. Belcher
Architect: Eden & Brown
Builder: Eden & Brown
T/A J.M. Rutter
Plans approved: 26 April 1932

233   *2, 9, 11, Ganghill (anti-clockwise from top left).*

234   12, 14, 27, Ganghill

235   *29, 32, 36, Ganghill.*

236 *37, 40, 42, Ganghill (clockwise from top left).*

Claude Burlingham applied to build five houses at the entrance to Ganghill and received approval on 21 May 1939, but he was advised that approval was subject to a proposed road improvement scheme that would provide for a service road where he intended to place the houses. He did not carry on with his plans, but the service road was never built. Had it been, 120ft would have been taken from the estate and it would doubtless have meant that the entrance walls and piers would have been lost. Instead, some 43 years later, a new by-pass was built.

In March 1937, Franks Harris, road contractors of Guildford, submitted plans for a road in the remaining part of Ganghill Copse at the other side of the railway line, on behalf of Burlingham. This referred back to the earlier plans of 1929, which had included the bridge over the railway. The plans called for a road from Boxgrove Lane, skirting the then Boxgrove School, along Merrow Copse, and into the road now called Merrow Woods.

Burlingham, at the same time as he attempted to get planning permission for the houses in Ganghill, used the same designs for an application to build four houses at Merrow Copse.

His intention was eventually to build seven houses, all of which were completed on behalf of Onyx Country Estates. They were built at different times. The builder of the initial four was W.F. Wilkinson & Sons and the plans were sanctioned on 16 May 1939. These numbered, 1, 3, 123, and 125. The designs had small variations in order to create interest. The final three houses were constructed from September 1939 by Mr W. Holt of Godalming. These were of a quite different design being somewhat narrower in width. Both types had three bedrooms. They are numbered 5, 115 and 117.

The development of the remainder of the estate was not started until the 1960s, long after Burlingham had left Guildford.

237 *Merrow Woods Design A.*

238 *Merrow Woods Design B.*

239 *Letterbox.*

And then came The Second World War …

A simple but apt reminder of this period is the letter box in Abbotswood situated at the 'triangle'. Like many, it is constructed of brick with a post box front, with the crest of arms for King George V moulded into the door. The interesting feature is the remnants of the white paint that was painted on each corner at the time of the Second World War. Many will recall that, when a Second World War film is shown, the cars have partly covered headlights, and white edges to the wings, and also that street furniture and pavement edges were also painted white. This was because full car lights were not allowed – just in case it helped the German Luftwaffe in their attempts to navigate from the air. By painting the letter boxes and the like, the white marks helped the drivers without full headlights to keep on the road! It was not always successful.

Thirteen

Notable Property Owners: Past and Present

A brief look into the lives of some of the owners in the estate of Abbotswood provides some most interesting tales. The descriptions of the houses lead to the conclusion that the early buyer was from a well-heeled background, perhaps an officer in the forces, a successful businessman, or someone from the professions. Was this indeed the case?

ADAMS

Mary Adams was born in 1928. She was adopted by Mr and Mrs Sydney Gotelee who, in 1926, had moved to White Gates. She remained there all her life, caring for her parents. After her father died in 1962, she married Jimmie Adams and they both then cared for her mother until she died. They remained there until 2004, when Mary passed away at the age of seventy-six.

She will be remembered for her encyclopaedic knowledge of the people in Abbotswood over the years. Her tales included knowing and playing with the children of the architect Claude Burlingham: Russell and Patricia, and curtseying to Mrs Kitchener from Iomhar. She attended school with Patricia, both at Tormead and subsequently at Clarendon. In her later years, she was often seen around the area on her bicycle, collecting newspapers for a greyhound charity. Her friendly approach to all she met has been much missed.

Mary was the encouragement to write this book, but sadly she was not able to enjoy the information discovered.

ADGEY-EDGAR

Mr and Mrs W.H. Adgey-Edgar of Hestercombe gave to the town the magnificent 16-ft angel that adorns the top of the cathedral. Weighing about a ton, it is made of copper and covered in gold leaf. As well as being a symbol for the cathedral, it also acts as a weather vane. Sometimes known as the Golden

Angel of Guildford, it was given in memory of their eldest son, Reginald, of the Intelligence Corps, who died on active service on 5 January 1944.

BETHELL

Colonel Alfred Bryan Bethell, C.M.G., D.S.O., D.L., served with the Royal Artillery, and lived at Brookdale from 1923 until 1950. He married Caroline Patience Nagle in 1913, and was made a Companion of the Distinguished Service Order in 1915, and made a Companion of the Order of St Michael and St George in 1918. Their only son was killed in Palestine in 1946.

Colonel Bethell's army career started in 1895, and he rose to the rank of Captain in 1901, Major in 1911, and Colonel in 1921. He was in South Africa for two years from 1900, when he was mentioned in dispatches, and received four clasps to the Queen's Medal. From 1901 to 1911 he was employed in the Egyptian Army. He was fighting in the Sudan from 1905, where he was again mentioned in dispatches and also awarded the Egyptian Medal with clasp. Major Bethell returned to fight in Europe from 1914 to 1918, when in addition to the awards mentioned above he received the Légion of d'Honneur. He spent most of his retirement in Abbotswood, when he was Deputy Lieutenant, before finally moving to Haselbury Plucknett in Somerset.

DASH

Sir Roydon Dash, D.F.C., Hon. L.L.D., F.R.I.C.S., F.A.I., and Lady Dash lived at The Cottage from 1942 until 1966.

Born in 1888, Roydon Englefield Ashford Dash served in the Royal Flying Corps during the First World War and was awarded the D.F.C. He married Joan Harrison in 1933. He was a chartered surveyor by profession and a chartered auctioneer. His career took him into the Inland Revenue. He was knighted in 1945 and retired from the service as Chief Valuer, Board of the Inland Revenue in 1951. He then became Vice-Chairman of the Bracknell Development Corporation and was a Director of the London Chamber of Commerce.

DORESA

From 1963-7 Peter Doresa lived with his wife Coral at Hillcrest. His family had owned the property since 1923, shortly after it was built.

Peter has the distinction of being awarded an immediate Military Cross, whilst a Second Lieutenant at the age of 19½ in The Queen's Own Royal West Kent Regiment. He was involved with the campaign on the India and Burma border, and in particular the defence of Kohima between 4 and 20 April 1944. This was the turning point of the war, when the Japanese were rebuffed in their attempt to take India. The Allied force of 3,500 was attacked

240 *Peter Doresa.*

by a Japanese force of 13,500 and, whilst the allies lost 1,350, the Japanese lost considerable more.

In one action, Doresa was ordered to take his platoon across open land and lead an assault 'with bayonet and grenade against the unsuspecting bashas'. Whereas Doresa's company commander, Captain Easten, had estimated that a Japanese platoon of 25 men was held up, there was in fact a company of 90 Japanese. They were protecting the forward supply depot in which food, equipment and ammunition was stored. The Japanese were pinning down 'C' Company, and with few qualms Peter led the attack. In all they killed 44 Japanese for the loss of none of the platoon.

The citation for Peter Doresa's Military Cross reads:

> At Kohima on 8th April, 1944, the enemy had infiltrated under cover of darkness between two company positions. 2nd Lieutenant Doresa's platoon was ordered to counter-attack an enemy bunker position surrounding and inside an ammunition dump.
>
> Ordering his platoon to give covering fire, 2nd Lieutenant Doresa led a small party forward and personally bombed these positions, driving the occupants into the open where they were shot by the remainder of the Company, causing heavy casualties to the enemy. 2nd Lieutenant Doresa himself shot at least 12. During the engagement the ammunition dump was set on fire and shells, mortar bombs, grenades and small arms ammunition were exploding in all directions.
>
> In spite of all this, 2nd Lieutenant Doresa carried on with his counter-attack and throughout the engagement showed a high standard of courage and devotion to duty, which was an inspiration to all those around him.

A member of Peter Doresa's platoon, Lance Corporal John Harman, had been outstanding. He, single-handed, attacked a Japanese machine gun post that was holding up the assault. To do this he ran across 35 yards of open land while machine gun bullets were all about. The citation reads 'Without hesitation he went forward, and using a grenade with a four second fuse, which he held for two of those seconds to get maximum effect, threw it into the Jap position and followed up immediately. He not only annihilated the post but also returned with the machine gun.' He was killed the following day during another heroic attack on an enemy position. He died just short of Peter as he tried to get back to the platoon. Peter recommended him for the Victoria Cross, which he received posthumously. This was the only Victoria Cross to be won by the Royal West Kents during the Second World War.

Peter was later shot through the leg. The battle is recorded in the book, *Not Ordinary Men*, by John Colvin.

Peter Doresa recalled to the author a more mundane fact about Abbotswood. When he lived at Hillcrest, there was a general agreement that a call would go out on Friday afternoon for anyone who wished to go to Guildford or Burpham, that they should do so before 4 p.m. It was recognised that after that time it would be almost impossible to get out onto the London Road. At the best of times, the traffic was such that to turn right was nigh impossible, and the only way was to turn left and go around the roundabout at the *Green Man* inn, the nearest available roundabout at the time.

Evill

From 1923 to 1927 Henrietta and Douglas Evill lived at Westward Ho. He was born in 1892, and in 1920 married Henrietta, who was the daughter of Sir Alexander Drake Kleinwort and brother of Sir Alexander Santiago Kleinwort,

2nd Baron. They had one son and two daughters. Douglas was educated at the Royal Naval Colleges, Osborne and Dartmouth.

He was serving in the Royal Flying Corps as a major when he won a D.S.C. in 1916 and the A.F.C. in 1919.

Evill became the Head of the Royal Air Force Delegation to Washington in 1942, and Vice Chief of the Air Staff between 1943 and 1946. He was created K.C.B. in 1943, and G.B.E. in 1946 when he became Air Chief Marshal Sir Douglas Claude Strathern Evill. He retired in 1947 and in 1953 was living at Brendon, Winchester.

FRANKS

The Franks family ran various businesses in Guildford at the beginning of the 20th century, including those of builder and coal merchant. Frank Harold Franks, the coal merchant, lived at The Gate House from 1919 to 1930. Franks Harris, contractors, were employed by Taylor and Burlingham in developments at Guildford and Cheam.

GATES

The Gates family are well known in Guildford as the family firm that sold dairy products from a small shop between the Abbot's Hospital and *The Three Pigeons* public house in the High Street, which eventually became Cow & Gate and ultimately merged with United Dairies to form Unigate.

The name Gates first appeared in connection with Abbotswood in 1915 when A.G. Taylor sold land to Ernest Gates of 'Pedwell', Guildford, on 26 February. This new house became known as The Croft.

Bramwell Gates lived at The Gate House from 1915 to 1919. This was undoubtedly one of the finest in Abbotswood. Bramwell owned several other fine houses in Guildford such as that at 24, Clandon Road, Guildford, which was designed by Peter Stoneham of Eastbourne in 1936. Whilst only having three main bedrooms and a dressing room, there were two separate maid's bedrooms, a double garage, and other facilities that are similar to the best in Abbotswood. The oak panelling is a light colour, and the ceiling embossed with roses, portcullis' and other figures. Externally, the house is part tile hung, and part half-timbered, with extensive lead lights to front and rear. Clearly no expense was spared to impress. Afterwards, Gates lived in Hillier Road.

GOODEVE

Many will remember Vernon Goodeve as the owner of a sweet shop in the Upper High Street. His mother purchased and ran a shop from 1914, the year he was born. This was at the other side of the road, near the

241 Vernon Goodeve, with the Maundy money.

Allen House. At that time his father worked in the city. Having health problems, Mr Goodeve senior ceased his daily commute and joined his wife running the shop. He died at the end of the Second World War.

When the Upper High Street was widened, the shop, along with several others, was demolished, and his mother purchased 244, High Street. This is now a restaurant that revels in the name of 'Jo Shmo's'. Allen House was later to befall the same fate, and facilitated the extension to the Grammar School. In 1962 Vernon eventually took over control of the shop from his mother, and that same year he purchased Sunnymead with his wife, Vera. The business eventually closed in 1984.

Vernon Goodeve was educated at Guildford Grammar School and served in the North African campaign, mainly in logistics, and in particular munitions. After the war he worked for Dennis Brothers, before helping his mother in the shop. Around this time, he was approached by a Captain Bowey. The captain told him that he was the sort of chap that he wanted to lay the wreath each year in memory of the 300 or so boys from the Grammar School who fell fighting for their country. Vernon readily agreed, and has been privileged to do the task for the last 60 years.

Vernon was honoured by the Queen in 2006, when he was one of the chosen Guildford residents to receive Maundy money at Guildford Cathedral.

HOPEWELL

The Hon. Mrs Hopewell arrived at Churston in 1917 with E.W. Hopewell. He died two years after they arrived but she remained in Abbotswood until 1928. She was a founder member of the Burpham Women's Institute.

Their son Alan Hopewell attended the Hereford Cathedral School before going up to Cambridge to study Classics. After attaining a commission in the Duke of Wellington's Regiment he was seriously wounded at Gallipoli and was invalided out of the army – he took up teaching and eventually became headmaster of his former school, the Hereford Cathedral School.

HUNT

From 1957 Mike and Audrey Hunt lived at Brookdale. Whilst known as Mike, his full name was Bernard Francis Hunt. Hunt, too, was invalided out of the army in 1917 and began a successful career as a produce broker with a Dutch firm in Java, eventually becoming a senior partner.

When Japan invaded Java during the Second World War, Mike escaped from the country and joined the Netherlands Indies Government in exile. Based in Australia, he was a director of public relations. During the last phases of the war, he became the Netherlands Indies Government Liaison Officer, with the headquarters of Lord Mountbatten in Ceylon. He returned to Java after the war and after resuming the same business was later invited to become the Dutch Government's Trustee for barter goods between Singapore and Indonesia. One suspects this was a type of avalising, whereby one set of goods was exchanged for another set of goods at pre-arranged prices. He retired in 1955, and later suffered from heart trouble, from which he died in 1971.

Mike was recognised for his services to the Netherlands during the war, when he was made an Officer of the Royal Order of Orange Nassau, equivalent to a British knighthood. Peter and Olivia Harwood, good friends of the Hunts, recall that Mike received a letter from Downing Street confirming that if he so wished, he could use the title 'Sir'. Whether or not he preferred Sir Bernard, or Sir Mike, we shall never know.

KITCHENER

Mr Elliott Kitchener lived with his wife, Bessie Maud at Iomhar.

His father was Phillip Elliott Kitchener, who had addresses at Little Walden Park, Essex, and Adare, Co. Limerick. Phillip was uncle to both the 1st Earl Kitchener, and his elder brother the 2nd Earl. The 1st Earl, who had no children, was The Secretary of State for War, when he was killed during the sinking of HMS *Hampshire* off the Orkneys on 5 June 1916, whilst en route to Russia.

Thus Elliott Kitchener was a first cousin of both the 1st and 2nd Earls Kitchener.

The current and 3rd Earl, Henry Herbert Kitchener, was the grandson of the 2nd Earl. His niece Emma, being the daughter of his late brother Charles, is Lady-in-Waiting to H.R.H. Princess Michael of Kent and is married to the actor Julian Fellowes. In 1998 he changed his name by deed poll to Julian Kitchener-Fellowes.

Elliott Kitchener was born in Adare, Co. Limerick, Ireland on 25 December 1865, and left Ireland when he was four years old. He was educated at Bedford, and at Christ's College, Cambridge. In 1906 Elliott married Bessie Maud MacIver. In 1892 he had a scholastic career, beginning as a master at Dulwich College and from 1895 he took the Army Class at Rugby School. He was headmaster at Greenbank School, Liverpool, and afterwards headmaster at the Golden Parsonage Preparatory School, near Boxmoor, Herts.

He retired and came to Guildford in 1922, when he purchased his Abbotswood property overlooking the Wey valley. He did examining work for the Board of Education, and London University, and took temporary mathematical work at Charterhouse. During the First World War he was a member of an Appeals Tribunal, and a section leader of special constables. Being an active churchman, he was co-editor of the 'Diocesan Gazette' in Guildford. He held various posts on Diocesan committees and was a lay preacher. He preached at Stoke church the day before he took ill in August 1929, eventually dying in October that year at the age of sixty-three. His widow continued to live in Abbotswood until 1940.

Elliot's interests had included art and music. He was a member and Honorary Secretary of the Guildford Art Society, which he co-founded.

The 1st Earl Kitchener won national fame on his second tour in the Sudan. After becoming Sirdar of the Egyptian Army he headed the victorious Anglo-Egyptian army in the Battle of Omdurman in 1898, a victory made possible by the massive rail construction programme that he had instituted in the area. Kitchener quite possibly prevented war between France and Britain when he dealt firmly, but non-violently, with the French military expedition to claim Fashoda.

The house in Abbotswood was named as Iomhar, which is a Gaelic reference to an army warrior with a bow. It also was the name of a Lochlonnach Chief who did battle in Ireland. It is believed that Elliott decided on the name to reflect the warrior qualities of his cousin, and also his own Irish links.

Manley

Dr David Michael John Picton Manley Ph.D, B.Sc (Hons), M.I.E.E., F.Inst. P., C.Dip. A.F., F.I.C.D.D.S., C.Eng. (1933-2006) was a renowned scientist. Michael Manley attended Charterhouse but left before his studies could be completed. He lived with his parents and sister Erica at Homewell. His father, as master at the school, died early. He had been a major in the First World War and had been gassed. Due to resulting financial constraints Michael continued his studies at Guildford Technical College and eventually achieved an honours degree at London University.

Michael worked for the Admiralty Research Laboratory, the Royal Aircraft Establishment and was a lecturer at Farnborough Tech and Hendon Tech. He was a scientific adviser to many large businesses and hospitals and also the Micro-seismology Department of Liverpool University. He was an expert in many aspects of nuclear, biological and chemical warfare.

Michael's main attributions included the design of the world's first blood bubble detector, an invention for measuring oil flows in pipelines which was adopted by the oil industry, and the setting up of the 'Welsh Marches Radiation Monitoring Team'. As an acoustics expert his later work included research into the noise and vibration caused by wind farms, and the adverse affect on people's health. He did not see this work come to fruition as he died in 2006.

NOBLE

The novelist Elizabeth Noble, better known in Abbotswood as Lizzie Young, has only recently left Abbotswood, and was a member of Abbotswood Women In Touch (AWIT) and the Abbotswood ladies reading club. Whilst living at Craig Cottage Lizzie wrote *The Reading Group*, which was published in 2003 and became a best seller in 2004. She later lived with her husband and children in Wonersh, near Guildford.

Lizzie was a committee member and once said that one of the best things about AWIT was that it provided an opportunity to meet women of all ages, united by the common bond of neighbourhood rather than the more usual segregation of age and stage in life. One will always wonder how many of the Abbotswood ladies, or their character traits, featured in some small way in her novels.

ONSLOW

William Hillier, 4th Earl of Onslow may be considered the first 20th-century owner in Abbotswood. He acquired Stoke Park Farm, on which the estate is built, as a descendant of Nathaniel Hillier.

William Hillier inherited the title at the age of just seventeen. He attended Eton where his Classics master described him as 'pretty well the tallest, least embarrassed, and most self-possessed young man whom I had ever had the pleasure of meeting'.

Much of his early life was spent trying to restore Clandon House to its former glory after years of neglect, and in doing so he had to sell parts of his large estate. He still found time for his sports of hunting, shooting, and was a frequent player at Guildford Golf Club.

The Earl was keen on dogs and was a founder of the Battersea Dogs' Home. He kept a pack of basset hounds and dachshunds, and it was he who promulgated the introduction of quarantine laws to eradicate rabies from the British Isles.

He became Lord-in-Waiting to the Queen in 1880, and later Under-Secretary to the Colonies, and in 1888 at the age of 34, Governor of New Zealand. Here, he made a name for himself as his enlightened attitudes greatly helped to improve relations between European settlers and the Maori. Four years later he became Under-Secretary of State for India, Privy Councillor and then President of the Board of Trade.

242   *William Hillier, 4th Earl of Onslow.*

William Hillier died in 1911 at the age of 58 and his eldest son Richard succeeded to the title, retiring from the Foreign Office to look after Clandon House and his estates.

Rickinson

William Rickinson lived at Rosedene from 1953. He was an engineer by profession. One former resident can recall that, as now, the garden was always beautifully maintained, and that it had a water feature in the centre of the front lawn. After his wife died, Mr Rickinson, a wealthy man, decided to retire to Bermuda. His son worked out there and had married a local girl. Some years later, his son called at the bungalow with a strange request. He wanted to take back to Bermuda the ashes of his mother. Unbeknown to the subsequent owners, William Rickinson had placed the urn in the water feature in the front garden, just in front of a stone bench. The request was enthusiastically allowed.

Rogers

In 1968 Bryan and Gerry Rogers moved to 2, Abbotswood Close.

The house had been built on the tennis court of Iomhar. Bryan travelled daily to London and the Head Office of the Inland Revenue, Somerset House.

Bryan was born in 1929 in Wrexham, North Wales, and was educated at Grove Park and University College, London where he graduated in the Classics. In 1953 he joined the Inland Revenue as an Inspector of Taxes with a first posting to Kendal. In 1955 he married Gerry. On completion of his exams he was transferred to Aberdeen in 1956, and in 1958, to Sheffield. In 1976 he became a Senior Principal Inspector. Promotion to Under Secretary and Director of Operations followed in 1978 and in 1981 he became Deputy Secretary and Director General of the Board of the Inland Revenue. In 1983 Bryan became a member of the Council of University College, and in 1984 was made a Companion of the Order of the Bath.

For Bryan, it was a great privilege to conduct H.R.H. Prince Charles on a tour of Somerset House one day. Bryan's daughter Frances, who was a medical student in London, came to join the crowd which had congregated in the Strand. She got a place right outside Somerset House by the royal car, and in the crush was pushed onto the rear door of the car, just as the Prince, escorted by Bryan, arrived to go home.

Prince Charles smiled at her and asked 'Who are you?', 'Mr Roger's daughter', she replied. H.R.H. retorted 'Who is Mr Rogers?'

Great family joke, retold many times.

Retirement came in 1989, presenting Bryan with more time for his love of music. He not only sang, but was deputy organist of Guildford Methodist Church. As a great thrill, Bryan was once allowed to play the organ of Westminster Abbey.

Bryan was Chairman of Abbotswood Residents Association (North Spur), until his death in 2006.

243 *Brian Rogers, with H.R.H. The Prince of Wales, and Frances.*

Simpson

Between 1972 and 1999 Gladys and Harry Simpson lived at The Corner House. Harry, a Commander of the British Empire, died in 1988.

Harry was Chairman of Abbotswood Residents Association. He suffered a heart attack a few days before he and Gladys were to celebrate their diamond wedding. The festivities were called off and he died shortly afterwards following a massive stroke.

John Major, then Foreign Secretary, was to have provided the address at the wedding celebration. The connection was that Harry, a mandarin in the Greater London Council, was very much the mentor of John Major, and indeed there was a family connection in that Gladys was the godmother of the daughter of John and Norma Major. After his death, the Harry Simpson Memorial Library was formed and Gladys was the guest of honour at its opening. She was very proud of the event and displayed a myriad of photographs in her living room, showing her with the hierarchy of the British cabinet of the time, including Lord Howe, Kenneth Clark, and Lord Hurd. When commenting on the opening of the library, Penny Junor, the columnist, was asking just who this diminutive, yet clearly influential female, was!

The story goes that after Margaret Thatcher stepped down from office, and the winner of the contest for her successor had been announced as John Major, the first telephone call that Norma Major made was to Gladys, with the words, 'Harry would have been so proud of John.'

Sir John Major had known both Harry and Gladys very well since 1968, when Harry was Director of Housing at Lambeth Borough Council. When asked, Sir John commented that 'Harry and Gladys were not only two of the nicest people that I have ever met but Harry was the most far-sighted and efficient Government official that I ever had the pleasure of working with. He was a visionary in housing matters and I learned a great deal under his tutelage.' A compliment indeed.

STEWART

John and Geraldine Stewart lived at Ederline.

In 1944, at the age of 17, John tried to join the Grenadiers, and succeeded for just two weeks until his blindness in one eye, caused by a childhood illness, was discovered. Desperate to 'join up', he was accepted into the R.N.V.R. and rose to Midshipman. He was wounded twice. The first time was when, as beach commander for a landing in the Far East, he was up a tree attaching a signal flag when a Japanese sniper shot at him. He fell from the tree and, whilst the bullet missed, the landing was severe. On the second occasion, he was on the bow of his ship leaving harbour, when a limpet mine attached to the bow went off. It raised the bow out of the water, and John with it, damaging both legs. Had he been in the American forces he would have received a couple of purple hearts for his pains.

After the war, John returned to education, gaining a first at University College, Cardiff, and went on to do post-graduate work at St Catherine's College, Cambridge. He joined the Colonial Geological Survey Service, Somaliland Protectorate, and rose to become Chief Geologist. With his first posting he was told what his area was, to purchase a dozen camels, hire numerous porters, take guns with ammunition for food and protection, and return in six months. What an adventure. He became Senior Liaison Officer, Somaliland-Ethiopian Ogaden, where he commanded a gendarmerie of some six hundred men, raised to protect the nomads from Ethiopian guerrillas.

He met Geraldine at that time, but at base rather than in the desert! They married in 1960. John had a number of postings, including District Commissioner, Northern Rhodesia. He retired from the Colonial Service in 1966, and returned to the UK for a course at Ashridge Management College. John and Geraldine purchased 10, Abbotswood that year for just £10,000, and stayed there until 1993.

After two years in the Home Office, John Anthony Benedict Stewart C.M.G., O.B.E., joined the Diplomatic Service, which took him away from Abbotswood with Geraldine for long periods of time. He was Head of Chancery and Acting High Commissioner in Barbados, and then in Uganda, when Idi Amin gave Asians 90 days to leave the country. John successfully arranged the evacuation of some 17,000 Asians. A lot of his time was spent looking after the ex-pat community and British business interests during the period of turmoil. He was awarded the O.B.E. at the end of the posting. Later, he spent a year at the Royal College for Defence Studies in London.

244 *John and Geraldine Stewart, at a St Andrews Ball, Colombo 1986.*

In 1974, John was made the first British Ambassador in Hanoi, North Vietnam. This appointment covered the fall of Saigon, and for a time he was responsible for the whole of Vietnam. In 1978 he became Ambassador in Laos, and in 1980 he was promoted to Minister, and became H.M. Ambassador to Mozambique. Finally, he was British High Commissioner in Sri Lanka. He was pleased to entertain Margaret and Dennis Thatcher at the opening of the Victoria Dam. For his further service he was awarded Companion of St Michael and St George.

In Abbotswood John and Geraldine were much respected, and well known for their lavish Christmas gatherings for the neighbours. John was fluent in six foreign languages, mainly Portuguese and French, but also Somali, Thai, Urdu and Swahili. Both he and Geraldine were keen fly fishermen, and would bring home trout for friends from Lord Onslow's lake at Clandon.

Geraldine and John moved for final retirement to the countryside at East Grimstead in Wiltshire, where John died on 12 September 1995 at the age of sixty-eight.

Author's Recollection: Geraldine and John were good friends of ours. John took over from me as Chairman of the Residents Association when I became involved with the Archways Appeal. One of my everlasting memories concerned a dinner party at Hillcrest. We were entertaining, along with the Stewarts, friends from Rhodesia, Iraq, and South Africa. The conversation was flowing very well, in fact too well, and a delay in serving the vegetables meant that they were a touch overdone. John, spotting Georgina's dilemma, let his monocle drop and lent over to say that they were the best vegetables he had tasted for many a while. A true diplomat indeed. To this day, should the vegetables be over cooked, which is a rarity in Georgina's kitchen, they are referred to as 'the Ambassador's vegetables'.

Thompson

Herbert Thompson J.P., and Mrs Clara Thompson lived at Aoetearoa from 1926 to 1952. Their granddaughter, Mrs Shirley Hewett, recalls her visits to see them:

> My Grandparents were Herbert and Clara Thompson, of Milestones, Abbotswood, who died both well into their nineties, just after the Second World War. They had spent most of their lives in Cumberland. Grandpa was manager on the Midland Bank in Workington, but spent most of his time growing carnations in his greenhouse and showing caged birds! They moved to Guildford in retirement, I suppose in the 1920s.
>
> During the 1930s they had a fire at the house. This had been started by a maid airing clothes in front of the fire. It was partly rebuilt after this. My two spinster aunts continued to live there for some time but eventually moved to Lansdown. My aunt kept chickens at the bottom of the garden during World War Two, and I remember an air raid once when staying there.
>
> I was at boarding school in those days and my mother did not visit often as she was so far away.
>
> I remember that there was a rather eccentric Lord living next door. I just remember Abbotswood as a nice leafy suburb, quiet and in easy reach of the bus to Guildford where we enjoyed shopping – so different from home in the depths of the Cumberland countryside.

These early photographs (facing page) show the front of the house, with a wicker gate. To the fore is Mrs Clara Thompson, and on the left, her daughter Joyce, who was a member of the A.T.S in Guildford during the Second World War. She had a very good voice, and joined ENSA, travelling to Egypt to entertain the troops. Her sister, Katherine, is in the background. Mr Thompson, who probably took the photographs, was a Justice of the Peace.

Thorp

Thorps bookshop in the former Constitutional Hall, close to the statue of George Abbot in the High Street, was once a much loved as a place to go for a browse through books new and old. From 1955 to 1969 Thomas Colebrook Thorp, the owner, lived at Eaglehurst.

Trickett

Jean and John Trickett came to live at 1, Westward Ho in 1971 where Jean still lives.

John was educated at Bradfield College, and served as a 2nd Lieutenant with the Royal Artillery. He and Jean met while they both worked in the editorial department at the *Sheffield Telegraph* and *Star*. John later became the sports editor for the *Manchester Evening News*.

He moved to Fleet Street in 1964 and became the sports editor for the *Daily Mail*, and later the racing editor for the *Daily Herald*, which became

The Sun. John wrote a weekly column for the *Sunday Mirror*, and finally rejoined *The Sun* as the horse racing columnist and tipster 'Trick Tips', before retiring in 1988.

John died in 1992, but before that completed his book *World Horse Racing.*

245 *The Thompson ladies, outside Aoetearoa and at the archways.*

VINEALL

Sir Anthony and Lady Vineall currently reside at Waysend.

Having held various senior positions at Unilever where he worked for 37 years, Tony's retirement was followed with involvements in a number of aspects of public sector remuneration and career structures involving doctors, dentists and the armed forces. Latterly Tony was Chair of the School Teachers Pay Review Body. He was also Chair of the Tavistock and Portman NHS Trust, and is currently the Vice-Chair of Governors of the Guildford Royal Grammar School.

In 2002 Tony was knighted as Sir Anthony Vineall.

VOKES

The name Vokes is well known in Guildford for the factory in Henley Park, Normandy. The founder was Cecil 'Gordon' Vokes, of Vokes Filter fame. His then former wife, Mrs Edith 'Edair' Vokes, and his only son Gordon Heatherton Vokes (Tony), moved to The Lair in July 1952 where Tony still resides. In 1972 Edair died.

Vokes supplied filters of all sorts for most types of transport; aircraft and ships, tanks and other vehicles. It was maintained that he did a great deal to help the allies win in North Africa during the Second World War when he supplied air, oil and fuel filters for aircraft, tanks and other military vehicles.

246   *Tony Vokes, as shown in an article from the Sunday Times in 1971.*

He was called on to produce filters for the 50 lend-lease destroyers from the United States as soon as they arrived in the U.K.

Of perhaps a lesser note, but of great significance to the author, is the fact that Gordon was a lifelong admirer of Lagonda cars. He proposed the first Lagonda Car Club in 1932, and became the first Club Secretary. He ran a stable of over six Lagondas, on which he tried and tested his many filters. To the chagrin of his salesmen, he insisted that they used these then old cars when travelling around the country. Some of the original prototype filters for oil, petrol and air remain with these very cars today and are much prized by their owners.

247   *The last of the Vokes Lagondas; a 1935, 3.5 litre tourer, taken in 1952.*

Fourteen

Developments: 1945 Onwards

The number of houses on the estate has not remained constant. It has been explained that the first land to be developed was that most suitable for the prestigious houses of the 1910s and 1920s. These utilised the good land on the relatively flat plateau, overlooking the valley of the River Wey. This left the marshy fields in the river flood plain and the orchards and shrub on the slopes rising from the river bed to the plateau. After the Second World War there followed a surge in demand for additional cheaper accommodation. Inevitably, not only local builders, but the residents of some of the older houses looked for profit.

The Widow's Plot

The infilling between houses was initially facilitated by the famed widow's plots. Most houses were built on a plot of no less that half an acre. In many cases the house was built to the side of the plot; some became thus when the owner purchased a second plot next door. Either way, this left a large garden to the side of the house, which often became an orchard.

It is thought that the purpose was to give the owner the option of building a further property in the garden. Some say that it could be used to provide a pension for the widow. She could down-size by building a smaller house, moving in and selling the former family home. Walking around the estate, one will see that frequently the older houses alternate with newer ones.

New Housing Developments

There have been three major inroads for Abbotswood.

The first major building work was that of Abbotswood Close, which took place at the northern end of Abbotswood, using the gardens of Nos. 32-3 in the late 1960s, and that of No. 34 in the seventies. The 11 houses were built to a more modest budget and some were constructed on the hillside. The development did not maintain the character of the old Abbotswood at a time when planners seemed to worry little about the environs affected by such works.

A second area was off the western spur. Parts of the gardens of 13-17 Abbotswood were sold off and the Westward Ho road was constructed. Initially, in 1965 permission was given for Nos. 1-3 Westward Ho which were built from 1967 in the garden of the house of that name. Over the years, the council tried to resist over-development by turning down applications for seven dwellings to the rears of 14-15, Abbotswood in August 1967 and even a planning application for 26 houses which was put before the council in 1975 by W.J. Burrill Ltd and Larchpine.

Nevertheless, development was allowed and 10 houses were initially constructed and, later, more in the garden of West Hill House by Mr Burrill. Westward Ho was again extended and further developed from 1984, this time by Bovis Homes, when another nine houses were constructed in low fields partly belonging to 13, Abbotswood. The houses were larger, having up to five bedrooms and three garages. Some were built on the hillside with the resulting additional building costs. There are now 29 houses in Westward Ho.

Thirdly, 11, Abbotswood, a 1950s building on the drive to Ederline, was pulled down in the early 1990s for the erection of four further properties.

County Hall

Although Guildford is regarded as the county town of Surrey, and the Assizes were generally held at the Guildhall in the High Street, the Surrey County Hall had been established in Kingston Upon Thames since 1889. The assizes were then held alternately at Guildford and Kingston but, due mainly to inadequate facilities, the Surrey sessions of the Assizes were held only in Kingston from 1930 onwards.

In the late 1960s until the mid-1970s there was every intention that the County Hall at Kingston, which had become situated outside the county boundary due to boundary changes, should be moved back to Guildford at a site on Stoke Park, where the Spectrum Sports Centre now stands. For a number of reasons, including strong local opposition, this was not proceeded with. The recently aborted attempt to transfer the County Hall to Woking has no doubt provoked memories.

How different the Abbotswood area would have been today, had County Hall been in place of the Spectrum. One can only imagine.

The Spectrum Sports Centre

In the late 1980s it was proposed that a sports centre should be built on the open land and allotments on the higher ground to the north of Parkway. Protest groups from all over Guildford fought against this on the basis that it would spoil their beautiful Stoke Park. At a protest meeting in the church hall at Christchurch, one of those speaking from the floor was Miss Phyllis Powell, a teacher who had retired in 1979 and lived in Burpham. She had been Deputy Head at George Abbott School, later teaching English at the Grammar School. She gallantly stood up to speak against the building, challenging the comment that it was 'an unused piece of land and should be built on'. She explained very eloquently that she and many others had used the land for years as somewhere to walk and enjoy the air. She made the poignant remark that she used its beauty each time she went passed on the way to Guildford. Sadly, shortly after she had sat down, she collapsed and died later in hospital.

The residents of Abbotswood expressed concerns about the noise from the cars and the running tracks, as well as the lights from the stadium and the track. On one occasion a developer, who was putting forward his plans as a short-listed contender, received an adverse comment that standing on the hill, with bright lights highlighting the building, it was like a beacon visible for miles. He commented that if that is not what people wanted, they could turn off the lights! Initially, it was planned to have the main building abutting Thorneycrofts, but at the suggestion of the residents it was moved to a central location.

The Spectrum was opened in 1993. Most of the initial fears have been well managed, and after several years even the most ardent objector has to admit that as a sports centre it has become a great success and is enjoyed by tens of thousands of Guildfordians each year. This, after all, is one of the purposes for which the Council purchased Stoke Park in the 1920s.

The noise from the car park was initially a concern but is largely unfounded. However, at one point the noise from starter guns on the athletics track became annoying. A full investigation was carried out at the request of the Residents Association. Peter Gunn, then Manager of Spectrum, assured residents that the weapons in use were standard .22 issue, and were not linked to the amplification systems.

A few weeks later, an embarrassed Mr Gunn reverted, commenting that, although the report had generally been correct, occasionally visiting officials bring their own starting guns. The previous weekend he had been at the stadium, and was alarmed not just at the noise of the starter's gun, but the sight of the weapon, which looked like a colt .45 from a Wild West movie. He had found the culprit and the source of annoyance. Problem solved.

The Mormon Church at Woodways
(The Hurst, 46)

To date, none of the Burlingham houses in Abbotswood has been totally lost to developers. Long may that continue. However, from 1996 to 1998 it was a 'close run thing'.

The Hurst at the Southern entrance had been lived in by Colonel and Mrs Coupland for many years. The Colonel died in the 1980s, leaving Joy. She had lived in the house with her parents and always said that 'I will only leave this house when they carry me out in a box'. This they sadly did in 1994 after Joy passed away. In December 1995 the house was sold through Clark Gammon, and the contents were auctioned off.

At that time the Church of Jesus Christ of Latter-Day Saints was looking for a plot to erect a church. They eyed The Hurst to the chagrin of local residents, providing the real possibility that the largest and most imposing house in Abbotswood would fall to the bulldozer.

The first thing residents did was to have a protection order placed on the trees by Guildford Borough Council and enlist the help of the local councillors. This started alarm bells ringing, and the church accepted that to pull the house down might be a problem. After much debate the new owners considered altering the house, but found that, whilst it might appease the neighbours, it would not suit their own requirements.

The Mormon leaders called a public meeting, which turned out to be less than good tempered, particularly when they displayed a drawing of the intended building which was more like a Tesco superstore than a church. Through a committee of residents, and with a great deal of the investigative work being undertaken by Carol Stevens of Hestercombe, English Heritage took an interest and listed the building for its high architectural qualities reflecting the later style of the Arts and Crafts Movement in Surrey.

The Hurst was subsequently bought from the Mormon Church by a local builder, trading as Borme Homes Limited, who carried out a superb restoration.

Residents Associations

The local authority did not adopt the entire road in Abbotswood, creating a need for house owners to club together to attend to road repairs and other issues. To this end there are three associations, each having a quite separate and distinct remit. Abbotswood Residents Association Limited covers 52 properties at the western end, including Westward Ho; the Abbotswood Residents Association (north spur) with 25 properties covers the north end including Abbotswood Close, and Abbotswood Residents Association (central crescent), covers the adopted road.

The quite different remits make it quite impossible to merge each association. For example, Abbotswood Residents Association Limited obtained a possessory title to the road it controls on 20 October 2004 and its members legally own the road through shareholdings. Residents in the private roads all contribute towards maintenance, repair and resurfacing of the roads and pavements.

Both the private road associations have been around since the 1960s when not only was there a need to co-ordinate road repairs, but a collective voice was required to challenge the developers wishing to extend the estate. Later on they were partly successful in challenging projects outside the estate such as realignment of the A3 trunk road and the Spectrum, and the building of Weylea Farm estate.

In 2005 the association covering the central crescent was formed. Unencumbered by the need to collect funds to maintain the road, this association was founded as a campaigning vehicle to address external threats to the quality of life of its residents, and to safeguard the character of the area, which includes ensuring that those organisations responsible for infrastructure do a satisfactory job.

Furthermore, recent threats from developers together with the need to be proactive in dealing with the Borough and County Councils have made it clear that a communal approach covering all of Abbotswood was now required. Additionally, there was a perceived need for a body to enable residents to express views on issues affecting Guildford as a whole, including, but not restricted to, environmental matters, traffic and noise reduction, and government planning guidelines.

All three residents associations are well supported by their respective members.

Abbotswood Women in Touch (AWIT)

The idea for this organisation was conceived in the autumn of 1997 when three ladies from Abbotswood, who had recently arrived, had coffee together. They realised that in an era when the car had become king, and all the adults in the family ventured even to the local shops by car, neighbours were seldom seen other than through a windscreen. This was becoming a situation where neighbour rarely spoke to neighbour and it was difficult to get to know someone from another part of Abbotswood. They felt certain that the estate must contain many interesting women, living behind high hedges, who would enjoy meeting each other on a partly cultural basis.

These three ladies, Sian Gregory-Smith, Sue Hibbert and Ros Hampson, formed a ladies' group, which would meet twice-monthly, in the evening and during the day, in each other's homes. The purpose would be chiefly to create a social gathering and to enable the members to get to know each other, and, at the same time, to expand their interests. Thus the meetings had a different topic each time, including visiting speakers, an annual tennis morning in the garden at Hillcrest, and visits to the Spectrum Leisure Centre for bowling. Trips to the local theatre and cinema were arranged and a book reading group was started.

Men were not allowed to these meetings. However, in order to help partners to feel part of the community, too, annual summer and Christmas parties were instituted which have proved to be most popular.

AWIT continues to thrive and, at the start of its 11th year, it is run by a committee of four, including two of the original founders. The membership is reasonably constant at around forty. People have said that the organisation makes Abbotswood feel like a village, where those that have lived there for a while and those that are newcomers have the opportunity to easily to get to know each other.

248 *Just a make-over, Sir?*

Fifteen

What Future for Abbotswood?

Somehow, despite the growth of the estate, Abbotswood has not lost its character and remains a pleasant area where the professionals of Guildford want to live. It is true that the number of houses has more than doubled, but still the original houses remain, be they mostly in smaller gardens. Still one can wander around the estate and imagine what it was like 70 years ago.

Some may fear that it is no longer 'out of town', and that the town now envelops the estate. This is not so. The amount of traffic on the London Road is probably not much more than it was in the late 1950s, and certainly a great deal less than it was in 1965. Yes, there is an element of noise from the A3, but that should be greatly reduced by the promised new road surface. Where in Surrey do you not get noise, from the town, from roads, or from aeroplanes?

We still have our 'green lung' at Stoke Park and continue to defend this open space. In 2005 a local entrepreneur attempted to obtain planning permission for an 8,000-spectator football stadium, surrounded by an eight-foot wall. This was rejected by the Guildford Borough Council Planning Committee, and also on appeal. Doubtless, this will not be the last attempt to add further concrete to the historic parkland. We must be thankful that, apart from the Spectrum stadium, the Guildford Technical College and the associated parking with both, and the Parkway by-pass, the park remains much as it was when planted over 200 years ago. Long may this be the case.

The biggest problem that could come for Abbotswood itself, would be if local residents bow to the temptation of avarice, and sell their houses collectively for destruction and thence the building of a greater number of houses or, worse still, apartments. Only then would the ambience of Abbotswood be destroyed forever. We must rely on English Heritage and our local authority to prevent such an occurrence. After all, Abbotswood, the only estate containing two listed properties, is unique to Guildford, and Guildford is unique to Surrey. Who dares despoil such a treasure?

Perhaps this book will help to preserve Abbotswood as we know it?

Appendix One

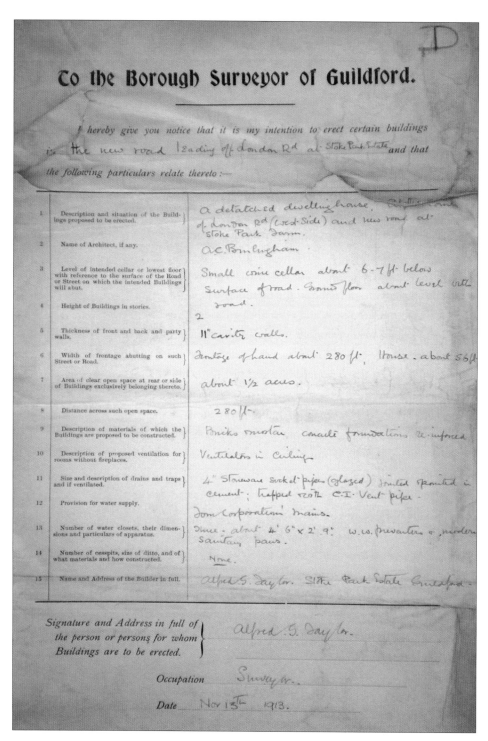

249 *Planning application.*

Appendix Two

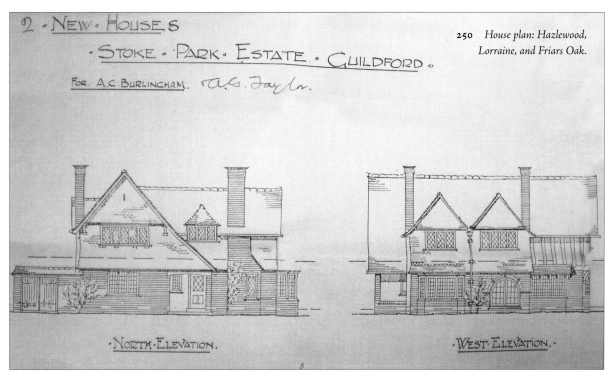

250 *House plan: Hazlewood, Lorraine, and Friars Oak.*

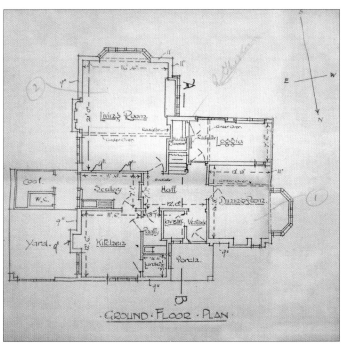

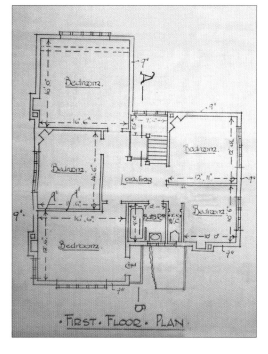

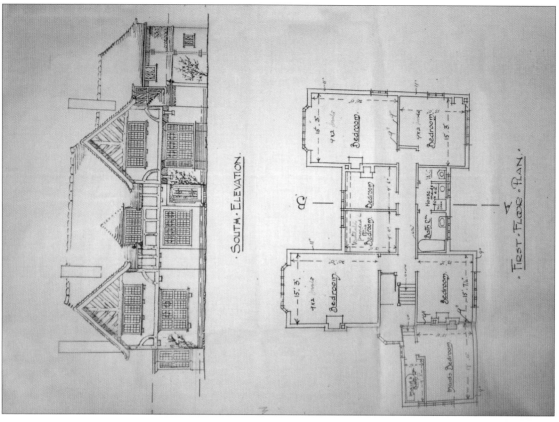

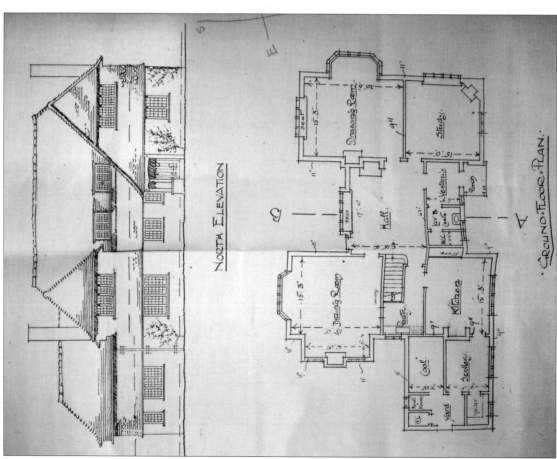

251   *House plan: The Gate House.*

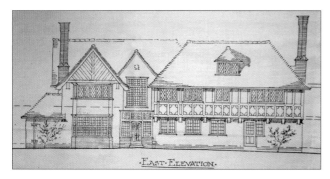

·EAST·ELEVATION·

WEST·ELEVATION·

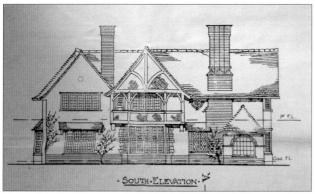

·SOUTH·ELEVATION·A·

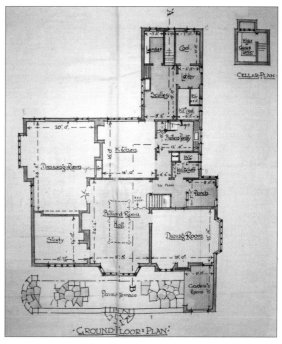

·GROUND·FLOOR·PLAN·

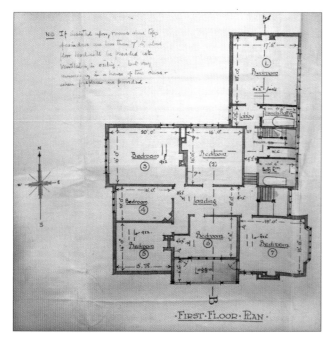

·FIRST·FLOOR·PLAN·

A.Claude.Burlingham ARIBA

Oct 1913. Archt

252 *House plan: The Hurst.*

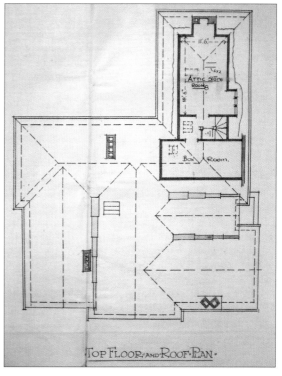

TOP·FLOOR·and·ROOF·PLAN·

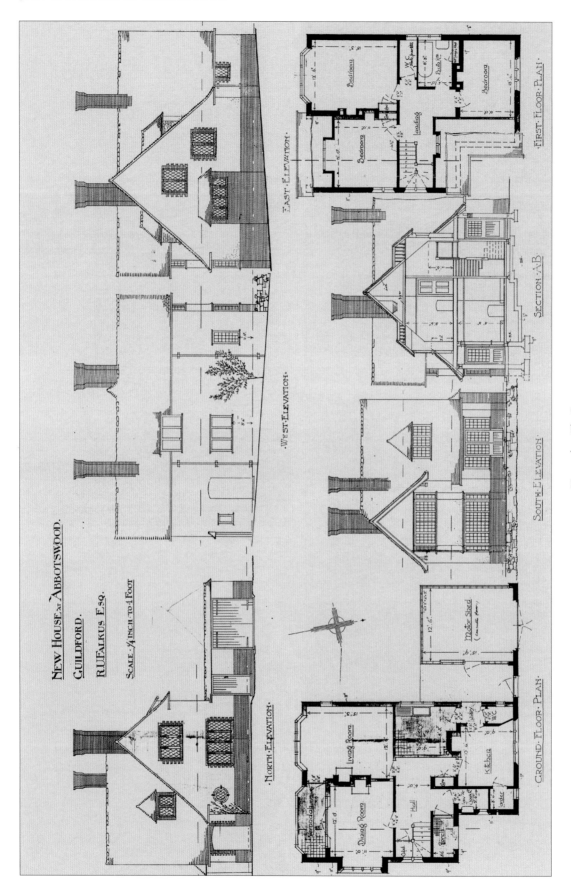

253 *House plan: The Cottage.*

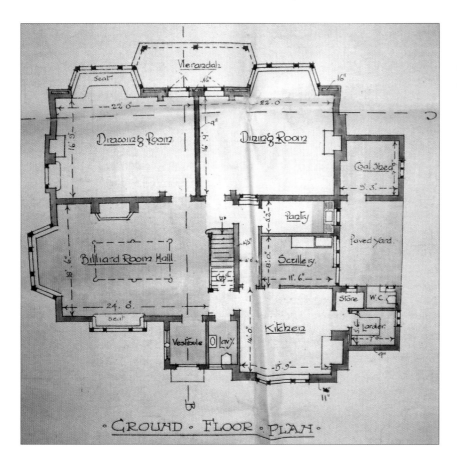

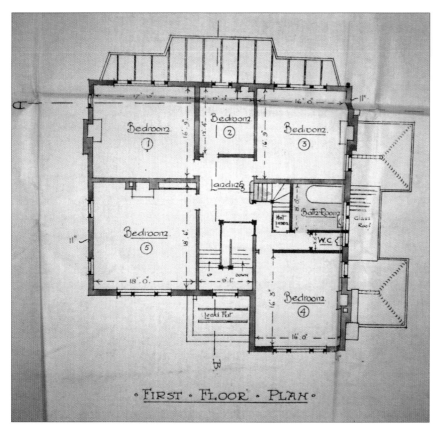

254 *House plan: Hestercombe and Upmeads.*

255   *House plan: Homewell,*
Brookdale, Red Cottage, Oakdene
and Crossways.

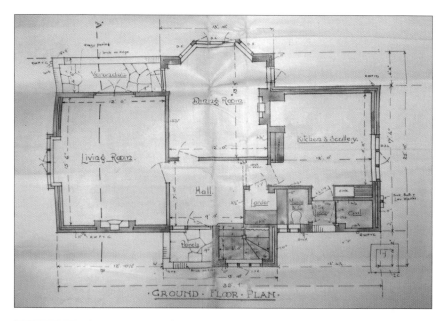

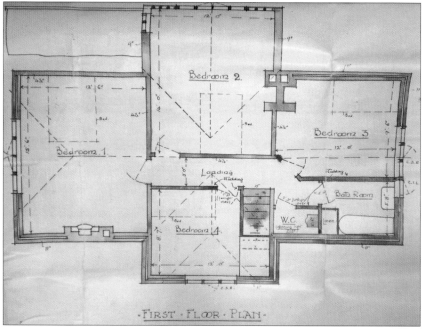

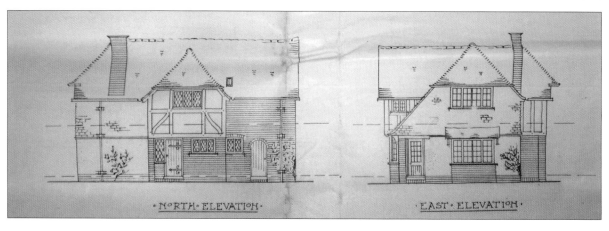

Appendix Three

Luss Cottage—
   Dalton, Chas. Fitz-gerald, esq., B.A.
Delaford—
   Berryman, Mrs.
Redbraes Nursing Home—
   Allard, Miss
Waterden Crescent—
   1 *Kirkton—*
      Johnston, J. L. esq
   2 Patrick, Mr. E. C.
   3 Corrie, Miss and Miss C. G.
   4 Taylor, Mrs. D.
   5 Smalley, Mrs.
Field View—
   Strudwick, Miss
   here is Waterden road
The Cottage—
   Horstfield, Mr.
Aldersey Place—
   1 Jeffries, H. H. esq. M.R.C.V.S. (Lond.)
   2 Lacy, Maurice H. esq.
   3 Upton, A. R. esq.
   4 Squires, A. L. J. esq.
   here is Clandon road
*Cross Lanes—*Smallpeice, F. F. esq. J.P.
   here is Cross lanes
The Glebe House—
   Edge, Mrs.
   Edge, Cyril T. esq., M.A., A.C.B.
Abersky—
   Howden, R. A. esq.
*Rostrevor—*Hill, W.
Glenthorpe—
   Davidson, A. esq.
   here is Ennismore avenue
Hereward—
   Streatfeild, C. E. esq.
St. Margaret's—
   Macleod, The Hon. Mr. Justice N. C.
*Newlands—*Grimshaw, Mrs. O. Donald
Eversleigh—
   Campbell, N., esq.
*Elmdon—*Willmott, H. esq.
   here is Avonmore avenue
St. Mildreds—
   Colvile, Lt.-Gen. Sir Fiennes Middleton K.C.B.
   *Stables—*Puttock, W.

Abbotswood.
The Gate House—
   Gates, Bramwell, esq.
Hazlewood—
   Jacobs, G. J. esq.

The Croft—
   Gates, E. R. esq.
Westwood Cottage—
   Hopewell, the Hon. Mrs.
Florence Lodge—
   Morse, H. esq.
Ths End House—
   Jacobs, C L. esq.
Littlefield—
   Burningham, A. esq.
The Hurst—
   Oldham, Comdr. R.N.
Hestercombe—.........
Milestones—
   Colthurst, Mrs.
Friars Oak—
   Morgan, C. esq.
*Upmeads—*Johnson, Miss
Sunnymead—
   Lucy, Reginald H., esq.
Stoke Park (east entrance)
*East Lodge—*Wheeler, J. J.
Avington—
   Trench, W. P. esq.
*Montana—*Willis, Mrs.
Greylands—
   Dashper, Mrs. C. G.
High School for Girls—
   Head Mistress, Miss Simmons, B.A.—Hon. Sec. P.T. Fairbrother, esq. M.A.
   Caretaker—Guy, Miss
CAB STAND & SHELTER
   here is York road
Trevor — Graham - Jones, John L. esq. B.A. M.B. B.C. (Cantab) M.R.C.S., L.R.C.P. (Lon.)
Drs. H. Branson Butler and J. L. Graham-Jones
Stringhams — Godwin-Austen, the Misses
Rathcoole—
   Simpson, Mrs.
North Dene—.........
Belhaven—
   Symes, Mrs. Colmer
Dene Lodge—
   Pierce, Dr. R. W. C. M.D., B.SC., M.R.C.S. L.R.C.P. (Lond)
   here is Dene road
*Stoke Lodge—*Levick, P. esq. M.B., B.C., B.A.
   Drs. Gabb and Levick
The Limes—
   Trained Nurses Home Supt.—Whyte, Miss
The Firs—
   Butler, T. M. esq. M.R.C.S., L.S.A.

LUDLOW ROAD

Genyn road

1 Looker, E. R.
3 Hoare, H.
5 Figgins, A.
7 Larby, J.
9 Taylor, F. W.
11 Underwood, C. J.
13 Huntingford, W.
15 Digweed, W.
17 Barter, T.
19 Toefield, —
21 Walter, C.
23 Haydon, W.
25 Stubington, F.
27 Moon, G.
29 Matthews, J.
31 Darnell, A.
33 Goodeve, W. J.
35 Hilton, W. H.
37 Edmunds, G.
39 Heney, Mrs.
41 Dunn, D.
43 Sims, F. G.
45 Bishop, H.
47 Dye, R.
49 Gyatt, J.
51 Martin, R.
53 Kett, —
55 Piggott, —
57 Sibley, J. A. T.
59 Goddard, H. G.
61 Spooner, H.
63 Mullens, Mrs.
65 Giles, A.
67 Burrow, W.
69 Cole, Miss
72 Kirkman, J.
70 Dance, A. G.
68 Hale, R. M.
66 Bigmore, F.
64 Jeanes, T.
62 Parsonson, H. G.
60 Carpenter, G.
58 Penfold, C.
56 Perkins, H.
54 Gardinor. F. T.
52 Crawford, H. B.
50 Cooper, B. G.
48 Matthews, Mrs.
46 Russell, A.
44 Bristow, E. A.
42 Merritt, H.
40 Cobbett, A.
38 Bier, J.
36 Johnson, Mrs.
34 Ballam, G.
32 } Boxall, R. Confectioner
30 }
28 Cole, Mrs.
26 Lee, L.

256 Guildford Street Directories, *1917. Abbotswood is highlighted.*

Guildford Street Directory.

ABBOT ROAD

From Warwick's Bench.

Highcliffe—Hooke F. J.
Ridgmount—Tyler J. F.
Withnoe—Palmer, Miss
Highlands—Fenn H. E.
The Gap—Manton The Misses
Valparaiso—Quittenton M.
Bella Vista—Mills A. J.
Broc Holt—Brooke Rev. T. L. M.A.
Quarry Edge—Senior Mrs.
Four Winds—Hawkins Mrs. E. R.
Chalk Bank—Gill R. H.
Benchway—Williamson W.

ABBOTS CLOSE

(Onslow Village)

From Manor Way

Brookdell—Waddell S.
Uplands—Russell Rev. G. H.
Killimani—Tilley E. A.
Haldon—Hills E. K.

ABBOTSWOOD

Gate House—Thorpe W. B.
Hazlewood—Gammon W. A.
Orchard Neville—Neville Rev. W. M.A.
Westwood Cottage—Hopewell Hon. Mrs.
Abbot's Lodge—Langtree Mrs. O.
Milestones—Thompson H., J.P.
Homewell—Bryant R. H.
Abbot's Cottage—Saunders C. L.
Hawksheid—Ross G. F.
Westward Ho!—Hunt Maj. A. F. D.S.O.
Wykeham Lodge—Crosby A. P.
The Odd House—Webb —
West Hill—Chambers A.
Penn Kenna—Maligny C. E.
Westcott—Burke J. W.
South Stoke—Murphy W. L.
Hillcrest—Hughes Major H.
Long Hayes—Woodward G. E.
Postland—Furnass J. E.
Albury—Leighton W. T.
Aysgarth—Touzel J. S. P.
St. Valery—Curtis E. H.
Hutton Ambo—Stainforth Major W. R.

Tyrol Lodge—Horstmann, Mrs. F.
Brookdale—Bethell Col A. B. C.M.G.
D.S.O.
Erles Dene—Alder R. L.
Eaglehurst—Hobbs B.
Iomhar—Kitchener Mrs
The Hazard—Finnimore B. K.
Waysend—Billinghurst Dr.
Littledene—Savage Major F. R.
Birch Tree Cottage—Gotelee S. T.
The Red Cottage—Butler Mrs A. S.
The Orchard—Manley W. B.
Abbotsmead—Gross Mrs
Holybourne—Complin Mrs. M. H.
Friars Oak—Archer J. H.
Abbots Trace—Wright Miss.
Rosedene—Medwin Mrs Florence
Oakdene—Tyler W. C. H.
Crossways—Peebles P.
Ardenholm—Clavering Miss
Woodways—Bullock H. S. M.A.

ACACIA ROAD

From Recreation Road

1 Mullard G.
2 Peirson Mrs
3 Woollard A. E.
4 Ward D.
5 Stephens C.
6 Bennett J.
7 Balchin W.
8 Tinham F.
9 Barnes L.
10 Burdett A. J. W.
11 Thorne W. H.
12 Cooper J.
13 Stevens E. A.
14 Pearce T.
15 Smith Mrs
16 Blake A. A.
17 Englefield H.
18 Deane H.
19 Pullen A. T.
20 Sharp G.
21 Greenfield F.
22 Thurgood, A. E.
23 Ponner Mrs
24 Stilwell E.
25 Guildford and District Window
Cleaning Co.—G. Hart

257 Guildford Street Directories, 1931 and 1933 (p.315-16). Abbotswood is highlighted.

THE
GUILDFORD
STREET DIRECTORY

EXPLANATION.

To account for missing Numbers in Streets, it may be understood that either the house was empty at the time the revision was made, or let in weekly tenements, or that the information was refused.

Early closing day, Wednesday.

ABBOT ROAD, from The Great Quarry to Warwick's Bench rd.

Fenn Harold Edwin (Highlands)
Hooke Fras. J. (Highcliffe)
Tyler Jas. F. (Ridgmount)
Williamson Wm. (Benchway)
Gill Hy. Raymond (Chalk Bank)
Hawkins Mrs. E. R. (Four Winds)
Palmer Miss (Withnoe)
Quittenton Maurice, sen. (Valparaiso)
Mills Arth. J. (Bella Vista)
Brooke Rev. Thos. Lionel M.A. (Broc Holt)
Shaw Miss (Quarry Edge)
Senior Mrs. (Quarry Edge)

ABBOT'S CLOSE (Onslow Village), from Manor way.

Tilley Edwin Arth. (Kilimani)
Waddell Jas. S. (Brookdell)
Hills Edwd. K. (Haldon)
Russell Rev. Geo. Herbt. (priest in charge, All Saints' church, Curling Vale) (Uplands)

ABBOTSWOOD, from London rd.

Archer John Harold (Friar's Oak)
Bethell Col. Alfd. Bryan C.M.G., D.S.O., D.L. (Brookdale)
Bryant Robert Henry (Homewell)

Bullock H. Somerset M.A. (Woodways)
Burke John William (Westcott)
Saunders Chas. Lewis (Abbot's cott)
Butler Mrs. A. S. (Red cottage)
Complin Mrs. (Holybourne)
Crosby Andrew Percvl. (Wykeham lodge)
Curtis Edwd. H. (St. Valery)
Gammon Wm. A. (Hazelwood)
MalignyChas. (Penkenna)
Manley William Bernard, barrister-at-law(The Orchard). Telephone, Guildford 1544
Thorpe Wilfred B. (Gate ho)
Furnass John Edwin (Postland)
Gotelee Sydney T. (Birch Tree cott)
Hopewell Hon. Mrs. (Westwood cot)
Horstmann Mrs. (Tyrol lodge)
Hunt Maj. Arth. Fredk. D.S.O. (Westward Ho!)
Langtree Mrs. O. (Abbot's lodge)
Leighton William Todd (Albury)
Medwin Mrs. Florence (Rosedene)
Murphy Wm. E. (South Stoke)
Neville Rev. Wm. M.A. (Orchard Neville)
Peebles Philip (Crossways)
Ross Geo. Fullerton (Hawksheid)
Stainforth Maj. W.R (Hutton Ambo)
Symes Samuel, farmer (Stoke Park farm)
Hughes Maj. Hy. (Hillcrest)

2 ACA   GUILDFORD

Abbotswood—continued.

Thompson Herbt. J.P. (Milestones)
Touzel Capt. J. S. P. (Aysgarth)
Tyler Wm. C. H. (Oakdene)
Way Rupert (The Croft)
Webb Algernon E. (The Odd ho)
Woodward Geo. Ernest C.B.E. (Long Hayes)
Wright Miss M. (Abbots Trace)

(For the remainder see Worplesdon.)

ACACIA ROAD, from 35 Recreation road.
(No thoroughfare.)
West side.

1 Mullard George
2 Peirson Mrs
3 Woollard Albt
4 Ward Daniel
5 Stephens Chas
6 Bennett John
7 Balchin Mrs
8 Tinham Fredk
9 Barnes Leonard
10 Burdett Albt. Jas. Wm
11 Thorne William Henry
12 Cooper James
13 Stevens Ernest Alfred
14 Pearce Tom
15 Smith Mrs
16 Blake Albert Arthur
17 Englefield Hermon
18 Deane Harry
19 Bullen Arthur

East side.
20 Makings Jn. Jsph
21 Greenfield Fredk
22 Thurgood Albert
23 Bonner Mrs
24 Stillwell Ernest
25 Guildford & District Window Cleaning Co
25 Hart Rt. Wm
26 Tomlinson George
27 Dance George
28 Ede Arthur
29 Woods Mrs
30 Lawrence Chas
31 Barnes Frederick
32 Young Hy. S. bookbinder
33 Marriott Lawrence
34 Jones Edwd
35 Hickley William Edgar
36 Pack Mrs
37 Bridger Mrs. E
38 Avery Mrs

ACACIA VILLAS.
See Woodbridge road.

ADDISON RD. from Harvey rd.
West side.
Harvey gardens.
2 Combridge Danl. Jn
3 Tull Wm. J. L
5 Jeffery Mrs
6 Butt Stanley E. A
———
5 Gyatt Bros. motor garage
5 Russhent Wm. Albt
7 Boxall William James. sen
7 Boxall Harry E. insur. agt
9 Harding Wilfred
11 Baigent William S
13 Tubbs Charles
15 Thompson Miss E
17 Pulling Edward James
19 Bunker Frederick
21 Hockley Jn
23 Feist William Henry
25 Drew Edwin James
27 Reeve Wm
29 Gyatt Henry
31 Brooker Albert
33 Cooper Miss
35 Stenning Willie Jesse, grocer
37 Durbridge Charles
39 Grafham Chas
41 Razzell Alfd. Jn
43 Simmonds Miss
43 Hutchins Miss
45 Laws Miss A
47 Eade Harry James
49 Bookham Edwin Fredk. fishmngr
51 Capp Mrs
53 Lyon Mrs
55 Belchamber Basil
57 Ede Ernest
59 Parker Walter
61 Bishopp Robert George
63 Watts Miss
65 Parker Chas
67 Ayling Fredk. Jas
69 Capon Sam, boot repairer
71 Mitchell Stanley Cyril
73 Benjamin Wm. E. J
. . . . here is road leading to allotments . . . .
77 Wise Jonas Harry
79 Stanford David
81 Steer George
83 Mitchell Mrs

Bibliography

Barrett, H. and Phillips, J., *Suburban Style: The British Home 1840-1960*, new edn (1993)

Briggs, A., *A Social History of England* (1983)

Clarke, L., *Stoke next Guildford* (1999)

Collyer, G. and Rose, D., *Images of Guildford* (1998)

Colvin, J., *Not Ordinary Men*, reprint (1995)

Corke, S., *Guildford: A Pictorial History* (1990)

Gradidge, R., *The Surrey Style* (1991)

Haigh, D., *Baillie Scott: The Artistic House*, reprint (1995)

Hitchmough, W., *The Arts and Crafts Home* (2002)

Marjoribanks, R., *Burpham: Norman Manor to Suburban Village* (1997)

Newman, S., *Guildford, The Changing Face* (2002)

Rose, D., *Guildford and District* (2000)

The Arts and Crafts Movement in Surrey, *Nature and Tradition*, new revised edn (2002)

Tinniswood, A., *The Arts and Crafts House* (1999)

Yorke, T., *The Edwardian House Explained* (2006)

Index

Numbers in **bold** refer to illustrations.